AMPHIBIANS & REPTILES

NATIVE TO MINNESOTA

The University of Minnesota Press
gratefully acknowledges
the generous assistance provided
for the publication of this book
by
Wallace C. Dayton,
the Hamilton P. Traub University Press Fund,
the Nongame Wildlife Program
of the Minnesota Department of Natural Resources,
the Margaret W. Harmon Fund,
and the Minnesota Herpetological Society

Funding for writing this book and partial funding for publication
have been provided by donations to the Nongame Wildlife Checkoff
on Minnesota tax forms

Barney Oldfield and John J. Moriarty

AMPHIBIANS & REPTILES
NATIVE TO MINNESOTA

Foreword by W. J. Breckenridge

UNIVERSITY OF MINNESOTA PRESS

Minneapolis / London

Published by the University of Minnesota Press
2037 University Avenue Southeast, Minneapolis, MN 55455-3092
Printed in Canada on acid-free paper
Jacket and book design by Diane Gleba Hall

Library of Congress Cataloging-in-Publication Data
Oldfield, Barney.
    Amphibians and reptiles native to Minnesota / Barney Oldfield,
    John J. Moriarty ; foreword by W. J. Breckenridge.
        p. cm.
    Includes bibliographical references and index.
    ISBN 0-8166-2384-8 (hc : acid-free).
    1. Amphibians—Minnesota.   2. Reptiles—Minnesota.
    3. Amphibians—Minnesota—Identification.   4. Reptiles—Minnesota—
    Identification.   I. Oldfield, Barney   II. Moriarty, John J.   III. Title.

QL653.M55O45   1994   93-45018
597.6'09776—dc20

The University of Minnesota is an equal-opportunity educator and employer.

CONTENTS

FOREWORD

W. J. Breckenridge

Public interest in, and concern for, the welfare of our natural environment has experienced a remarkable increase in Minnesota and elsewhere during the past few decades. People are eager to learn and understand more about the plants, animals, and habitats that surround them. Oftentimes their interest is sparked initially by the ability to identify different species of plants and animals. Authoritative natural history reference books are one of many avenues for furthering their knowledge of the natural world.

Among reference books, regional field guides are a primary first source of information for beginning naturalists. Little had been done on the reptiles and amphibians of Minnesota when I undertook a treatise covering these species as my Ph.D. thesis subject in the late 1930s. Later this material was reedited to meet the needs of the general public, and my book *Reptiles and Amphibians of Minnesota* was published by the University of Minnesota Press in 1944. This source book served its purpose for nearly 50 years. Now it seems appropriate to update the material covered by that book, and Barney Oldfield and John Moriarty have done just that in this new volume *Amphibians and Reptiles Native to Minnesota,* also published by the University of Minnesota Press.

The excellent color photographs reproduced here add considerably to the reader's ability to identify specimens quickly and correctly. A few name changes have been made during the past half century, and numerous changes in species' ranges are recorded. The latter are, of course, in part due to the increased number of field workers. In a few instances, however, significant differences in ranges are noted that could have been missed by me and my limited number of reliable reporters. On the other hand, these differences may represent actual range extensions or constrictions due to human disturbances of the habitats. One innovative approach to field identification is the authors' use of practical circular keys. The expanded introductory section also adds welcome information to the general subject of herpetology.

This attractive new volume will be a very valuable and timely addition to the libraries of both amateur and professional herpetologists who might be initiating studies both in Minnesota and in neighboring states.

PREFACE

I *t was chilly—downright chilly. My breath formed billows of vapor under-*
neath the headlamp. The chest waders kept me reasonably warm, but frustra-
tion was setting in. I had been standing in the middle of the sedge swamp
in a foot of water and mud for well over an hour. I was there to photograph
the Spring Peeper. There were hundreds of them, but I couldn't find a single
frog. The males resumed their deafening chorus shortly after they had accepted
me as a harmless lurking shadow. Even with their piercing screams surround-
ing me, locating one of these thumbnail-sized treefrogs was nearly impossible.

I finally spotted the characteristic shine of the inflated vocal sac. The little
male frog was hanging on to a leaf of vegetation on the surface of the water.
Even with my bright light shining into his eyes, he continued calling undaunted.
I raised my camera and attempted to focus. After readjusting the headlamp,
I was able to fire off some shots. I continued to creep closer until I was squat-
ting within 2 feet of the tiny frog. I took the photographs I wanted. With less
difficulty I was able to spot several more callers before leaving the swamp close
to midnight.

Only an intense interest in amphibians and reptiles like that
shared by the authors is likely to compel a person to spend a night
in a frog swamp as the senior author (Oldfield) recounts. Our lifelong
interest in amphibians and reptiles began as children, with Barney
pursuing lizards in New Mexico and John catching Bullfrogs in
Connecticut. This herpetological curiosity has driven us to vault
from canoes, wade waist deep in muck, and spend hours turning

over rocks and logs in search of these interesting vertebrates.

We have a combination of 25 years of experience studying and observing Minnesota's amphibians and reptiles. We have, jointly and independently, conducted numerous herpetological projects in Minnesota, including herpetofauna surveys of the southwest and southeast regions, county biological surveys, and various field research projects on individual species (Blanding's Turtles, Wood Turtles, Gopher Snakes, and Timber Rattlesnakes). This book embodies countless hours of working with and learning about our favorite Minnesota animals.

Nearly 50 years have passed since Dr. Walter Breckenridge's excellent book *Reptiles and Amphibians of Minnesota* was published. The extensive habitat loss and alteration during this time has had considerable impact on our wildlife. During this same period there has been a substantial gain in information on the distribution and natural history of our native amphibians and reptiles. Two additional reptiles, the Ouachita Map Turtle and the Lined Snake, have been added to the state list during the past 20 years. With this new information comes a need for a Minnesota amphibian and reptile book with up-to-date distribution maps, current nomenclature, and contemporary life-history information.

This book's purpose is to provide a contemporary account of the 48 species of amphibians and reptiles found in Minnesota. Naturalists, hunters, fishermen, gardeners, and nature photographers should find opportunity to use this book as an aid to the identification of the occasional snake, toad, or salamander that they may encounter. Distribution maps, keys, and natural history data in the book will be useful to natural resource managers, field biologists, and serious students of herpetology. *Amphibians and Reptiles Native to Minnesota* will be of value to people in bordering states and Canadian provinces since many of their species are shared with Minnesota.

John Moriarty authored the history of Minnesota herpetology, the section about amphibian and reptile habitats, the summary of common amphibian and reptile problems, the identification keys, the amphibian species accounts, and the description of species of possible occurrence. He also compiled the distribution maps. Barney Oldfield provided photographs (unless otherwise credited) and the remaining text.

It is our hope that this book will promote a genuine interest, understanding, and concern for these remarkable animals. Curiosity and fascination with amphibians and reptiles often begin when one is a child, and they frequently blossom into a lifelong interest. This book will stimulate and help educate the younger set as well as the young at heart.

ACKNOWLEDGMENTS

The concept to write a new amphibian and reptile book for Minnesota was initiated by Dr. Jeff Lang in 1982. Unfortunately, Jeff was not able to pursue this project because of research commitments. We are very grateful to him for allowing us to continue the project and for use of his distribution records.

Over the past several years many friends, colleagues, and herpetological enthusiasts have provided us with information and assistance used in writing this book. They helped by collecting distribution and natural history information, providing pertinent literature, supplying specimens for photography, and reviewing earlier versions of the manuscript.

Persons who provided us with distribution records include employees of the Minnesota Department of Natural Resources: Richard Baker, Ed Brecke-Kramer, Jon Cole, Carol Dorff, Elaine Feikema, Joan Galli, Jack Heather, Jeff Hines, Mary Miller, Gerda Nordquist, Dave Palmquist, Pam Perry, John Schladweiler, and Welby Smith. Many members of the Minnesota Herpetological Society and the general public contributed: Dr. Phillip Cochran, Dr. Bruce Cutler, Jamie Haskins, Tom Jessen, Greg Kvanbek, Dr. Jeff Lang, Glenn Lewis, John Meltzer, Dr. R. Earl Olson, Gloria Peterson, and Dr. Dwain Warner.

Distribution records were also collected by reviewing the amphibian and reptile collections at the James Ford Bell Museum of Natural History. We would like to thank Drs. Elmer Birney, Donald

Gilbertson, David Merrell, Phillip Regal, and James Underhill for providing access to the collections and natural history information. Dr. Regal also provided the original idea for developing a circular identification key.

Several people generously provided loan of live specimens to be photographed for the book or patiently assisted with animals during photography sessions. These people include Jim Gerholdt, Pam Gerholdt, Ted Hoberg, Dr. Dave Hoppe, Don Johnson, Tom Johnson, Del Jones, Dr. Dan Keyler, Greg Kvanbek, Dr. Donn Leaf, John Meltzer, Ken Mueller, Dan Nedrelo, Casey Oldfield, Ann Porwoll, Blake Sheldon, and Eric Thiss.

A small group of colleagues provided a great deal of assistance in all aspects of the book, including field work, literature citations, and manuscript review. We would like to thank Jim Gerholdt, Dr. Dave Hoppe, Del Jones, and Dr. Dan Keyler for their efforts.

We are very grateful to Dr. Daryl Karns for reviewing the complete manuscript and providing many helpful comments. Dr. Dick Buech reviewed the Wood Turtle account, Tom Klein produced the computer version of the circular keys, and Julie Janke drew the key figures. Barbara Coffin, Carl Conney, and Judy Melander assisted in getting the book to the press and into production.

The preparation of this book was partially funded by the Minnesota Department of Natural Resources Nongame Wildlife Program. We would like to acknowledge Carrol Henderson for his efforts and support with contract and funding negotiations for the book. Lee Pfannmuller served as our editor during the various drafts and development of the book. We greatly appreciated her assistance and patience.

Dr. Walter Breckenridge graciously wrote the foreword to this work. We are indebted to Dr. Breckenridge for writing the original amphibian and reptile book for Minnesota. We will be greatly honored if our book is as well accepted as his was and stands the "test of time" as his did.

Lastly and most importantly, we would like to thank our immediate families for their support, beginning years ago with the patience and tolerance of our parents. Jack Oldfield, Mercedes Oldfield, William Moriarty, and Carol Moriarty allowed an endless procession of biological "specimens" (alive and dead) through their homes. Our wives (Linda Oldfield and JoAnne Wetherell-Moriarty) provided support and encouragement through many years of writing and editing "The Book." Casey and Sherilyn Oldfield assisted with numerous field surveys, including wading through "frog swamps" at night. Caitlin and Daniel Moriarty waited until the book was near completion before showing up on the scene.

INTRODUCTION

Minnesota's amphibians and reptiles are an interesting and diverse group of vertebrates. There are 48 species native to the state, and their variety in form, size, and color is indeed remarkable. Minnesota has 19 species of amphibians including 5 salamanders and 14 anurans (frogs and toads). Of the 29 species of reptiles inhabiting the state there are 9 turtles, 3 lizards, and 17 snakes. Many of the species native to Minnesota are at the northern limits of their range. Frequently, a species' range extends into the state along the Mississippi River valley; thus the southeastern portion of the state offers the greatest numbers and varieties.

Several Minnesota species are habitat generalists and are relatively common throughout the state. American Toads, Common Garter Snakes, Painted Turtles, and Northern Leopard Frogs are examples. Other species have special habitat requirements, and their distribution is limited to localized areas. Species such as the Western Hognose Snake, Wood Turtle, Five-lined Skink, and Mink Frog fit this category. A third group includes extremely rare species (Northern Cricket Frogs, Massasaugas, Lined Snakes, and Rat Snakes), whose ranges just barely extend into Minnesota from neighboring states.

WHAT IS A HERP?

Herpetology is the discipline for the study of amphibians and reptiles, and a person who studies these animals is a herpetologist. *Herp* is a popular colloquial term that refers to either an amphibian or a reptile and has become popular during the past ten years. Derivatives of the word *herp* that are in widespread use include *herper* (someone interested in amphibians and reptiles), *herping* (searching for amphibians and reptiles), and *herp societies* (organizations devoted to the study and captive care of amphibians and reptiles).

Amphibians and reptiles are not close relatives, but placing these two classes of animals into one group for study is convenient for several reasons. Characteristics of animals in both classes include cold-bloodedness, extended periods of dormancy, secretive lifestyles, and dependence upon crawling or hopping for transportation. In addition, both amphibians and reptiles are often greatly maligned and misunderstood by humans.

Ectotherm is a better term than cold-blooded to describe the dependency of amphibians and reptiles on the environment to regulate their body temperature. Amphibians and reptiles must actively seek out warmer or cooler areas to sustain a relatively constant body temperature during periods of activity. When climatic conditions are unsuitable, they become inactive. Amphibians and reptiles in Minnesota may overwinter up to six months, generally extending from mid-October through mid-April. During this period both amphibians and reptiles substantially reduce their physical activity and cease to feed. Metabolic rates slow to conserve stored fat deposits. Some species also enter a period of dormancy called *estivation* during arid or hot conditions. Dormancy may also occur during periods of water or food shortage, even if climatic temperatures are suitable for activity.

Amphibians and reptiles normally lead secretive lives. Although seasonal breeding and migration activities make them more apparent at certain times of the year, they generally spend much of the time hidden from view under logs, leaf litter, or rocks, or in burrows. Many amphibians and reptiles are masters of camouflage. While they remain motionless, their cryptic coloration allows them to blend into the surroundings.

Another common denominator of amphibians and reptiles is the restrictions imposed by their size and modes of locomotion. Generally, amphibians and reptiles are small animals that crawl, hop, or swim. Many are capable of surprising bursts of speed, but these peaks of speed are of short duration when compared to birds or mammals.

Because amphibians and reptiles are primarily restricted to surface travel, they remain within relatively small territories, and they are highly vulnerable to habitat changes.

Amphibians and reptiles suffer greatly from human ignorance and prejudice. Their secretive nature and their methods of movement provoke fear and hate in many people. Many amphibians and reptiles (especially snakes) are killed needlessly each year by well-meaning but poorly informed people. These animals are an important segment of our biological diversity, and they deserve the protection that we provide our more "likable" wildlife. As the public becomes more informed, acceptance of amphibians and reptiles will grow, and attitudes toward them will improve.

HISTORY OF HERPETOLOGY IN MINNESOTA

Before the 1900s, historical accounts of Minnesota's herpeto-fauna are scarce. Early travelers to the state mentioned finding turtles or snakes, but few details accompanied their reports. Herpetological works before 1900 were regional with only a passing reference to Minnesota (Baird 1858; Cooper 1859; Cope 1889, 1900). Breckenridge (1941) gives a detailed listing of these historical accounts.

In the early 1900s, however, several individuals began studies of Minnesota's amphibians and reptiles. The "famous" snake trainer Grace Wiley began her career at the Minneapolis Public Library and Museum. Although much of her work was with captive animals, she was the mentor for several associates who worked on the biology of Minnesota species (Friedrich 1934; Stiles 1938). Gustav Swanson (1935) undertook the first herpetological study with a statewide perspective, preparing a checklist of Minnesota's amphibians.

Walter Breckenridge began his career at the University of Minnesota in the 1930s. His work on Minnesota's amphibians and reptiles began as a sideline to his ornithological studies but later expanded into a graduate project (Breckenridge 1941). Specimens collected for his study became the foundation of the amphibian and reptile collection at the James Ford Bell Museum of Natural History. His graduate project resulted in the publication of *Amphibians and Reptiles of Minnesota* (Breckenridge 1944) and numerous shorter articles (Moriarty and Jones 1988). The book marked the beginning of modern herpetology in Minnesota and has been the standard herpetological reference for the state and the entire Upper Midwest since its publication. Breckenridge's herpetological research continued with studies on softshell turtles (Breckenridge 1960) and toads (Breckenridge and Tester 1961; Tester and Breckenridge 1964; Tester et al. 1965). The latter work pioneered the use of radioactive tagging in the study of amphibian movements (Tester 1963, 1964) and resulted in two theses (Ewert 1969; Williams 1969).

From the late 1950s to the early 1970s almost all of the amphibian and reptile work in Minnesota was conducted by graduate students at the University of Minnesota. Studies included the ecology and natural history of Wood Frogs (Bellis 1957; Fishbeck 1968), Green Frogs (Fleming 1976), Mink Frogs (Hedeen 1970), and Prairie Skinks (Nelson 1963). Two important studies were conducted at other institutions. James (1966) worked on the habits of softshell turtles in the Mississippi River, and Lang (1971) studied the use of ant mounds by overwintering snakes in northern Minnesota.

Extensive research on Northern Leopard Frogs in Minnesota also began during this period. Drs. David Merrell and Robert McKinnell conducted the majority of the work. Their research, totaling 30 publications (Moriarty and Jones 1988), focused on the genetics and the biology of cancerous tumors in Northern Leopard Frogs. Merrell (1977) also provided a very useful account of the ecology and life history of this species.

Begun in the late 1970s, the Minnesota Department of Natural Resources' Nongame Wildlife Program and Natural Heritage Program have promoted interest in and research on Minnesota's amphibians and reptiles. The Nongame Wildlife Program (Henderson 1979a–c; 1980 a–f) prepared a series of pamphlets on their distribution, and the Natural Heritage Program began keeping computer records on the rare species. Together this information was used by the reptile and amphibian group of the Minnesota Endangered Species Advisory Committee. This group was responsible for developing the state's first list of endangered, threatened, and special concern amphibians and reptiles (Coffin and Pfannmuller 1988; Lang et al. 1982).

The Minnesota Herpetological Society (MHS) was founded in 1981 following the symposium "Ecology of Reptiles and Amphibians in Minnesota" (Jones 1981; Elwell et al. 1981). The society has been a source of information on the conservation, natural history, and care of amphibians and reptiles. The Minnesota Nongame Wildlife Program has worked with the society on several studies in southeastern and southwestern Minnesota (Moriarty 1985, 1986). The society has also published distribution maps of the state's native amphibians and reptiles and publishes papers of regional interest in an occasional paper series.

The study of herpetology has been particularly active in Minnesota during the past decade. Two hundred and ninety-five articles were published on Minnesota herpetology between 1900 and 1985; 107 have been published since 1980 (Moriarty and Jones 1988). Cochran (1981, 1982a–d, 1983a–c) published several papers and notes on the natural history and distribution of Minnesota amphibians and reptiles. Schmid (1982) reported on the survival of amphibians below freezing temperatures. Lang (1982a, 1983) studied the endangered Five-lined Skink population in western Minnesota. He (1982b) also completed a report to the Nongame Wildlife Program on the distribution and habitat preferences of and selected references for Minnesota amphibians and reptiles, a study that was used as a foundation for this book. Karns (1983, 1984, 1992a, 1992b) studied the ecology of amphibians in the peatlands and authored "Field Herpetology: Methods for the Study of Amphibians and Reptiles in Minnesota" (Karns 1986).

Over the last five years, the Nongame Wildlife Program has continued to be involved in amphibian and reptile research and management. The small grants program has funded studies on Wood Turtles (Buech et al.1990), Blanding's Turtles (Dorff 1989; Linck 1988), Timber Rattlesnakes (Keyler and Oldfield 1992), Gopher Snakes (Moriarty 1991), Five-lined Skinks (Matthews 1990), Northern Leopard Frogs (Hoppe and McKinnell 1989, 1991a, 1991b) and Northern Cricket Frogs (Whitford 1991). A pamphlet on the snakes and lizards of Minnesota (Perry and Dexter 1989) was also published. Initiated in 1987, the County Biological Survey (Natural Heritage Program 1988) has further promoted the study of Minnesota's amphibians and reptiles (Moriarty 1988).

The Minnesota Herpetological Society continues to be an important supporter of amphibian and reptile conservation in the state. The MHS and the Nongame Wildlife Program succeeded in erecting turtle-crossing signs at Weaver Dunes in 1988 to protect Blanding's Turtles. In 1989, the society led the effort to remove the bounty on rattlesnakes.

As herpetology in Minnesota heads into the 1990s, there is growing interest in reptiles and amphibians. The Nongame Wildlife Program continues to support amphibian and reptile research and management. The MHS has grown to over 300 members with a strong interest in Minnesota species. The James Ford Bell Museum of Natural History has moved to a larger building with expanded space for the collection containing 15,000 specimens of amphibians and reptiles. These organizations are strongly committed to the investigation and advancement of herpetology in Minnesota.

HABITATS

Amphibians and reptiles depend on a diversity of ecologically healthy habitats. Information about these habitats combined with knowledge of the geographic distribution of species tells herpetologists where to look for amphibians and reptiles. Herpetologists know from this information, for example, that exploring granite or limestone outcrops in southeastern Minnesota for Five-lined Skinks is likely to be successful, whereas searching for this species in northern Minnesota would be a waste of time.

Climate affects the distribution and abundance of amphibians and reptiles. Generally, amphibians are less tolerant of arid climates and thus are less abundant in western Minnesota, where the climate is drier. Reptiles do not adapt well to colder environments; thus there is a sharp decline in the number of species in northern Minnesota. A comparison of the number of species in the southeast (Houston County, 22 reptiles and 12 amphibians) to the number in the northwest (Kittson County, 7 reptiles and 10 amphibians) demonstrates the large decrease in reptile species due to colder and drier conditions.

Most of Minnesota's amphibians and turtles live in aquatic habitats, whereas lizards and the majority of snakes live in terrestrial habitats. Amphibian and reptile habitats in Minnesota can be divided into eight types, four aquatic and four terrestrial, which cover the spectrum of natural vegetation in the state. Each habitat has its own diversity of amphibians and reptiles (Table 1). Aquatic habitats include rivers and streams, lakes and ponds, marshes, and peatlands. Terrestrial habitats include three forest types and one grassland type. Amphibians and reptiles are not equally distributed within each habitat type. Food, cover, and the availability of breeding sites affect their distribution and abundance.

AQUATIC HABITATS

Rivers and Streams

Minnesota has a large network of rivers in the drainage basins of the Minnesota River, the Mississippi River, the Red River, and Lake Superior. Rivers and streams have various physical characteristics.

Rivers and streams, Beaver Creek, Houston County, Minnesota

Rivers with bottom substrates of bedrock and gravel, such as trout streams, provide habitat for Wood Turtles. Rivers with thick sand and organic bottoms, such as the lower Mississippi River, are used by Mudpuppies and are the major habitat for map turtles and softshells.

Rivers and streams may have a network of backwaters and coves. These areas of limited current and dense vegetation provide important habitat for amphibians and reptiles. The backwaters of the

Table 1. Distribution of amphibians and reptiles by habitat type

AQUATIC HABITATS

Rivers and Streams (24 Species)	Lakes and Ponds (21 Species)	Marshes and Prairie Wetlands (23 Species)	Peatlands (8 Species)
Mudpuppy	Blue-spotted Salamander	Blue-spotted Salamander	Blue-spotted Salamander
Eastern Newt	Tiger Salamander	Tiger Salamander	American Toad
American Toad	Eastern Newt	Eastern Newt	Gray Treefrog
Great Plains Toad	American Toad	American Toad	Spring Peeper
Canadian Toad	Great Plains Toad	Great Plains Toad	Green Frog
Northern Cricket Frog	Canadian Toad	Canadian Toad	Northern Leopard Frog
Cope's Gray Treefrog	Northern Cricket Frog	Northern Cricket Frog	Wood Frog
Gray Treefrog	Cope's Gray Treefrog	Cope's Gray Treefrog	Common Garter Snake
Bullfrog	Gray Treefrog	Gray Treefrog	
Green Frog	Spring Peeper	Spring Peeper	
Pickerel Frog	Western Chorus Frog	Western Chorus Frog	
Northern Leopard Frog	Green Frog	Green Frog	
Mink Frog	Pickerel Frog	Pickerel Frog	
Smooth Softshell	Northern Leopard Frog	Northern Leopard Frog	
Spiny Softshell	Mink Frog	Mink Frog	
Snapping Turtle	Wood Frog	Wood Frog	
Painted Turtle	Spiny Softshell	Snapping Turtle	
Wood Turtle	Snapping Turtle	Painted Turtle	
Blanding's Turtle	Painted Turtle	Blanding's Turtle	
Common Map Turtle	Blanding's Turtle	Northern Water Snake	
Ouachita Map Turtle	Northern Water Snake	Plains Garter Snake	
False Map Turtle		Common Garter Snake	
Northern Water Snake		Massasauga	
Massasauga			

TERRESTRIAL HABITATS

Floodplain Forest (19 Species)	Big Woods and Oak Forest (20 species)	Conifer Forest (11 Species)	Prairie (18 Species)
Blue-spotted Salamander	Blue-spotted Salamander	Blue-spotted Salamander	Tiger Salamander
Tiger Salamander	Tiger Salamander	Tiger Salamander	American Toad
Eastern Newt	American Toad	Redback Salamander	Great Plains Toad
American Toad	Cope's Gray Treefrog	American Toad	Canadian Toad
Canadian Toad	Gray Treefrog	Gray Treefrog	Northern Leopard Frog
Cope's Gray Treefrog	Northern Leopard Frog	Spring Peeper	Six-lined Racerunner
Gray Treefrog	Wood Frog	Northern Leopard Frog	Five-lined Skink
Green Frog	Five-lined Skink	Wood Frog	Prairie Skink
Northern Leopard Frog	Prairie Skink	Ringneck Snake	Racer
Wood Frog	Racer	Redbelly Snake	Ringneck Snake
Wood Turtle	Ringneck Snake	Common Garter Snake	Fox Snake
Rat Snake	Rat Snake		Western Hognose Snake
Fox Snake	Fox Snake		Milk Snake
Eastern Hognose Snake	Eastern Hognose Snake		Gopher Snake
Smooth Green Snake	Milk Snake		Plains Garter Snake
Brown Snake	Brown Snake		Common Garter Snake
Redbelly Snake	Redbelly Snake		Lined Snake
Plains Garter Snake	Plains Garter Snake		Timber Rattlesnake
Common Garter Snake	Common Garter Snake		
	Timber Rattlesnake		

Mississippi River are the only habitat in Minnesota where Bullfrogs and Massasaugas naturally occur.

Lakes and Ponds

Lakes and ponds are bodies of water that range in size from Lake Superior to ponds less than 1 hectare (2.5 acres). Smaller lakes and shallow bays of large lakes provide better habitat for amphibians and reptiles than deep, open water. Shallow water supports more vegetation, both emergent and submergent, which provides cover and food. Warmer water temperatures in shallow areas promote the development and growth of amphibian larvae. Small ponds that lack predatory fish provide good habitat for tadpoles and salamander larvae.

Marshes and Prairie Wetlands

Marshes are large areas of shallow water with thick emergent vegetation, mainly cattails (*Typha*), sedges (*Carex*), and bulrushes (*Scir-*

Lakes and ponds, Scenic State Park, Itasca County, Minnesota

Marshes and wetlands, Wild River State Park, Chisago County, Minnesota

Peatlands, Warner Nature Center, Washington County, Minnesota

pus). These areas are commonly associated with prairie lowlands in the western half of the state. Cattail marshes are scattered throughout the state in association with lake systems. Prairie wetlands are important breeding sites for Great Plains Toads and Canadian Toads. Marshes provide good amphibian and reptile habitat for a variety of species because they provide cover, water, and food.

Peatlands

Peatlands can be divided into bogs and fens. Sphagnum beds in bogs are normally water saturated and sometimes contain floating mats of vegetation. Bog water is very acidic (pH < 4.5) and nutrient poor. These characteristics may limit the number of amphibians that can use the habitat. Wood Frogs, Mink Frogs, American Toads, and Blue-spotted Salamanders are common bog inhabitants. Calcareous fens are scattered across the state but are very rare. Blanding's Turtles are found in association with these calcareous habitats in southwestern Minnesota.

TERRESTRIAL HABITATS

Floodplain Forests

Floodplain or bottomland forests are associated with the floodplains of large rivers. Their moist rich soils, which may be seasonally flooded, promote a lush growth of vegetation. Major tree species associated

Floodplain forest, Chippewa River, Buffalo County, Wisconsin

with this community are elms (*Ulmus*), maples (*Acer*), ash (*Fraxinus*), and cottonwood (*Populus*). Willows (*Salix*) are normally found along the riverbanks. Wood Turtles are found in bottomland forests that border streams, where their favorite foods, raspberries and strawberries, are common. Redbelly Snakes and Brown Snakes are also found in this forest type because of large earthworm populations.

Big Woods and Oak Forest

Big Woods and oak forest, Nerstrand State Park, Rice County, Minnesota

Big Woods and oak forests are the two deciduous forest types found in central and southeastern Minnesota. These forests differ in soil

conditions and topography. The southeastern region of the state, where oak (*Quercus*) forests dominate, lies in the "driftless zone," an unglaciated area of steep hills and rock outcrops. These outcrops are an important habitat component for many southeastern species including the Timber Rattlesnake, Five-lined Skink, and Rat Snake.

The Big Woods are on a glacial plain with rolling low hills dominated by elms (*Ulmus*), maples (*Acer*), and basswoods (*Tilia*). Woodland species of amphibians and reptiles, including American Toads, Wood Frogs, garter snakes, and Redbelly Snakes, are dependent on logs and downed branches in these forests for cover. Many forest stands, however, are no longer viable habitat for amphibians and reptiles because most of the undergrowth and downed logs have been removed for firewood.

Conifer Forests

Conifer forests, including red and white pine, jack pine, and spruce-fir, are found in northern Minnesota. Dominated in presettlement

Conifer forest, Gunflint Lake, Cook County, Minnesota

time by spruce (*Picea*), fir (*Abies*), and some pine (*Pinus*), large areas of this forest type have been converted as a result of commercial logging to aspen (*Populus*) and birch (*Betula*) hardwood stands. Although conifer forests are generally poor habitat for amphibians and reptiles, Redback and Blue-spotted Salamanders are regularly found resting under logs and pieces of bark.

Prairies

Before European settlement, western Minnesota was dominated by vast expanses of prairie. Prairies are grasslands with a few scattered trees near streams and lakes. Found on various soils and substrates, prairies are dominated by bluestem (*Andropogon*), Indiangrass

Prairie, Pipestone County, Minnesota

(*Sorghastrum*), switch grass (*Panicam*), and a wide variety of forbs (wildflowers). Today 99% of Minnesota's original prairie grasslands have been converted to agricultural land. There are many open grassy areas throughout Minnesota that are not prairies because they have been seeded with nonnative grass species. Amphibians and reptiles that are restricted to prairies, including the Western Hognose Snake, Gopher Snake, and Canadian Toad, generally do not use nonnative grasslands. Bluff prairie, a special type of prairie that occurs on steep slopes and near rock outcrops in the southeastern corner of the state, is the preferred habitat of Racers, Ringneck Snakes, Timber Rattlesnakes, Milk Snakes, and Six-lined Racerunners.

DISTURBED HABITATS

During the last 150 years many of Minnesota's natural habitats have been converted to agricultural land and, more recently, to urban areas. Most of these disturbed habitats are devoid of amphibians and reptiles because they lack cover, prey, or water. Where these three items are available, some of the hardier, more adaptable species, such as American Toads, garter snakes, or Painted Turtles, may be present.

OBSERVING, STUDYING, AND PHOTOGRAPHING AMPHIBIANS AND REPTILES

ETHICAL FIELD METHODS

How does a person find amphibians and reptiles in their indigenous habitats? Turtles are readily spotted at a distance basking on logs in ponds or along riverbanks. Frogs are often seen leaping into the water from the edges of ponds. Nearly every child at one time or another has caught a toad near a doorstep, in a garden, or at a local park. Nevertheless, many Minnesota species are secretive and not easily found. Even people who spend a great amount of time outdoors rarely see snakes, lizards, or salamanders. The only snake most Minnesotans ever see roaming free is a garter snake. Lizards and salamanders are secretive and remain hidden much of the time. How does a person go about finding and studying these interesting animals?

Successful herping requires patience, diligence, and time. Obviously, selecting suitable areas to search is the first consideration. Abandoned farmsteads, old rock quarries, woodlots, ponds, and marshes are good spots to investigate. Good sites for looking for amphibians and reptiles may be on private property, and permission from the owner should be acquired before beginning the hunt.

Walk slowly through promising locales, and keep an eye out for movement. Carefully pull aside rocks, logs, shingles, tin, and boards to see what is underneath. Hay hooks and potato rakes are helpful for turning this material over. Pull ground cover toward you to provide a shield in case a wasps' nest, a skunk, or a venomous snake is uncovered. The likelihood of uncovering a venomous species in Minnesota is quite rare, but stinging insects are not scarce. Carefully look at the undersurfaces of logs and boards, as well as at the exposed ground. Small animals often remain still and are difficult to see. Replace cover objects in their original location to preserve the microhabitat of the organisms using this living space. Searching for amphibians and reptiles is destructive if not conducted in an environmentally conscientious manner. Treat the habitat kindly!

Swamps, marshes, streams, and sloughs are excellent areas to hunt. Amphibians and reptiles that are likely to be found in and near wet areas include turtles, water snakes, frogs, and amphibian larvae. Waders or hip boots give protection in cool weather; cutoffs and old tennis shoes work well in warm weather.

For those seeking adventure, the investigation of breeding congregations of frogs or toads is an exciting and rewarding experience. During the night use a good flashlight; a headlamp is ideal because it frees both hands. Calling amphibians pay little or no attention to a flashlight, so it is easy to observe their calling and breeding behavior. If they stop calling, wait until the vocalizations begin again before proceeding with the search. Toads display little fear during courtship activities, and in no time the males will be calling unabated within hands' reach. Small treefrogs require more diligence to locate because of their size and concealing color patterns. Scan the area slowly with the flashlight, and look for a reflection from their inflated vocal sacs.

Road driving is another useful technique for finding amphibians and reptiles, particularly at night. During periods of spring and fall migrations, road driving can provide success in Minnesota, but at other times of the year very few amphibians and reptiles are found on roads. Choose a rural blacktop road with little traffic. Drive slowly, and keep an eye on the road for small animals. Watch out for other traffic when making a hasty stop. Unfortunately, many of the amphibians and reptiles found on roads are dead. One quickly gains an appreciation for the large numbers of animals that are run over. Roadkills may be of scientific value, especially to establish locality records. Refer to the maps in the species accounts for the currently known distribution. Road-killed specimens from new localities or remains of rare species should be frozen and delivered to the James Ford Bell Museum of Natural History. Include an accurate location description and map with the specimen.

Proper timing contributes to the success of a herping trip. Spring is the best season to find amphibians and reptiles because of their increased visibility in association with overwintering emergence and subsequent breeding activities. Summer is less rewarding because of decreased activity levels. Also, heavy vegetation provides cover for the animals, which makes them more difficult to locate. One notable exception during midsummer is the movement of large numbers of newly transformed amphibians away from breeding ponds. Road driving on warm summer evenings may be helpful in finding nocturnal species. Many species become more conspicuous in the fall as they migrate to overwintering sites.

Amphibians and reptiles become active by mid-morning during warm months. Air temperatures from 21° to 32° C (70° to 90° F) are preferable, especially for reptiles. Amphibians are active at somewhat cooler temperatures and during rainy weather.

Successful searching requires experience and patience, but luck is a key factor. Even a seasoned veteran has days of failure. An excellent publication with detailed herpetological techniques is "Field Herpetology: Methods for the Study of Amphibians and Reptiles in Minnesota" (Karns 1986).

Frequently it is necessary to have an animal in hand to make an identification. Care should be taken to prevent injury to the animal during capture and handling. Small amphibians and reptiles may accidentally be killed by overturning rocks, and big hands can unintentionally crush small, wiggly salamanders and lizards. Small amphibians and lizards can be held for examination by gently pressing one of their rear legs between thumb and forefinger while the animal remains free to cling to the remainder of the hand. Large frogs should be grasped around their abdomens with their rear legs extended. Large snakes should be held with both hands to keep the frightened animal from injuring itself by thrashing. One hand should keep the head under control while the other supports the snake's body. A Snapping Turtle should be held by its rear legs or by the back edge of its shell with the head of the turtle pointed away from the handler's body. Suspending a Snapping Turtle solely by its tail may permanently damage the turtle's spinal cord. A Softshell turtle can be restrained by grasping the rear edge of its upper shell while staying clear of its sharp beak and claws. Conant and Collins (1991) and Karns (1986) illustrate proper methods of handling amphibians and reptiles.

After the animal is identified, observed, and photographed, it should be released at the capture site. Many amphibians and reptiles are territorial with specific home ranges and die or do poorly in a different locality. Nonnative species and long-term captives should not be released; in most cases these animals quickly perish. On rare occasions, an exotic species may become established in an area and be detrimental to the native fauna. For example, Bullfrogs were intentionally introduced into several western states with devastating effects on native frog populations.

The best method of transporting snakes and lizards is a well-sewn cotton sack such as a pillowcase. A snug overhand knot in the neck of the sack will prevent escape. Amphibians are best placed in small bottles or self-sealing plastic bags with damp moss or vegetation to prevent desiccation. Amphibians and reptiles trapped in containers in the direct sun perish quickly from overheating. Extreme care must be taken to prevent such unfortunate accidents. Sacks and containers with occupants should be placed in a picnic cooler in the shade. These coolers make ideal transportation boxes in automobiles because they provide protection from temperature extremes and substantially decrease the possibility of an escape inside the car.

Three species of reptiles native to Minnesota have legal status in the state and are fully protected. The Five-lined Skink is on Minnesota's endangered species list. The Blanding's Turtle and the Wood Turtle are classified as threatened. All amphibians and reptiles are protected in national parks, state parks, and state scientific and natural areas. There are restrictions on and license requirements for capturing frogs to be used as fishing bait. Possession and collection of Snapping Turtles is regulated because large numbers of these turtles are used for human food. The Minnesota Department of Natural Resources can provide current rules and regulations concerning Minnesota's amphibians and reptiles.

Searching for amphibians and reptiles can be a rewarding and interesting venture. Genuine curiosity about the natural world and a good deal of patience are the key ingredients for countless hours of enjoyment.

FIELD STUDY

There is a tremendous lack of information concerning the secretive lives of amphibians and reptiles. Information is needed on population dynamics, habitat requirements, predator-prey relationships, reproduction, and ecology. Resource managers have difficulty implementing beneficial short- and long-term conservation programs without sufficient knowledge about the natural history of a species.

Before going out in the field, take some time to study background materials on species of interest. Such preparation saves time and makes observations more meaningful. The requirements for herpetological field study are simple—curiosity and a notebook are all that is needed to get started. In addition, binoculars are useful for observing difficult-to-approach animals such as turtles and lizards. Record the locality, weather information, and a description of the habitat when an amphibian or reptile is found. Make notes about the size and sex of the animal, unusual markings, and its behavior. As more information is accumulated, it becomes more useful. For example, recording the dates and weather conditions of Spring Peeper breeding congregations from year to year allows the observer to predict these activities in future seasons and note changes in populations.

There are various methods of keeping field records. A small, durable field notebook is simple and effective. A system using 3-by-5-inch note cards is also easy to use (see the accompanying example). After an amphibian or reptile sighting, a preprinted field card is filled out and later filed according to species in chronological order. These cards can be used to record roadkills, breeding congregations, egglaying activities, and migrational information. Simply type up a blank card with the desired headings and appropriate blank spaces. Then take the card to a printer and have a number duplicated. Carry a supply of cards in your vehicle and while you are in the field. A small dictation tape recorder is an alternative to a notebook or note cards, but tapes need to be transcribed to be useful.

```
Species......................................................................................................

Date................Time....................Weather...........................

State..................................................County............................

TWP#................Range#................Section

Habitat.........................................................................................

Observations..............................................................................

......................................................................................................

......................................................................................................

......................................................................................................

......................................................................................................

......................................................................................................

......................................................................................................
```

Personal computers can play a substantial role in amphibian and reptile field studies. A data-base program can be used to construct a computer analog of the note card system that allows quick information storage and retrieval. The computer has become an extremely important tool of the research herpetologist and is equally useful for anyone seriously interested in the field study of amphibians and reptiles.

Advanced field study may require marking individual animals for recapture studies. Mark-and-recapture programs are used to determine such things as territories, migration patterns, longevity, and population dynamics. These programs are best conducted by trained biologists with specific goals in mind. Indiscriminate marking of an animal does little to further research and may result in death of the individual if the mark draws inordinate attention to it. Any study requiring the marking of animals should be coordinated with the Minnesota Department of Natural Resources before the start of the program.

Field biologists use a variety of methods to mark animals. They include painting on numbers, shell notching (turtles), attaching metal or plastic tags, and toe clipping. A sophisticated and expensive marking technique has recently been developed for use in the field. A small electronic chip that requires no power source is injected under the skin of the subject. A hand-held instrument reads the chip code that identifies the individual.

Biotelemetry is a technique that allows the researcher to relocate an animal. A small radio transmitter powered by batteries is attached to or surgically implanted in the study specimen, and a receiver with an antenna is used to relocate the animal after its release. Biotelemetry has provided natural history information about animals that would otherwise be unattainable.

"Amateur" herpetologists have made valuable contributions to the field of herpetology, but advanced field research should not be undertaken casually. Expertise, time, patience, and coordination with knowledgeable authorities are demands of advanced methods. The welfare of the research animals must remain a high priority.

Field study provides hours of enjoyment and education without the responsibility of caring for captives. Information gathered about a species in the wild is generally more reliable than that gathered about captives. More information about field techniques can be found in Karns (1986), Seigel, Collins, and Novak (1987), and Harless and Morlock (1979).

CARE OF CAPTIVES

A fascination with amphibians and reptiles may compel a person to bring one home as a captive. For the sake of the animal, considerable forethought should go into this decision. Removing an amphibian or reptile from the wild means taking on the responsibility for the welfare of that animal. Make sure the animal can be legally taken (i.e., it is a nonprotected species from nonrestricted public or private lands). Prepare suitable escape-proof housing before the collecting trip. Keep the number of captives to a minimum. Many individuals are nervous and do not settle down in captivity. Others may languish and refuse to eat or drink. Animals that do not adjust to captivity should be released where they were collected before their physical condition deteriorates to the point that their continued survival is unlikely.

Providing a suitable cage environment and appropriate food are key requirements for successful keeping. Suitable warmth and lighting are necessary for animals to remain active and feed properly. Most species require a supplementary heat source during the cooler months. Provide an area of seclusion (such as a hide box) within the enclosure to help the animal better adapt to confinement. Keep cages and enclosures clean to reduce the buildup of disease organisms. Many species require live food such as insects, rodents, or other small animals. Providing a constant supply of these food items may be difficult or impossible. It is best not to feed live rodents to a caged snake because the snake may be attacked by the rodent.

Pet stores that specialize in amphibians and reptiles sell live and frozen food, cages, and accessories. Informed storekeepers can be helpful with husbandry problems, but it is best to rely on the advice of individuals thoroughly familiar with the care of captive amphibians and reptiles. Mattison (1987) provides reliable information about care of captive amphibians and reptiles. Additionally, the Minnesota Herpetological Society has many members knowledgeable about proper techniques of amphibian and reptile care.

Keeping venomous reptiles captive is highly discouraged. A person who maintains dangerous animals is legally liable if problems arise. Local ordinances may prohibit the keeping of such animals, and few neighbors or landlords accept or tolerate such practices.

Caring for and observing captive amphibians and reptiles can be rewarding and fascinating. Many youngsters have developed a lifelong interest in herpetology and a greater appreciation for wildlife from their first frogs or snakes, but the *best* place to observe and study amphibians and reptiles is in their natural environment.

AMPHIBIAN AND REPTILE PHOTOGRAPHY

Amphibian and reptile photography is an enjoyable and fulfilling endeavor. Compiling a collection of photographs of amphibian and reptile species can not only be personally rewarding but can also provide valuable documentation of field localities and herpetological events. In the past the only acceptable scientific record of a species from a locality was a specimen preserved in a museum jar. Many museums are now cataloging and using photographs for locality documentation. Many opportunities arise to photograph amphibians and reptiles found in the field and on roads.

A comfortable working knowledge of amphibian and reptile photography may require more information than can be provided in this book. Several photography books that contain in-depth information and useful ideas applicable to herpetological photography are listed in Resources at the back of this book.

Equipment

Amphibian and reptile photography is best served by the versatile 35-mm single-lens reflex (SLR) camera. The availability of close-focusing attachments, interchangeable lenses, and small electronic flash units makes 35-mm systems ideal for producing high-quality, frame-filling photographs of these interesting and colorful animals. SLR cameras allow the photographer to view the subject directly through the lens that records the image. In general, point-and-shoot and instamatic cameras are not suitable, because they do not allow focus at close range. Cameras larger than 35 mm may be too cumbersome in the field to be practical for photographing small, active animals.

Even with a 35-mm SLR camera and a 50-mm (normal) lens, it is not possible to focus close enough to get frame-filling photographs of small subjects (salamanders, treefrogs, lizards, etc.). Several methods are available to focus closer to the subject. A simple, inexpensive set of close-up lenses that attach to the front of the normal lens work quite well. Extension tubes that fit between the lens and the camera body give higher-quality images but are more tedious to use. Bellows can also be used between the lens and the camera body to allow close focusing, but they are too bulky and fragile for field work. Macro lenses focus from infinity to a 1:2 (image size = ½ subject size) or 1:1 (image size = subject size) reproduction, and they are ideally suited for close-up amphibian and reptile photography. Macro lenses are commonly available in two focal lengths—50 mm and 100 mm. Better results can be obtained with longer focal-length lenses when photographing frightened animals because longer focal lengths allow a greater working distance between camera and subject. When compared to the 50-mm macro lens, the 100-mm macro allows twice the working distance while giving the same image size.

Zoom lenses with a close-focusing capability in the 80-200 mm range are very useful. Zoom lenses furnish framing flexibility and useful working distances, but they do not focus as close as macro lenses. A close-up lens attached to the front element of an 80-200-mm zoom lens will give close-focusing capabilities that nearly match a macro lens (Shaw 1987). Wide-angle lenses are excellent for habitat photographs because of their expanded field of view. Wide-angle focal lengths that work well include 28 mm and 24 mm.

Additional useful accessories for amphibian and reptile photography include a day pack or fanny pack for carrying camera equipment in the field, including extra film, spare batteries, and cleaning supplies for cameras and lenses. Tripods are ideal when tack-sharp photographs are desired, but they can be difficult to use when following an active animal. A shoulder support or a monopod increases camera stability while allowing the photographer to quickly reposition to follow a moving subject.

Film

Choosing film need not be difficult. If the desired result is photographs for an album, then the best choice is print film. Medium-speed film such as Kodacolor 100 provides pleasing color saturation and allows for a moderate degree of enlargement with good results. If the photographer intends to give public programs, to have high-quality enlargements made, or to pursue publishing, then slide film is the preferred choice.

A slow- or medium-speed slide film gives the best color saturation and the least amount of grain. All photographs in this book were taken with Kodachrome 25, Kodachrome 64, Kodachrome 200, Ektachrome 100 Plus, or Fujichrome Velvia. Kodachrome is the film of choice for museum catalogs because of its archival storage properties.

Flash Photography

Large snakes and adult turtles can be successfully photographed using natural lighting. A small hand-held electronic flash unit is desirable for photographing small subjects up close. When photographing at close range, it is best to use apertures of $f/11$ to $f/22$ to get adequate depth of field (i.e., more of the subject in sharp focus). Electronic flash gives off enough light so that small apertures can be employed, and the short duration of light gives sharp photographs with a hand-held camera. Night photography of calling frogs and toads is exciting and becomes possible with electronic flash. A headlamp or an assistant with a flashlight is needed to light the subject while the photographer focuses.

Mounting the flash on the camera hot shoe is not suitable for close-up photography because the flash beam overshoots the subject. The flash must be taken off the camera and aimed at the subject. The flash can be hand-held with the proper electronic cord connecting the flash to the camera, but this arrangement is cumbersome. An adjustable bracket that allows independent aiming of the flash works well. Two excellent flash brackets marketed by Saunders (21 Jet View Drive, Rochester, NY 14624) are the Naturalist Macro Flash Bracket (single flash) and the Lepp Dual Flash Macro Bracket (two flash units). An accessory block for an additional flash can be purchased separately for the Naturalist Macro Flash Bracket. Two flash units provide more pleasing lighting by softening the shadows and decreasing contrast, but high-quality photographs are obtainable with a single flash.

Correct flash exposure has been greatly simplified by the lens flash (TTL) metering that is available on the majority of newer camera models. A TTL meter measures the light from the flash at the film plane and shuts off the flash unit as soon as enough light is received for accurate exposure. Before modern flash metering systems, measurements, calculations, guesses, and failures were common companions of flash photography. To obtain correct flash exposure with older units that lack TTL metering, shoot a trial roll of slide film at various flash-to-subject distances and various aperture settings. Keep records and choose the best exposure from the developed slides. Then, apply these exposure guidelines to future photography sessions. Many hand-held flash units allow for an aperture of $f/16$ or $f/22$ with ISO 64 film at a distance of 12 to 18 inches from the subject. Set the electronic flash to manual mode because the automatic setting may result in overexposure at close flash-to-subject distances.

Animal Handling

Properly handling amphibians and reptiles during photography sessions notably improves photograph quality. When amphibians and reptiles are encountered in their natural environment, their secretive character and their attempts to escape make photography difficult or impossible. Generally, the animals must be captured and moved to a suitable site, preferably an open area with a minimal amount of distracting elements such as grass, leaves, and sticks. Also, an assistant to help handle the animal can be an enormous asset.

Amphibians and reptiles placed on the ground to be photographed immediately crawl, hop, or run away. One useful method is to have an assistant place cupped hands or a hat (or similar object) over the animal until it quiets down. The photographer prefocuses on the spot. On cue, the assistant removes the cover. Frequently, the surprised animal remains still long enough for several photographs to be taken.

Some photographers cool down amphibians and reptiles in a refrigerator before the session. The animals become more tractable, but the resulting photographs are of animals with abnormal body postures and moribund stares. None of the photographs in this book are of chilled animals.

The use of a captive set (an enclosure that restricts animal movement) is a technique that gives controlled working conditions for photographing amphibians and reptiles. An aquarium can serve as a simple ready-made set, but shooting through glass can be tricky because of unwanted reflections. A Plexiglas enclosure with an open top and front works nicely. Three panels of Plexiglas can be held together with duct tape or small hinges. The set should be about 12 inches high, 20 inches wide, and 16 inches deep. A 16-by-20-inch film developing tray makes a practical bottom. Soil, bark, and plants can be arranged inside to furnish a natural-appearing background. Again, an assistant can be indispensable for controlling and positioning the animal while the photographer concentrates.

Photography of venomous snakes should be done at a safe distance with a telephoto lens in the 200 mm range. A companion to keep an eye on the snake is an essential safety precaution. Handling of these animals is best left to professionals.

A nice feature of amphibian and reptile photography is that the reward is the image on film. Once the "photo trophy" is taken, the animal is free to go. Natural history photography is a nondestructive form of nature study with educational, scientific, and recreational value.

CONSERVATION

Preventing the extinction of species is a compelling reason for the conservation of our native amphibians and reptiles. An element of natural history is lost forever with extinction. Unfortunately, the human species has contributed to the rapid loss of many kinds of plants and animals throughout the world. The disruption of the balance of nature and the destruction of biodiversity are ongoing processes occurring at an accelerated pace throughout much of Minnesota, especially in the more populated areas. The following statement by the senior author (Oldfield) presents a personal viewpoint on the meaning of amphibian and reptile conservation and how it is related to ongoing environmental changes due to human activities.

Conservation can be selfish. I liked to turn rocks at an old quarry and find Milk Snakes. I derived great pleasure from canoeing a local river and seeing large numbers of Spiny Softshells and an occasional Wood Turtle. Every spring I climbed into my waders and slogged into the water at my favorite sedge swamp to observe Spring Peepers during their annual breeding frenzy. I delighted at finding a new individual or renewing an old acquaintance at a Timber Rattlesnake den that I have been studying for the past ten years. Nevertheless, those ten years have brought changes. The Milk Snake quarry was destroyed by road expansion. Pollution and silting have caused the river to become less suitable for Wood Turtles, and I find fewer each year. Frogs no longer call from the marsh that was converted to agricultural cropland. Two years ago a house was built on top of the rattlesnake hill, and last year snake hunters dislodged rock slabs and destroyed the den. The meaning of conservation to me is simple. I want my children, their children, and their children's children to be able to observe and enjoy amphibians and reptiles in their natural state as I have. Moreover, I feel that the conservation of amphibians, reptiles, and other plants and animals is ultimately tied to the survival of the human race.

HABITAT LOSS

Destruction and loss of habitat are the greatest threat to amphibian and reptile populations. Without a home these animals perish. Amphibians and reptiles have restrictive home ranges, and they lack the ability to wander great distances to locate new living space. Also, their ability to adapt to habitat change is limited. Obviously a shopping center and parking lot destroy the habitat, but alterations such as mining, agriculture, and housing developments have significant impacts. Recreational activities of humans may indirectly disrupt the habitat and normal activities of amphibians and reptiles. An example is the damage done to turtle nesting sites by unintentional trampling by boaters and campers along riverbanks. Mammalian predators (e.g., skunk, raccoon, and opossum) dig up turtle nests and consume the eggs. Since these mammals are attracted to human recreational areas in search of food, many more nests are found and destroyed.

The preservation of habitat is especially critical to rare species. If valuable natural areas can be identified, prime habitat for rare species can be protected. In recent years the Minnesota Department of Natural Resources has launched various habitat protection and inventory programs including the Scientific and Natural Areas Program, the Natural Heritage Program, the Nongame Wildlife Program, the Minnesota County Biological Survey, and the Reinvest in Minnesota Program. Together these programs have placed increased emphasis on inventorying the state's biological resources and protecting critical habitats. Recent wetland restoration efforts by both state and federal resource agencies have also benefited Minnesota's amphibians and reptiles. Private conservation organizations, especially The Nature Conservancy, have further contributed toward statewide habitat protection goals. With strong citizen support, these and other conservation efforts will help insure the preservation of Minnesota's amphibians and reptiles.

POLLUTION

Unfortunately, little information is available about the susceptibility of amphibians and reptiles to environmental contaminants. It is possible that an entire population or species could perish before the cause of the tragedy could be discovered. Pesticides accumulate in prey species and over time may poison predator species as well. The loss of Spring Peepers in the Twin Cities metropolitan area may be related to the intensive use of chemicals in the urban environment as well as to significant habitat loss. Research has shown that the water in ponds affected by acid rain can prevent successful breeding in some amphibian species. Effective methods of cleaning up contaminated areas are urgently needed. Humans must find ways to greatly reduce obvious and insidious forms of chemical pollution before it is too late for amphibians and reptiles.

HARVESTING PRESSURES

Our native amphibians and reptiles are at risk from excessive hunting and overcollecting. In Minnesota the Snapping Turtle is the only reptile that is commercially harvested for food to any substantial extent. Presently, the State of Minnesota does not monitor

Blanding's Turtle and turtle crossing sign, Wabasha County, Minnesota

populations of this species, although they do keep records of turtle harvests. Large numbers of frogs and larval salamanders are taken in Minnesota and sold as fishing bait. No limits on collection are imposed, and the extent of this harvest is unknown and largely unregulated. Painted Turtles and Northern Leopard frogs are collected by biological supply houses under license by the Minnesota Department of Natural Resources, but there are no restrictions. Finally, the pet trade generates collection pressures on native reptiles. Minnesota species favored as pets include Gopher Snakes (Bullsnakes), Western Hognose Snakes, Fox Snakes, Milk Snakes, and Wood Turtles. Currently, Minnesota law protects Wood Turtles and Blanding's Turtles.

PERSECUTION

Numerous snakes are deliberately killed each year because of fear, hate, and ignorance. Snake haters dispatch snakes on sight assuming they are ridding the world of dangerous pests. Uninformed people often kill harmless species because they mistake them for venomous species. The killing of a snake is seldom justifiable, with the possible exception of a venomous species found near human habitation. Even the life of the venomous species can be spared if a person knowledgeable about the species can be contacted. The local animal control officer or conservation officer can assist in contacting knowledgeable authorities.

Throughout history, humans have singled out and intentionally persecuted certain species. For more than 50 years, Minnesota had an active rattlesnake bounty. It was administered by local township boards in several southeastern counties. For the years 1967 through 1982, Houston County paid bounties on 28,685 rattlesnakes. Only 191 bounties were paid in Minnesota in 1987. A Minnesota statute removing the authority to pay bounties on rattlesnakes was signed into law in 1989. Bounty systems have repeatedly been shown to be biologically unsound as well as difficult to monitor and administer.

COMMON AMPHIBIAN
AND REPTILE PROBLEMS

A number of common amphibian and reptile "problems" are of concern to the general public. Some of the problems concern the well-being of the animal, but more often it is the well-being of the human that is at issue. Many problems are easily solved by the exclusion of amphibians or reptiles from areas where people do not want them. The problems or situations described in this chapter address the most common interactions between amphibians and reptiles and humans. The state wildlife extension specialist at the University of Minnesota or a nongame wildlife biologist at the Minnesota Department of Natural Resources can address other situations. They can provide additional information or a referral to someone who can help. This chapter does not include problems that might arise from captive maintenance of reptiles or amphibians. Those questions can be answered by members of the Minnesota Herpetological Society.

SNAKES IN THE HOUSE OR GARAGE

A frequent problem encountered in the spring is the unwanted appearance of snakes, especially garter snakes, basking on the patio or front steps. Home owners also frequently complain about snakes in their basements or garages. Both of these problems are usually due to cracks or holes in the house's foundation. Garter snakes overwinter behind concrete steps or patios because these spaces provide a warm (above freezing) place to spend the winter. Snakes in the basement or garage may be looking for a place to overwinter, but they may also enter while searching for food, specifically mice.

This problem can be eliminated by sealing the cracks between the house and stoop or patio and filling holes or cracks in the foundation. Most snakes can fit through a crack ½ inch wide. Another way to discourage snakes is to eliminate their food source. Mice like to nest in woodpiles stacked adjacent to or in the house or garage and can also come through the same cracks as the snakes. Mice can be controlled by using traps or poison baits. Standard procedures and chemicals used by pest control companies are generally ineffective for dealing with snakes.

SNAKES IN THE YARD

Snakes are regularly found in yards in rural areas, because they are attracted to cover and food resources (rodents) found near the yards. The easiest way to discourage snakes is to make the yard unattractive to them. These measures include removing woodpiles from the vicinity of buildings and areas used by humans, trimming shrubs and trees to create a space of at least 6 inches between the ground and first branches, and keeping grass short throughout the yard. The only way to keep snakes out completely is by fencing. A normal chain-link, picket, or split-rail fence can be made snake-proof by attaching 18–24-inch-high hardware cloth to the outside of the fence and burying the bottom of the hardware cloth 2 to 4 inches into the soil. Snakes tend to travel along a fence rather than go over it. This is the style of fence recommended for keeping rattlesnakes out of yards (Peterson and Fritsch 1986).

SALAMANDERS IN THE BASEMENT

Tiger Salamanders are commonly found in older basements made of stone or cement block where there are spaces between the stones or blocks. They are also frequently found in wells and cisterns in rural areas. The salamanders are searching for a place to overwinter. If they do not find a moist site, they will desiccate and die. Salamanders are totally harmless and will not cause any damage. The solution for controlling both salamanders and snakes is the same—seal the cracks in the home's foundation. Not only will this prevent their entry, it will also help reduce home heating costs.

TURTLES NESTING IN THE YARD

More and more houses are being built along lakes and wetlands. These shorelines are where turtles have been laying eggs for centuries. Turtles continue to nest in the same area even if it has been changed into a manicured lawn or a child's sandbox. Species commonly encountered in yards are Painted Turtles, Snapping Turtles, and Blanding's Turtles. All nesting turtles can cause damage to turf while excavating their nests. The only turtle that may be a safety problem (especially to young children) is the Snapping Turtle because of its size and temperament.

The best way to deal with these turtles is to leave them alone. If a turtle is seen nesting in a yard, it should be observed, and the nest should be marked when egg laying is completed. Marking may keep the nest from being accidentally disturbed by humans, and later on the hatchlings can be observed when they emerge. If a nest is not wanted in the yard, the turtle must be returned to its pond before it lays eggs. The turtle may have to be returned several times before she will go to a different area to nest. A fence around the perimeter of the yard will keep turtles out. The fence has to go all the way to the ground and be sturdy, or turtles will push under it.

If a turtle lays her eggs before she can be moved, the nest should be left alone. Turtle eggs are easily killed by inexperienced handling. We do not recommend that the general public attempt to transplant or hatch turtle eggs.

SNAPPING TURTLES EATING DUCKLINGS

The Snapping Turtle is a predator and scavenger by nature. It eats fish, frogs, snakes, other turtles, and ducklings. This is a normal occurrence in nature. Sometimes a turtle population becomes excessive in a lake or pond and can cause high duckling mortality. Turtles can be controlled by trapping. Commercial turtle trappers can be hired to remove the turtles, but since they can only keep turtles over 10 inches long, continual control measures may be necessary.

SALAMANDERS, FROGS, OR TOADS IN THE ROAD OR YARD

Spring rains initiate the movements of amphibians in search of breeding ponds. In some areas these migrations consist of thousands of individuals. When these migrations intersect a road, the outcome can be a massacre. The same situation occurs in the fall, when young frogs and salamanders are moving to overwintering sites. At some localities the migrations are so large that roads become slick with dead animals.

Protection of amphibian migrations has recently become a conservation concern. In some areas in Europe and the United States, tunnels have been constructed for the animals to pass under the road. In Massachusetts some roads are closed during salamander migrations.

Home owners sometimes get upset about all the frogs and salamanders in their lawn and on their driveways when a movement corridor of amphibian migration goes through a yard or residential area. The animals will not hurt the property and will be gone within several days. Grass mowing and other yard activities should be curtailed during the migration.

AMPHIBIAN AND REPTILE IDENTIFICATION

HOW TO USE THIS BOOK

A principal objective of this book is to enable the user to identify Minnesota's amphibians and reptiles. Making an identification will likely require having the animal in hand or located where it can readily be observed. After an identification is made, the reader can become more familiar with that species' distribution, habitat requirements, and life history.

To make an identification, refer to the circular keys and decide which taxonomic group the animal belongs to (i.e., salamanders, frogs, turtles, lizards, or snakes), and then go to the appropriate key to determine the species. Examine the photographs and carefully read the description of the species in question to support the identification. Checking the range maps can be helpful, but do not rule out identification by distribution alone, because it may be a new county record.

If an animal cannot be identified, expert help is available from the Minnesota Herpetological Society, the James Ford Bell Museum of Natural History, and the Minnesota Department of Natural Resources' Nongame Wildlife Program. An unusual animal may be an escaped captive or may have been transported to Minnesota by way of truck or train. Several commonly reported nonnatives are the Eastern Box Turtle (*Terrapene carolina*), the Ornate Box Turtle (*Terrapene ornata*), and the Green Treefrog (*Hyla cinerea*).

Several species found in adjacent states near the Minnesota borders may someday be verified as Minnesota residents. Brief descriptions and photographs of these neighbors and potential inhabitants are found in the chapter "Species of Possible Occurrence."

DESCRIPTION OF SPECIES ACCOUNTS

Each species account is subdivided into categories, which are described in this section. A minimum of one color photograph and a Minnesota range map is included with each account. The description and photograph aid in species identification, and the remainder of the material provides useful and interesting information concerning the natural history of the animal.

Name

Each species has a common and a scientific name. Generally people are comfortable using the common name of an animal. Confusion arises, however, when one person refers to a particular kind of turtle as a "mud turtle" and someone else calls it a "painted turtle." To avoid confusion, scientists assign a two- or three-part Latin or Greek name to each species when it is first described. This name is based on its relationship with similar species and is recognized as the name for that particular species worldwide.

With two exceptions the common and scientific names used in this book are taken from "Standard Common and Current Scientific Names for North American Amphibians and Reptiles" by Joseph T. Collins (1990). Conant and Collins (1991) treat the Boreal Chorus Frog (*Pseudacris triseriata maculata*) as a subspecies of the Western Chorus Frog (*Pseudacris triseriata triseriata*), whereas Collins (1990) elevates the Boreal Chorus Frog to a full species. We have chosen to retain the Boreal Chorus Frog as a subspecies of the Western Chorus Frog. With the recent publication of Vogt (1993), the Ouachita Map Turtle (*Graptemys ouachitensis*) has been given full species recognition, elevating it from a subspecies of the False Map Turtle (*Graptemys pseudogeographica ouachitensis*). (See the species accounts for an explanation.)

Photographs

Photographs were selected to provide a typical and overall view of each species and to demonstrate key diagnostic features. Additional photographs are used to demonstrate key features, unusual color variations, juvenile patterns, or behavior. All photographs, unless credited otherwise, were taken by Barney Oldfield.

Maps

The distribution maps are a composite of museum records, literature reports, and sightings. The museum records are mapped as pre-1960 (◒), post-1960 (●), and literature and sighting records (○).

The majority of the museum records are from the James Ford Bell Museum of Natural History. Other museums with records of Minnesota specimens include the Academy of Natural Sciences, American Museum of Natural History, Carnegie Museum, George Mason University, Milwaukee County Public Museum, Museum of Comparative Zoology (Harvard), Nebraska State Museum, Royal Ontario Museum, Science Museum of Minnesota, United States National Museum (Smithsonian), University of Colorado, University of Kansas, University of Michigan Museum of Zoology, and University of South Dakota. Vouchers at museums other than the James Ford Bell Museum of Natural History and the Science Museum of Minnesota were not examined unless they represented a range limit or rare species.

Literature reports were compiled by reviewing all of the Minnesota literature (Moriarty and Jones 1988) and other pertinent publications. Sight records were collected through the Minnesota Nongame Wildlife Program, Minnesota Herpetological Society, colleagues, and other interested persons. Records included in the distribution maps are those records from credible sources.

A Minnesota map with county names and a legend of the distribution symbols can be found at the back of the book. A new county record or a species not known from a county since 1960 should be reported to the James Ford Bell Museum of Natural History or the Minnesota Nongame Wildlife Program (addresses in Resources). To be an acceptable record, the actual specimen or a recognizable photograph accompanied with a detailed locality description is needed. Refer to the field record on page 17 for a suggested record form.

Description

This section gives a description of a typical adult found in Minnesota followed by information about sexual differences, subadult color variations, and average and maximum sizes. Generally, measurements for salamanders, lizards, and snakes are given as total lengths (nose tip to tail tip). Anuran measurements are given as snout-vent lengths (tip of nose to vent), and turtle measurements are given as a straight line from the front edge of the carapace to the rear edge (not following the curve of the shell). Total lengths and snout-vent lengths are given for lizards because they frequently lose their tails, and the length given for rattlesnakes does not include the rattle because of its propensity for breaking. Finally, characteristics are noted that distinguish this species from others that might be confused with it.

Distribution

A brief description of the North American range of the species is given followed by its range in Minnesota. Maps of the entire North American distribution of Minnesota species can be found in Conant and Collins (1991).

Habitat

Because many amphibians and reptiles have specialized living requirements, a description of each species' preferred habitat is included. Because overwintering requirements are directly related to habitat, information concerning overwintering sites is also included under this heading. Knowing the type of habitat in which a species is typically found increases the odds of finding a particular species.

Life History

This section provides information on periods of seasonal activity, daily activity, home range, food preferences, courtship and breeding behavior, egg development periods, number of young, defense strategies, predators, and general natural history information.

Because frogs and toads have distinctive calls that are useful in identification, descriptions of their vocalizations are included in this section. Written descriptions are helpful, but it may become necessary to track down calling anurans or listen to recordings to become competent in recognizing calls. Recordings that are useful for learning the breeding calls of resident frogs and toads are listed in Resources.

Information contained in this book concerning natural history comes from our experience, knowledgeable field personnel, and various references listed in Literature Cited. We have attempted to incorporate information that deals specifically with the amphibians and reptiles of Minnesota.

Remarks

Additional information regarding a species that is pertinent or interesting is included in this section. When applicable, subspecies are described (see the following section), and nonstandard common names known to us are provided. Unusual behavior, longevity, and additional items of interest are also included. Species that were legally classified as state endangered, threatened, or special concern at the time this book went to press are noted; however, the Minnesota Department of Natural Resources should be consulted for the most recent status information.

SUBSPECIES

During the early planning stages of this book, we decided to depart from the standard nomenclature hierarchy found in many state and regional books. In this book, all species accounts begin with the common and scientific names of the species, and subspecies are not used. The names of subspecies found in Minnesota, and their distinguishing features, are described in Remarks. Because species are considered to be the biological unit and because each account is organized the same way, this approach is logical. One shortcoming of our method is a lack of emphasis when only one subspecies is found in the state and it may be in need of protective status as that subspecies.

Subspecies are geographical races of species. They are designated by a three-part (trinomial) name that contains the two-part (binomial) name of the species (e.g., Western Painted Turtle, *Chrysemys picta bellii,* is a subspecies of the Painted Turtle, *Chrysemys picta*). Subspecies all belong to a particular species, but they differ from one another by subtle coloration differences, scale counts, geography, and voice analysis. Because many subspecies have not been adequately studied across their entire range, discrepancies in distribution information exist. Numerous nomenclature changes will likely occur in the next few years as additional taxonomy studies are completed.

CHECKLIST OF AMPHIBIANS AND REPTILES NATIVE TO MINNESOTA

AMPHIBIANS *(19 Species)*		
CAUDATA **Salamanders**	*Ambystoma laterale* Hallowell, 1856	Blue-spotted Salamander
	Ambystoma tigrinum Green, 1825	Tiger Salamander
	A. t. diaboli Dunn, 1940	Gray Tiger Salamander
	A. t. tigrinum Green, 1825	Eastern Tiger Salamander
	Necturus maculosus (Rafinesque, 1818)	Mudpuppy
	N. m. maculosus (Rafinesque, 1818)	Mudpuppy
	Notophthalmus viridescens (Rafinesque, 1920)	Eastern Newt
	N. v. louisianensis (Wolterstorff, 1914)	Central Newt
	Plethodon cinereus (Green, 1818)	Redback Salamander
SALIENTIA **Frogs and Toads**	*Acris crepitans* (Green, 1818)	Northern Cricket Frog
	A. c. blanchardi Harper, 1947	Blanchard's Cricket Frog
	Bufo americanus Holbrook, 1836	American Toad
	B. a. americanus Holbrook, 1836	Eastern American Toad
	Bufo cognatus Say, 1823	Great Plains Toad
	Bufo hemiophrys Cope, 1886	Canadian Toad
	B. h. hemiophrys Cope, 1886	Canadian Toad
	Hyla chrysoscelis Cope, 1880	Cope's Gray Treefrog
	Hyla versicolor LeConte, 1825	Gray Treefrog
	Pseudacris crucifer (Wied-Neuwied, 1838)	Spring Peeper
	P. c. crucifer (Wied-Neuwied, 1838)	Northern Spring Peeper
	Pseudacris triseriata (Wied-Neuwied, 1838)	Western Chorus Frog
	P. t. maculata (Agassiz, 1850)	Boreal Chorus Frog
	P. t. triseriata (Wied-Neuwied, 1838)	Western Chorus Frog
	Rana catesbeiana Shaw, 1802	Bullfrog
	Rana clamitans Latreille, 1801	Green Frog
	R. c. clamitans Latreille, 1801	Green Frog
	Rana palustris LeConte, 1825	Pickerel Frog
	Rana pipiens Schreber, 1782	Northern Leopard Frog
	Rana septentrionalis Baird, 1854	Mink Frog
	Rana sylvatica LeConte, 1825	Wood Frog

REPTILES *(29 Species)*		
TESTUDINES **Turtles**	*Apalone mutica* (LeSueur, 1827)	Smooth Softshell
	A. m. mutica (LeSueur, 1827)	Midland Smooth Softshell
	Apalone spinifera (LeSueur, 1827)	Spiny Softshell
	A. s. hartwegi (Conant & Goin, 1941)	Western Spiny Softshell
	A. s. spinifera (LeSueur, 1827)	Eastern Spiny Softshell
	Chelydra serpentina (Linnaeus, 1758)	Snapping Turtle
	C. s. serpentina (Linnaeus, 1758)	Common Snapping Turtle
	Chrysemys picta (Schneider, 1783)	Painted Turtle
	C. p. bellii (Gray, 1831)	Western Painted Turtle
	Clemmys insculpta (LeConte, 1830)	Wood Turtle
	Emydoidea blandingii (Holbrook, 1838)	Blanding's Turtle
	Graptemys geographica (LeSueur, 1817)	Common Map Turtle
	Graptemys ouachitensis Vogt, 1980	Ouachita Map Turtle
	G. o. ouachitensis Vogt, 1980	Ouachita Map Turtle
	Graptemys pseudogeographica (Gray, 1831)	False Map Turtle
	G. p. pseudogeographica (Gray, 1831)	False Map Turtle
LACERTILIA **Lizards**	*Cnemidophorus sexlineatus* (Linnaeus, 1766)	Six-lined Racerunner
	C. s. viridis Lowe, 1966	Prairie Racerunner
	Eumeces fasciatus (Linnaeus, 1758)	Five-lined Skink
	Eumeces septentrionalis (Baird, 1858)	Prairie Skink
	E. s. septentrionalis (Baird, 1858)	Northern Prairie Skink
SERPENTES **Snakes**	*Coluber constrictor* Linnaeus, 1758	Racer
	C. c. flaviventris Say, 1823	Eastern Yellowbelly Racer
	Crotalus horridus Linnaeus, 1758	Timber Rattlesnake
	Diadophis punctatus (Linnaeus, 1766)	Ringneck Snake
	D. p. arnyi Kennicott, 1859	Prairie Ringneck Snake
	D. p. edwardsii (Merrem, 1820)	Northern Ringneck Snake
	Elaphe obsoleta (Say, 1823)	Rat Snake
	E. o. obsoleta (Say, 1823)	Black Rat Snake
	Elaphe vulpina (Baird & Girard, 1853)	Fox Snake
	E. v. vulpina (Baird & Girard, 1853)	Western Fox Snake
	Heterodon nasicus Baird & Girard, 1852	Western Hognose Snake
	H. n. nasicus Baird & Girard, 1852	Plains Hognose Snake
	Heterodon platirhinos Latreille, 1801	Eastern Hognose Snake
	Lampropeltis triangulum (Lacépède, 1788)	Milk Snake
	L. t. triangulum (Lacépède, 1788)	Eastern Milk Snake
	Nerodia sipedon (Linnaeus, 1758)	Northern Water Snake
	N. s. sipedon (Linnaeus, 1758)	Northern Water Snake
	Opheodrys vernalis (Harlan, 1827)	Smooth Green Snake
	Pituophis catenifer (Blainville, 1835)	Gopher Snake
	P. c. sayi (Schlegel, 1837)	Bullsnake
	Sistrurus catenatus (Rafinesque, 1818)	Massasauga
	S. c. catenatus (Rafinesque, 1818)	Eastern Massasauga
	Storeria dekayi (Holbrook, 1836)	Brown Snake
	S. d. texana Trapido, 1944	Texas Brown Snake
	Storeria occipitomaculata (Storer, 1839)	Redbelly Snake
	S. o. occipitomaculata (Storer, 1839)	Northern Redbelly Snake
	S. o. pahasapae Smith, 1963	Black Hills Redbelly Snake
	Thamnophis radix (Baird & Girard, 1853)	Plains Garter Snake
	T. r. haydenii (Kennicott, 1860)	Western Plains Garter Snake
	T. r. radix (Baird & Girard, 1853)	Eastern Plains Garter Snake
	Thamnophis sirtalis (Linnaeus, 1758)	Common Garter Snake
	T. s. parietalis (Say, 1823)	Red-sided Garter Snake
	T. s. sirtalis (Linnaeus, 1758)	Eastern Garter Snake
	Tropidoclonion lineatum (Hallowell, 1856)	Lined Snake

SPECIES OF POSSIBLE OCCURRENCE IN MINNESOTA *(6 Species)*

Ambystoma maculatum (Shaw, 1802)	Spotted Salamander
Hemidactylium scutatum (Temminck & Schlegel, 1838)	Four-toed Salamander
Bufo woodhousii Girard, 1854	Woodhouse's Toad
B. w. woodhousii Girard, 1854	Woodhouse's Toad
Spea bombifrons (Cope, 1863)	Plains Spadefoot
Sternotherus odoratus (Latreille, 1802)	Common Musk Turtle
Ophisaurus attenuatus Cope, 1880	Slender Glass Lizard
O. a. attenuatus Cope, 1880	Western Slender Glass Lizard

KEYS TO
AMPHIBIANS AND REPTILES
NATIVE TO MINNESOTA

USE OF CIRCULAR KEYS

The following keys are designed to assist in identifying the amphibians and reptiles found in Minnesota. The circular format allows the user to move easily through a dichotomous (two-part) system. The first key guides the user to one of the five major groupings: frogs, salamanders, snakes, lizards, and turtles. These keys are designed to be used with adult specimens and may not work for juveniles.

Start at the center of each key and work to the outer ring. Drawings of certain features are referenced in the keys and found at the end of the keys. When a decision has been made, refer to the page numbers below the species name. If the photograph does not match the species, then back up to the previous ring and try again.

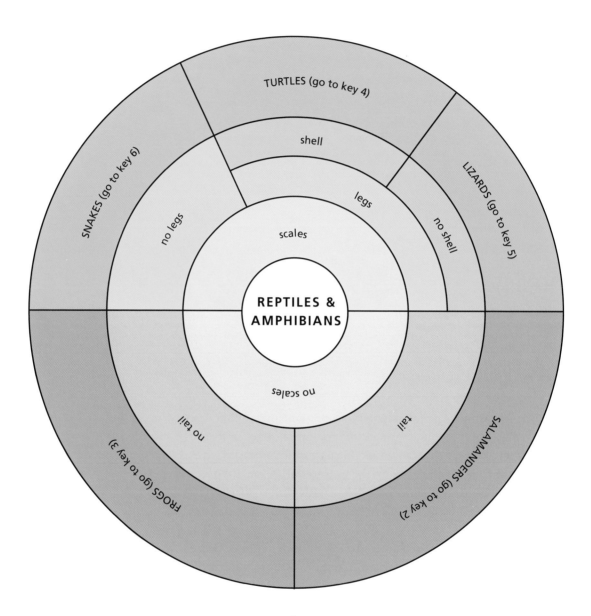

1

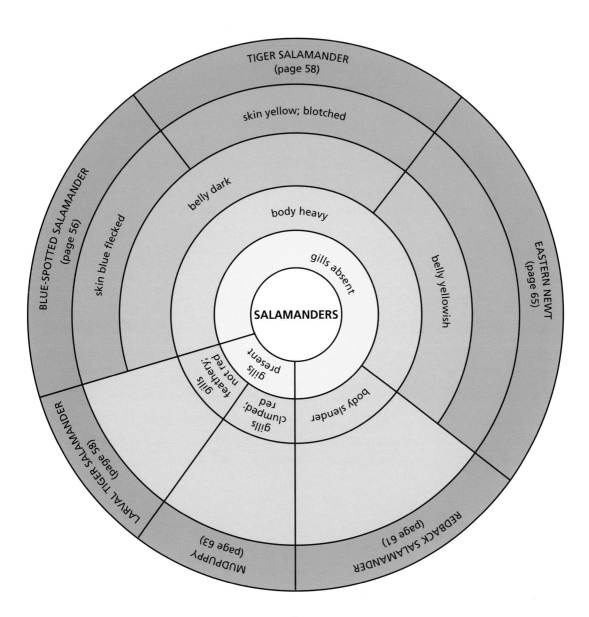

TIGER SALAMANDER
(page 58)

skin yellow; blotched

belly dark

body heavy

gills absent

BLUE-SPOTTED SALAMANDER
(page 56)

skin blue flecked

EASTERN NEWT
(page 65)

belly yellowish

SALAMANDERS

gills
present

gills
feathery;
not red

gills
clumped;
red

body slender

LARVAL TIGER SALAMANDER
(page 58)

MUDPUPPY
(page 63)

REDBACK SALAMANDER
(page 61)

2

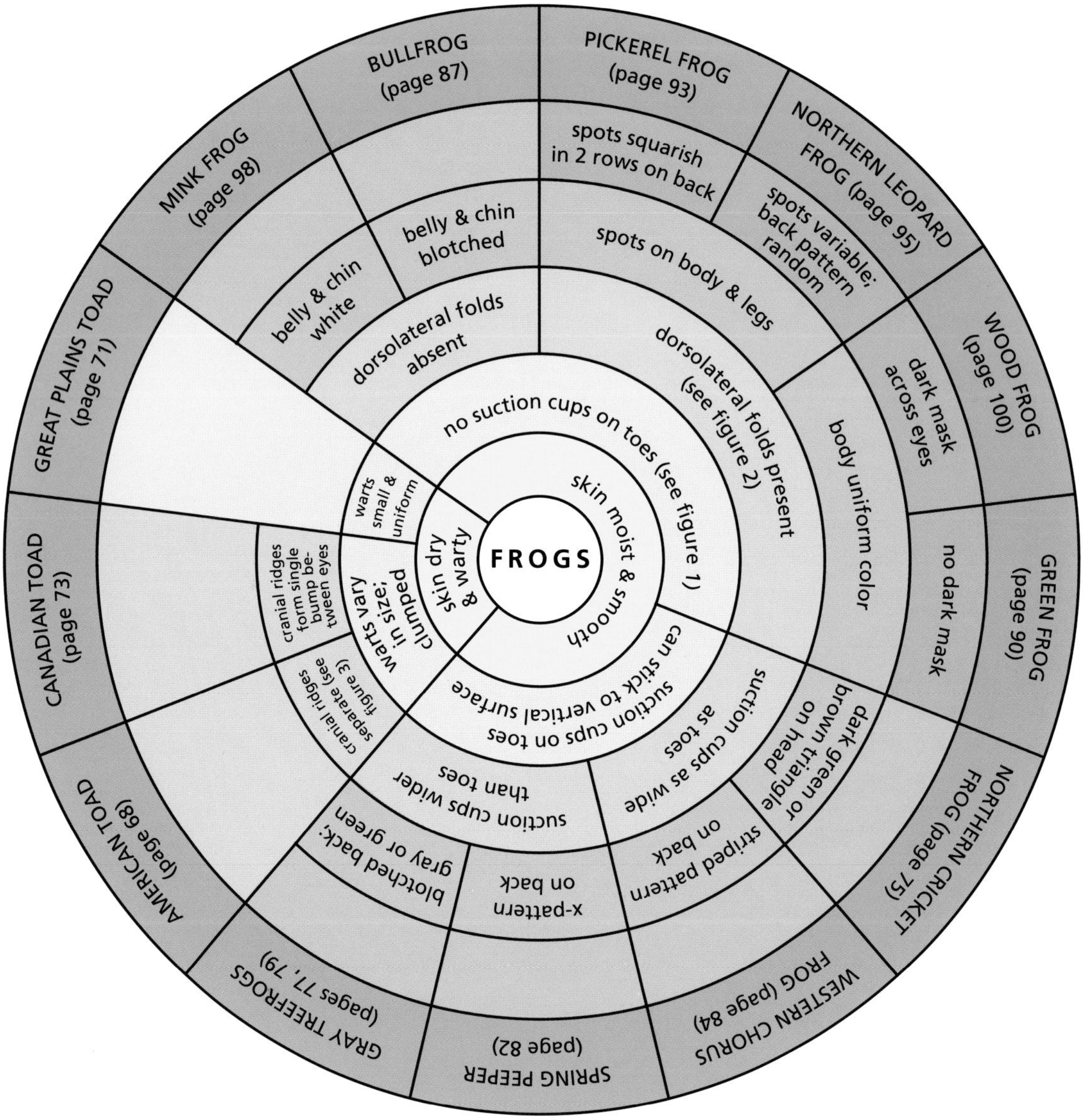

FROGS

Center: FROGS

Inner ring (skin characteristics):
- skin moist & smooth
- skin dry & warty

Second ring:
- no suction cups on toes (see figure 2)
- can stick to vertical surface
- suction cups on toes
- warts small & uniform
- warts vary in size; clumped

Third ring:
- dorsolateral folds present (see figure 1)
- dorsolateral folds absent
- suction cups as wide as toes
- suction cups wider than toes
- cranial ridges form single bump between eyes
- cranial ridges separate (see figure 3)

Fourth ring:
- spots on body & legs
- body uniform color
- belly & chin blotched
- belly & chin white
- brown triangle on head
- striped pattern on back
- x-pattern on back
- blotched back; gray or green

Fifth ring (detail):
- spots squarish in 2 rows on back
- spots variable; back pattern random
- dark mask across eyes
- no dark mask

Outer ring (species):
- BULLFROG (page 87)
- PICKEREL FROG (page 93)
- NORTHERN LEOPARD FROG (page 95)
- WOOD FROG (page 100)
- GREEN FROG (page 90)
- NORTHERN CRICKET FROG (page 75)
- WESTERN CHORUS FROG (page 84)
- SPRING PEEPER (page 82)
- GRAY TREEFROGS (pages 77, 79)
- AMERICAN TOAD (page 68)
- CANADIAN TOAD (page 73)
- GREAT PLAINS TOAD (page 71)
- MINK FROG (page 98)

3

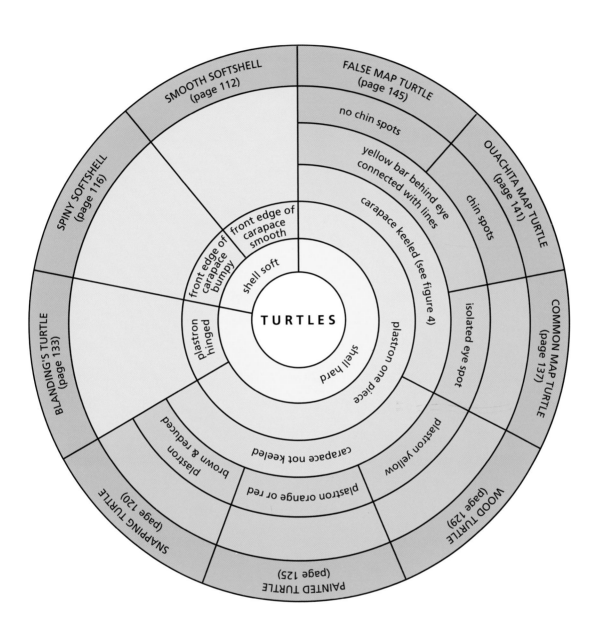

SMOOTH SOFTSHELL (page 112)

FALSE MAP TURTLE (page 145)

no chin spots

yellow bar behind eye connected with lines

OUACHITA MAP TURTLE (page 141)

chin spots

SPINY SOFTSHELL (page 116)

carapace keeled (see figure 4)

front edge of carapace smooth

front edge of carapace bumpy

shell soft

isolated eye spot

COMMON MAP TURTLE (page 137)

TURTLES

plastron hinged

shell hard

plastron one piece

BLANDING'S TURTLE (page 133)

plastron yellow

WOOD TURTLE (page 129)

plastron brown & reduced

carapace not keeled

plastron orange or red

SNAPPING TURTLE (page 120)

PAINTED TURTLE (page 125)

4

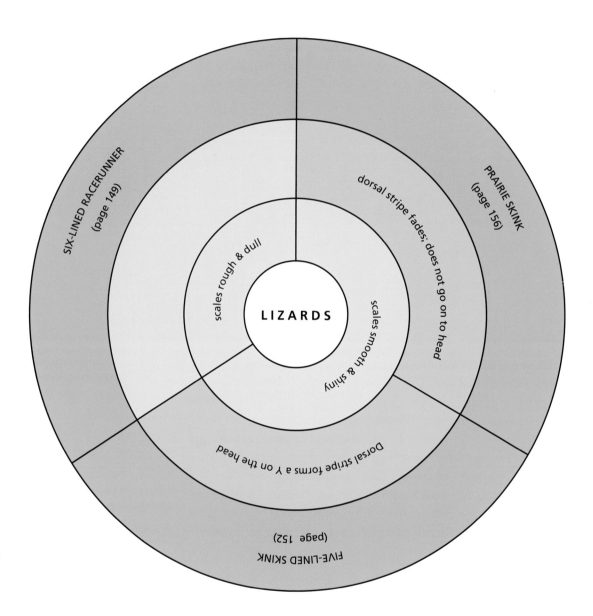

SIX-LINED RACERUNNER
(page 149)

PRAIRIE SKINK
(page 156)

dorsal stripe fades; does not go on to head

scales rough & dull

scales smooth & shiny

LIZARDS

Dorsal stripe forms a Y on the head

FIVE-LINED SKINK
(page 152)

5

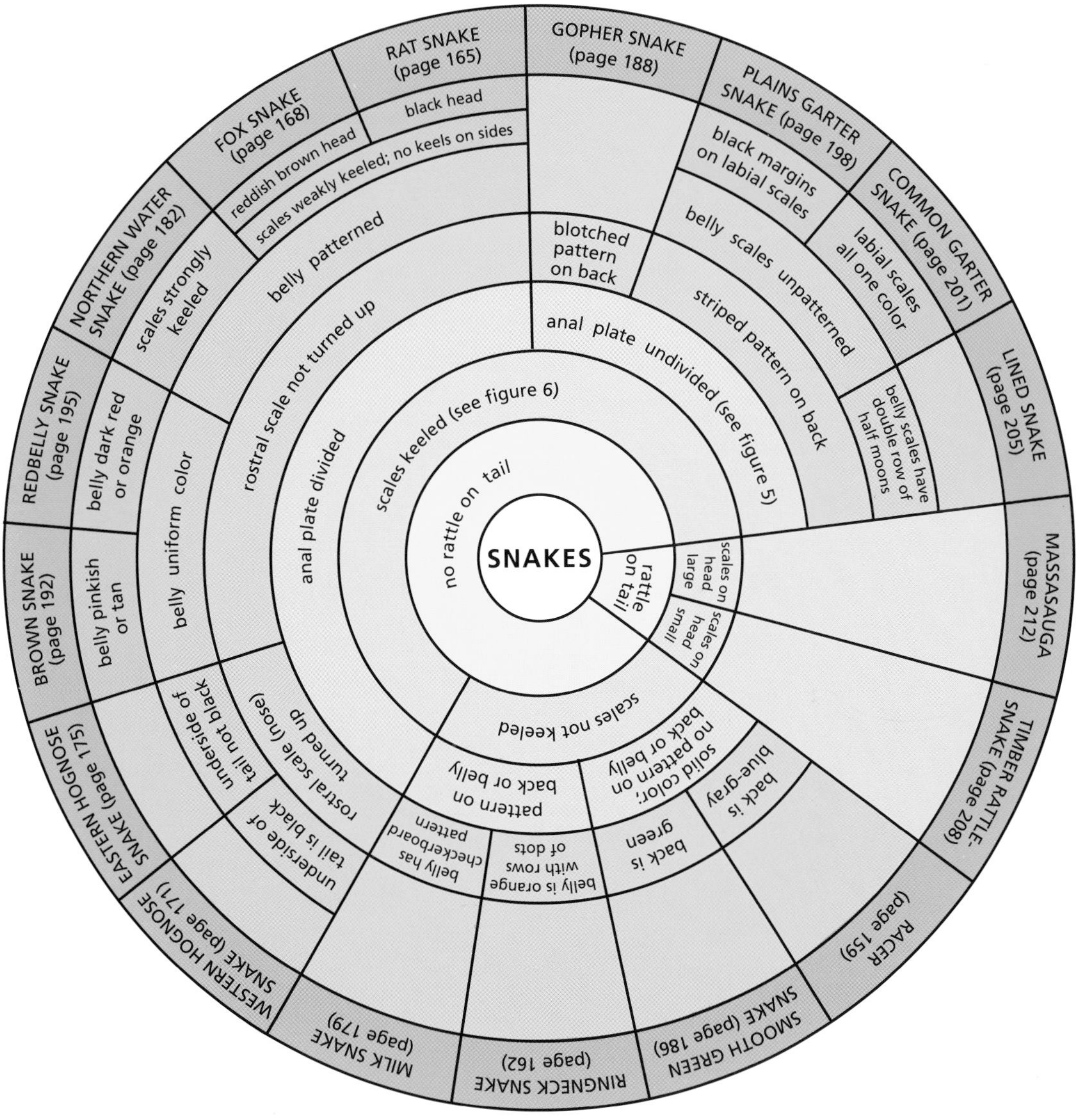

SNAKES

Central: **SNAKES**

Inner ring:
- no rattle on tail
- rattle on tail

Second ring:
- scales keeled (see figure 6)
- anal plate undivided (see figure 5)
- anal plate divided
- scales not keeled
- scales on head large / scales on head small

Branches and outer species:

- RAT SNAKE (page 165) — black head
- FOX SNAKE (page 168) — reddish brown head
- scales weakly keeled; no keels on sides
- GOPHER SNAKE (page 188)
- PLAINS GARTER SNAKE (page 198) — black margins on labial scales
- COMMON GARTER SNAKE (page 201) — labial scales all one color
- belly scales unpatterned
- blotched pattern on back
- belly patterned
- striped pattern on back
- NORTHERN WATER SNAKE (page 182) — scales strongly keeled
- LINED SNAKE (page 205) — belly scales have double row of half moons
- rostral scale not turned up
- REDBELLY SNAKE (page 195) — belly dark red or orange
- belly uniform color
- MASSASAUGA (page 212)
- TIMBER RATTLE SNAKE (page 208)
- BROWN SNAKE (page 192) — belly pinkish or tan
- EASTERN HOGNOSE SNAKE (page 175) — underside of tail not black
- WESTERN HOGNOSE SNAKE (page 171) — underside of tail is black
- rostral scale (nose) turned up
- pattern on back or belly
- no pattern on back or belly
- solid color; blue-gray
- RACER (page 159) — back is blue-gray
- SMOOTH GREEN SNAKE (page 186) — back is green
- RINGNECK SNAKE (page 162) — belly is orange with rows of dots
- MILK SNAKE (page 179) — belly has checkerboard pattern

6

Figure 1 **TOE PADS**

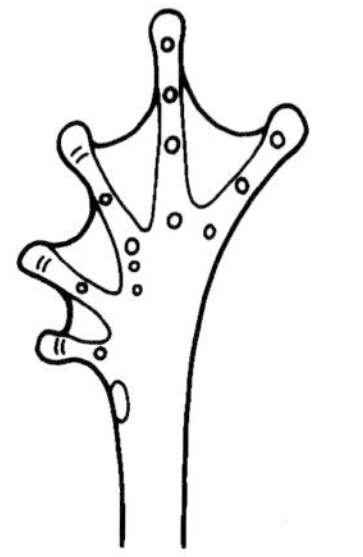

enlarged
(suction cups)

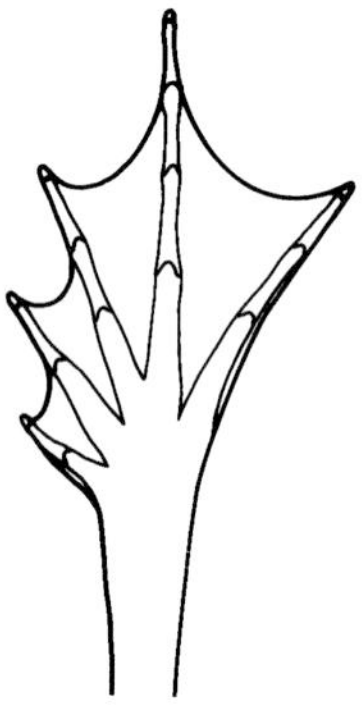

not enlarged

Figure 2 **DORSOLATERAL FOLD**

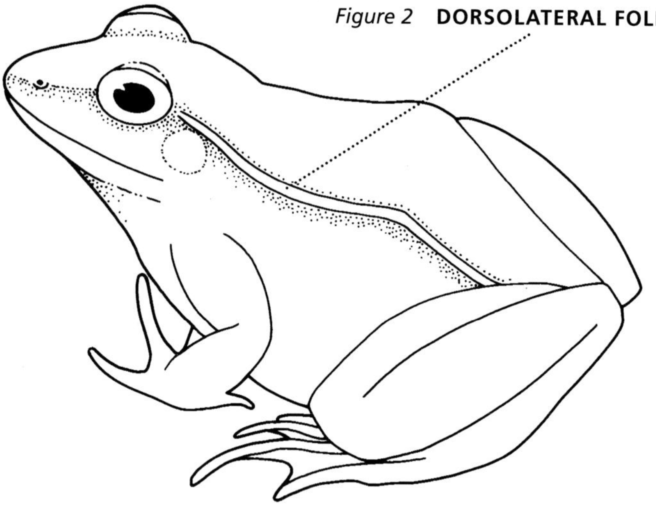

Figure 3
**CRANIAL
RIDGES**

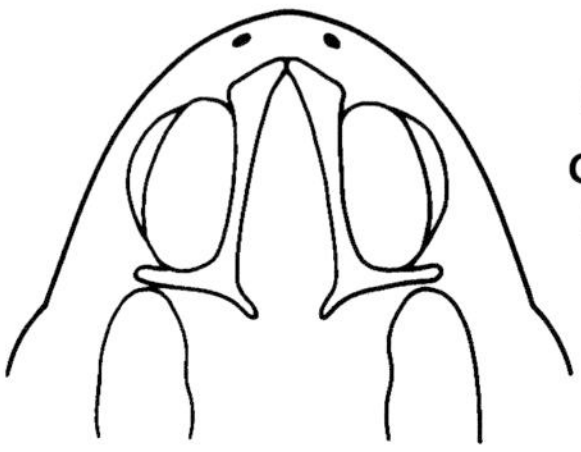

separate

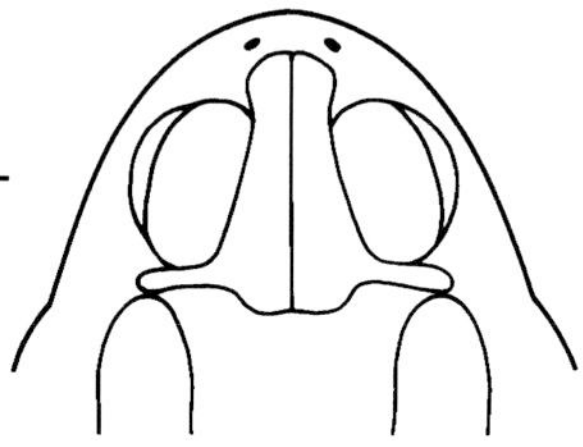

fused

Figure 4
CARAPACE

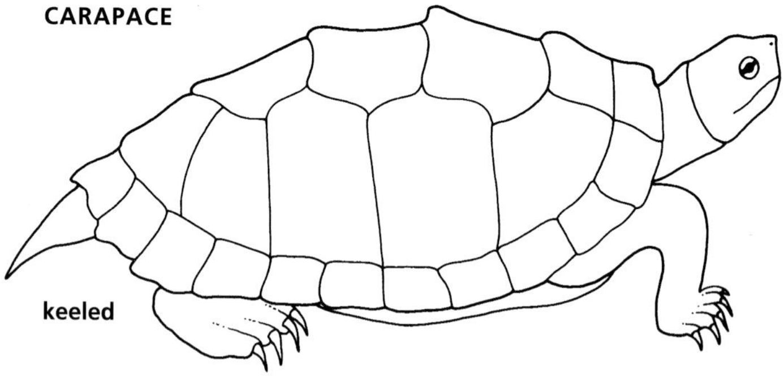

keeled

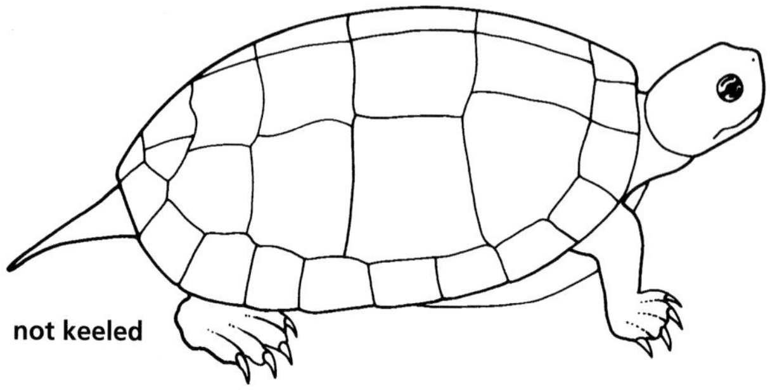

not keeled

Figure 5 **ANAL PLATE**

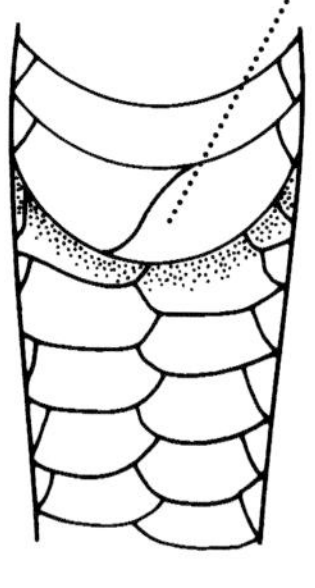

divided

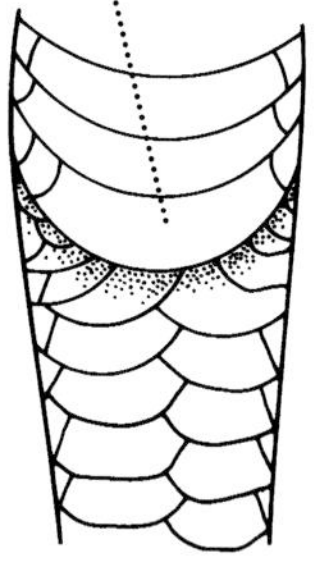

undivided

Figure 6 **SCALES**

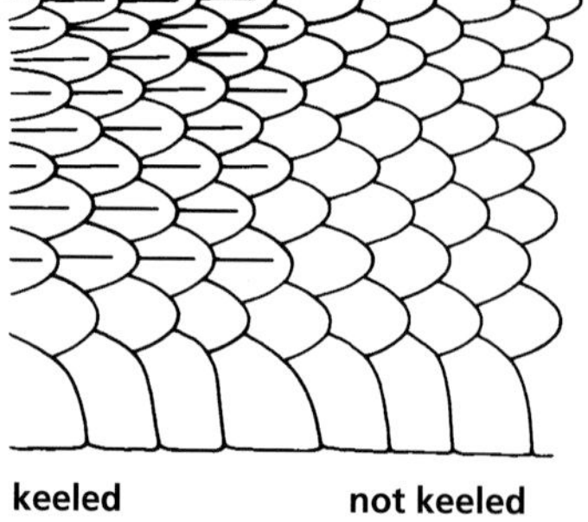

keeled

not keeled

AMPHIBIANS

CLASS AMPHIBIA

Amphibians evolved from fish ancestors around 400 million years ago. The evolution of lungs and limbs allowed ancestral amphibians to colonize land during the late Devonian period and to become the first land-dwelling vertebrates. Modern-day amphibians consist of 3,260 species in three orders. Restricted to the tropics, the order Gymnophiona (caecilians) contains 154 species of secretive, wormlike creatures. Members of the order Caudata (salamanders) have four legs, a relatively long tail, and a head distinct from the body. There are approximately 336 species of salamanders worldwide of which 100 are found in the United States. There are over 2,700 species of the order Anura (Salientia) (frogs and toads) of which 80 species are found in the United States. Frogs and toads are collectively referred to as anurans. They are tailless, lack a distinct neck, and have elongated rear legs adapted for jumping. Five salamanders and 14 anurans are found in Minnesota.

The name *amphibian* means double life, referring to the aquatic and terrestrial phases found in the life cycles of many species. Most amphibians must live in water or in a relatively damp environment to prevent dehydration. Their glandular skin lacks an outer covering, such as scales or water-impermeable skin, to retard water loss. This moisture requirement also explains their greatly increased activity during or shortly after rainfall. By far, the largest diversity and concentration of amphibians are found in regions with abundant rainfall.

All North American amphibians lay eggs. Lacking a protective shell, the eggs are generally laid in the water. They hatch into gill-bearing larvae that later transform into air-breathing adults. Two exceptions to this life cycle are found in Minnesota. Mudpuppies live an entirely aquatic life, and Redback Salamanders lack an aquatic larval stage.

Amphibians are the only class of land-dwelling vertebrates that have external gills during some phase of their life. Amphibian larvae always pass through a stage with external gills either during development in the egg or later as a free-living animal. Nearly all amphibians lack claws. They have blunt toe tips or toe disks. Some species of toads have spurs on their rear feet, which they use for digging.

Amphibian skin has several interesting features. Numerous mucus glands in the skin produce a slimy secretion that helps protect the skin, and the mucus itself is useful for slipping out of a predator's grip. Poison glands that are found in the skin of a number of species serve as another defensive mechanism. The large glands behind the eyes of a toad are called parotoid glands and are a congregation of poison glands. When handled roughly, toads release a whitish secretion from these glands that is extremely irritating to the membranes of the mouths of predators. Dogs have been fatally poisoned by chewing on certain species of tropical toads, which are not native to Minnesota.

Mudpuppy, head and gills,
Goodhue County, Minnesota

Several species of treefrogs are capable of remarkable color changes. A hormone released from the pituitary gland causes a pigment shift in special skin cells called melanophores. Environmental temperature and the emotional state of the animal affect the color displayed. Males often display bright colors during courtship. A skin color that matches or blends with the surroundings is useful for eluding predators. In Minnesota, the Gray Treefrog is capable of changing from dark gray to bright lime green.

Respiration is another important function of amphibian skin. Moist, highly vascular areas of their skin permit gaseous exchange with the environment. Salamanders of the family Plethodontidae are lungless and maintain a terrestrial existence by "breathing" through their skin and the lining of their mouth. The Redback Salamanders found in Minnesota are members of this family. Periodically, amphibians shed their outer skin layer and in many cases consume it.

Courtship and reproduction are an important and interesting aspect of amphibian life history. Most species mass into breeding congregations to carry out courtship activities and egg laying. Salamanders normally concentrate in the spring or the fall. During these congregations males court females by pushing, rubbing, and nudging them. Fertilization is internal, although copulation does not occur. Following courtship, females use their cloacal lips to pick up gelatinous, sperm-filled sacs (spermatophores) deposited by males.

Frog and toad breeding season tends to be a raucous affair. Male anurans reach the breeding ponds first and begin vocalizing. Each species has its own distinctive voice, and several species may call from the same pond simultaneously. Noise produced in the male's larynx is amplified and resonated with single or paired vocal sacs. After females arrive, there is much pushing and shoving between males to establish dominance over an individual female. Male anurans clasp females behind their front legs in what is called amplexus, and the eggs are fertilized externally as she lays them. Some male frogs and toads are nonselective of mates and will mount other males. Mounted males may emit a guttural noise to signal the other male to release. Some species set up territories, which reduce fights over individual females and extend the length of the breeding season. The number of eggs laid may vary from a few hundred eggs to several thousand, depending on the species.

The delicate amphibian egg, which requires high moisture for survival and development, is covered with a gelatinous coat and is generally darkly pigmented. Dark pigment absorbs sunlight and increases egg temperature, expediting development of the embryo.

After a short egg development period, many species of amphibians

Spring Peeper, male calling, Goodhue County, Minnesota

American Toads, amplexsus, Fillmore County, Minnesota

exhibit a free-living aquatic stage during which they use gills to obtain oxygen. Larval anurans are popularly called tadpoles or polliwogs. Their round bodies and flattened tails are familiar to almost everyone. Salamander larvae generally possess legs and external gills.

Amphibian transformation or metamorphosis is a fascinating and complex phenomenon. Rotund little tadpoles sprout legs, lose their tails, trade gills for lungs, develop large mouths, and hop out onto land. Salamander larvae undergo a similar change but with fewer outward physical alterations. In Minnesota, transformation may take a few weeks or as long as two years, depending upon the species. Most amphibians reach breeding age in 1 or 2 years. The average life span is 3 to 8 years, but some species are known to exceed 25 years in captivity.

The ecological significance of amphibians is just becoming appreciated. Adult amphibians are entirely carnivorous predators. They have voracious appetites and consume extraordinarily large quantities of arthropods and other invertebrates. Not only do amphibians consume large quantities of animal protein, they in turn serve as an important food source for native fish, birds, reptiles, and mammals. Amphibians command an important position in the natural food

web. There has been a sharp decline in the numbers of some amphibian species, especially anurans, during the last decade. Herpetologists have expressed a deep concern about this problem and they are trying to identify the causes of and find solutions to this compelling problem.

Green Frog, larva (tadpole), Goodhue County, Minnesota

AMPHIBIAN FAMILIES NATIVE TO MINNESOTA

Family Ambystomatidae—Mole Salamanders

Mole salamanders are restricted entirely to North America. Seventeen species are found throughout the United States. These salamanders are stout-bodied with short, wide heads and four well-developed limbs. There are four toes on the front feet and five on the hind feet. Generally the costal grooves are well developed. Eggs are laid in the water. Gill-bearing larvae transform into terrestrial adults, which spend most of their lives underground in mammal tunnels or under logs. Adults are most frequently observed during spring breeding activities and fall migrations.

The Blue-spotted Salamander and the Tiger Salamander are the representatives of this family found in Minnesota. A third species, the Spotted Salamander, is found in Wisconsin within 200 meters (219 yards) of the St. Croix River.

Family Plethodontidae—Lungless Salamanders

The plethodontids are the largest family of salamanders, with over 200 species worldwide. One-third of the plethodontid species are found in the United States. Two-thirds of the species are neotropical, found in South America and Central America, and three species are found along the Mediterranean coast of Europe. Plethodontids are the only group of salamanders to have successfully invaded tropical habitats.

This family is highly variable. The primary physical trait of this family is the lack of lungs. Respiration is accomplished through the moist skin. It is the only family that possesses a naso-labial groove that runs from the nostril to the upper margin of the lip. This groove is used for various chemosensory functions, such as courtship and searching for food. Body forms range from long and slender to short and stout. Most species have four front toes and five back toes.

Minnesota has one representative of this family, the Redback Salamander. A second species, the Four-toed Salamander, is found within 1 km (0.6 mile) of the state border in Wisconsin.

Family Proteidae—Waterdogs and Mudpuppies

The waterdogs are a small family of six species worldwide. Five species are found in the United States and southern Canada, and one species is found in southern Europe. The salamanders in this family are all neotenic. As adults, they possess both gills and lungs. They never leave the water, even under drought conditions.

Minnesota has one species, the Mudpuppy, which belongs to the only North American genus.

Family Salamandridae—Newts

The newts are a small family in the United States with only six species in two genera. Three species (genus *Notophthalmus*) are found in the eastern United States, and three species are found along the West Coast (genus *Taricha*). Most species in the family are found in Europe, and representatives are found in northern Africa, China, Southeast Asia, and Japan.

Terrestrial forms of these salamanders have rough skin, whereas aquatic forms have smooth skin. Costal grooves are absent in both forms. Breeding is variable, with some species breeding in the water and some on land. Subadult newts may spend several years as terrestrial salamanders, which are called efts.

Minnesota only has one species, the Eastern Newt, belonging to the newt family.

Family Bufonidae—True Toads

With over 340 species in the family, true toads are found on every continent except Antarctica. The toads found in Australia, however, were introduced. True toads are normally heavy bodied with wide heads and rough, dry-feeling skin, often covered with "warts." Their thicker epidermis slows moisture loss allowing them to withstand relatively dry environments compared to true frogs and treefrogs. Other characteristics include large parotoid glands behind the head, short legs, and reduced webbing between the toes. The eggs of North American Bufonids are laid in long, gelatinous strings.

Minnesota's three representatives of this family, all in the genus *Bufo*, are the American Toad, the Great Plains Toad, and the Canadian Toad. One additional species, Woodhouse's Toad, is found just across the Minnesota border in South Dakota.

Family Hylidae—Treefrogs

Treefrogs are found on every continent except Antarctica. With over 640 species, this family is one of the largest families of frogs. Treefrogs are slender bodied, with a flattened profile. Most have disks on their toe pads to assist in climbing. The majority of species are arboreal, but some species have evolved for terrestrial or semi-aquatic habitats.

Minnesota has five species of hylids in three genera, including the Northern Cricket Frog, Cope's Gray Treefrog, the Gray Treefrog, the Spring Peeper, and the Western Chorus Frog. In Minnesota the two *Hyla* species are primarily arboreal.

Family Ranidae—True Frogs

The family Ranidae, or true frogs, is another widespread family, with 610 species and representatives on all the continents except Antarctica. Generally, true frogs have large eyes and tympanums and large, highly developed hind legs. The world's largest frog, the Goliath Frog of central Africa, is a member of this family. Minnesota's largest frog, the Bullfrog, is also in the family Ranidae.

Minnesota has six representatives of the family Ranidae including the Bullfrog, the Green Frog, the Pickerel Frog, the Northern Leopard Frog, the Mink Frog, and the Wood Frog.

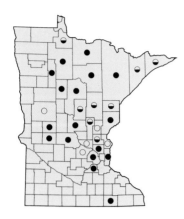

Blue-spotted Salamander

Ambystoma laterale

Description

The adult Blue-spotted Salamander has a black, blue black, or grayish black dorsal surface with a somewhat lighter belly. The sides are speckled with small bluish-turquoise spots. Some spots extend onto the back and belly. These salamanders have 12 costal grooves and attain a length of 7 to 13 centimeters (3 to 5 inches) (Conant and Collins 1991). During the breeding season males have swollen cloacas. Newly transformed larvae have yellow speckles instead of blue, but otherwise they resemble the adults.

Distribution

Blue-spotted Salamanders range across the extreme northeastern United States and southern Canada, west to Minnesota and Ontario. In Minnesota, this species can be found in the northeastern and east-central portions of the state from the Minnesota River northward. An isolated population occurs in Mower County near Austin, in southern Minnesota.

Blue-spotted Salamander, adult, Pine County, Minnesota

Habitat

These salamanders inhabit the forest floor of moist woodlands and boreal forests. Small ponds and woodland potholes that retain water until late summer are used for breeding (Wilbur and Collins 1973). Adults may be found in the summer under bark, logs, and moss. Rocks and logs at the edges of ponds are known to serve as over-wintering sites (Vogt 1981).

Life History

Blue-spotted Salamanders feed on a variety of invertebrates, including beetles, snails, earthworms, sow bugs, and spiders (Minton 1972). The larvae eat small aquatic crustaceans.

Courtship activity has been observed as early as 15 April in Wisconsin (Vogt 1981). Most activity occurs at night, and the elaborate courtship activity involves the male clasping the female from above while rubbing his nose over the front part of her body. Periods of thrashing about in the water are followed by the pair lying quietly on the pond bottom. After these courtship encounters cease, the male climbs off the female and deposits one to three spermatophores. The female picks these up with her cloacal lips, and fertilization occurs internally. Eggs are laid singly or in small clusters of six to ten at the bottom of the pond and are attached to vegetation. Larvae transform into subadults during August (Pfingsten and Downs 1989).

Remarks

The Blue-spotted salamander arches its tail and waves it slowly back and forth when approached by a predator. An apparently foul-tasting, sticky substance is excreted from glands at the base of the waving tail (Pfingsten and Downs 1989).

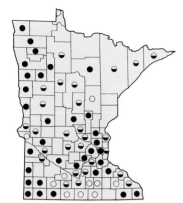

Tiger Salamander

Ambystoma tigrinum

Description

The Tiger Salamander is the largest land-dwelling salamander in Minnesota. Characteristic features of Tiger Salamanders include a stout body, a broad head, and small eyes. The back and sides of this amphibian may be dark brown, dark gray, dark green, or black with numerous yellow green to yellow gold bars, blotches, or spots. Tiger salamanders tend to become more blotched and less spotted with age. In Minnesota, some Tiger Salamanders are almost totally black. The belly surface is lighter, and belly spots are not as vivid as dorsal spots. There are 11 to 14 costal grooves. Adult Tiger Salamanders reach a total length of 18 to 33 centimeters (7 to 13 inches) (Conant and Collins 1991). The largest Minnesota specimen, from Douglas County, with a total length of 34.5 centimeters (13¾ inches) is the largest reported specimen for this species. Males have swollen cloacas during the breeding season. The larval form is yellowish green with small dark spots and has external gills attached to the base of the head. Larvae reach adult size before transformation.

Distribution

Tiger Salamander, adult, Goodhue County, Minnesota

The Tiger Salamander ranges throughout most of the United States excluding the extreme northeast and the western coastal states. The

salamander is found all across the state of Minnesota, although a number of counties lack verifiable records.

Habitat

Tiger Salamanders utilize many types of habitats, including marshes, prairie ponds, farm ponds, woodland ponds, and lakes. Except in

Tiger Salamander, larva, Minnesota

early spring and fall, adults spend most of their time underground in mammal burrows, crayfish burrows, or in self-excavated burrows. Breckenridge (1944) observed Tiger Salamanders living in gopher and ground squirrel tunnels.

Life History

Adults are commonly found above ground during spring and fall migrations to and from breeding ponds and upland habitats. Many are accidentally trapped in window wells and swimming pools during migration. They are also encountered crossing highways during rainy weather, especially during spring and fall. Overland movements are made nocturnally or on overcast days.

Tiger Salamanders are carnivorous during both larval and adult stages. Adults are known to eat earthworms, crickets, grasshoppers, other insects, small mice, and other amphibians, including their own larvae. Cannibalistic larvae develop grotesquely large heads (Hammerson 1982).

Warm nocturnal spring rain stimulates movements to breeding ponds. Eighteen to over 100 eggs are laid in loose masses in early to late April after a unique strutting courtship (Kumpf 1934) during which the male nudges and pushes the female around the breed-

Tiger Salamander, diaboli *subspecies*

ing pond and then leaves her. The female then follows the male to reinitiate breeding. Eggs are attached to vegetation near the pond bottom. Transformation to adults takes place during late August and September. The majority of salamanders found in the fall are newly transformed adults. They are sexually mature by their first spring.

The Tiger Salamander is capable of becoming sexually mature without transforming into a terrestrial form. The process of becoming sexually mature as a larval form is progenesis. Progenic salamanders have not been reported from Minnesota, but populations have been found in Michigan (Hensley 1964).

Skin secretions of the Tiger Salamander can be irritating to the eyes and mucous membranes. This secretion serves as a useful defense mechanism.

Remarks

Two subspecies of the Tiger Salamander are recognized in Minnesota (Conant and Collins 1991). The Eastern Tiger Salamander (*Ambystoma tigrinum tigrinum*), a dark animal with yellow markings, is found throughout most of the state. The Gray Tiger Salamander (*A. t. diaboli*), a light olive salamander with scattered small dark spots, has been reported in extreme west-central Minnesota.

Tiger Salamanders have been known to live 25 years in captivity (Bowler 1977). Adult Tiger Salamanders are often incorrectly identified as lizards. Salamanders superficially resemble lizards in body form, but lizards (reptiles) have scales and salamanders (amphibians) do not. Larval Tiger Salamanders are used as fishing bait and sold as "waterdogs," and they are sometimes misnamed "mudpuppies."

Redback Salamander

Plethodon cinereus

Description

The Redback Salamander is the smallest salamander in Minnesota. This salamander is appropriately named for its brick-red dorsal stripe, although some may have a dull brownish stripe. The sides and belly vary from brown to gray, with white flecking on the belly giving a salt-and-pepper appearance (Pfingsten and Downs 1989). A gray or "leadback" phase and an all-red or "erythristic" phase are also known, but they have not been documented in Minnesota. A large specimen is 10 centimeters (4 inches) in length and the average range is 6 to 8 centimeters (2½ to 3 inches); males are slightly smaller than females (Conant and Collins 1991).

The body is long and slender with four small, delicate legs. There are 18 to 19 distinct costal grooves. The Redback Salamander has five toes on the hind feet. The Four-toed Salamander is similar in its dorsal appearance to the Redback Salamander, but it has four toes on the hind feet. The Four-toed Salamander has a bright white belly with black spots.

Distribution

The Redback Salamander is found in the northeastern United States and southeastern Canada from southern Quebec and Ontario to North Carolina and Indiana. There are disjunct populations in sev-

Redback Salamander, adult, Cook County, Minnesota

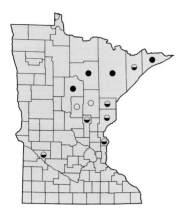

eral southern states, and their taxonomic status is currently under study (Highton 1989).

Most of the records of Redback Salamanders in Minnesota are from the northeast region of the state from Cass County east into the northeast corner. There is one disjunct record from along the Minnesota River near Montevideo in Chippewa County.

Habitat

Redback Salamanders are completely terrestrial salamanders closely associated with forested habitats. Breckenridge (1944) reported that specimens collected in northeastern Minnesota are commonly associated with pockets of hardwoods. In deciduous forests the salamanders are found under logs, rocks, human debris, or leaf litter. The Chippewa County record is from a floodplain forest along the Minnesota River that extends into former prairie habitat (Breckenridge 1944). They are also found in coniferous forest habitat. Redback Salamanders overwinter in animal tunnels up to 1 meter (3 feet) below the surface (Caldwell 1975).

Life History

Redback Salamanders deposit their eggs in damp substrates such as in rotten logs or in soil under rocks and logs. They are the only Minnesota salamanders that do not lay their eggs in the water. The female guards her 3 to 14 eggs and the young for up to three weeks after hatching (Pfingsten and Downs 1989).

The Redback Salamander spends its life in a very humid environment. They are rarely found when the humidity is below 85% (Heatwole 1962). Seasonal variations in humidity are correlated with salamander activity. In the spring and fall, when damp conditions normally occur, adults are more easily found. The Redback Salamander has a small home range of less than 25 square meters (270 square feet) (Kleeberger and Werner 1982).

When Redback Salamanders are active, they eat a wide variety of small invertebrates including worms, sow bugs, centipedes, and spiders (Bishop 1941). In Indiana, Caldwell (1975) found Redback Salamanders with stomachs full of ants during December while overwintering in ant mounds. Redback Salamanders are preyed upon by small snakes, shrews, and larger salamanders.

Remarks

Burton and Likens (1975) found the biomass of salamanders to be twice that of birds in a New Hampshire study site. Redback Salamanders made up 94% of the salamander biomass, with 2,950 salamanders per hectare (1,200 per acre).

Mudpuppy

Necturus maculosus

Description

The Mudpuppy is the only fully aquatic salamander in Minnesota. An adult Mudpuppy is a brownish color with dark blotches over the entire body. Juveniles are dark brown with broad, lateral yellow stripes. The deep-red gills are the most striking feature. The large, squarish head has small eyes and nostrils. Front and hind legs have four toes. The tail is laterally flattened with a dorsal and ventral fin. The Mudpuppy is the largest salamander in Minnesota with an average length of 33 centimeters (13 inches). Some specimens have been recorded up to 40 centimeters (16 inches) (Bishop 1941).

Mudpuppy, adult, Goodhue County, Minnesota

The sexes are similar, but males have a crescent-shaped groove on the front of the vent (Bishop 1941). Larval Tiger Salamanders, which are sometimes confused with Mudpuppies, have five toes on their hind legs.

Distribution

Mudpuppies are found in the east-central United States from the Great Lakes south to northern Alabama. They are found west of the Appalachian Mountains through Missouri and north to Minnesota.

Mudpuppies are restricted in Minnesota to the Minnesota, Red, St. Croix, and Mississippi (south of St. Anthony Falls) river drainages.

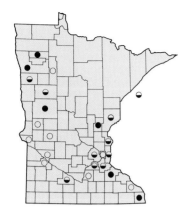

St. Anthony Falls acts as a barrier to the upper Mississippi River (Cochran 1991).

Habitat

The Mudpuppy is found in large to medium rivers and large lakes. In Minnesota, Mudpuppy habitats range from swift gravel-bottom streams to slow, muddy rivers. Rivers with high turbidity are used if there are silt-free gravel areas for nesting (Pfingsten and Downs 1989). Mudpuppies prefer some cover and may use rocks, sunken logs, or submerged abandoned tires. Young Mudpuppies stay in shallow water or riffles, whereas adults use deeper water (Pfingsten and Downs 1989).

Life History

Adult Mudpuppies spend the entire year in the same habitat, and they are active year-round. They are the only Minnesota salamanders that do not exhibit some form of winter dormancy. Mudpuppies are regularly caught by people ice fishing on the St. Croix River (John Almendinger, personal communication).

Mudpuppies breed in the fall and early winter. Their courtship ritual is similar to that of other salamanders (Bishop 1941). The female lays her eggs in late spring and summer under rocks or logs in silt-free areas, where she guards them during development. The eggs, laid in groups of 50 to 100, take one to two months to hatch depending on water temperature. Warmer streams and lakes allow for faster development.

Size at hatching is 22 millimeters long (⅞ inch) (Bishop 1941). Young Mudpuppies are very secretive, and there are very few records of juveniles from Minnesota (Philip Cochran, personal communication). The color pattern changes during the five years it takes the Mudpuppy to reach maturity. Bishop (1941) details changes in both color and morphology.

Mudpuppies are carnivorous and eat nearly anything that fits into their mouth, including crustaceans, insects, worms, fish, and even other salamanders (Bishop 1941). A sample of 340 Mudpuppies from New York revealed that crayfish and aquatic insects comprised the major volume of food items (Hamilton 1932). Mudpuppies feed year-round.

Remarks

The Mudpuppy was once considered vile and poisonous. Local fishermen would cut them off their lines because they believed Mudpuppies had dangerous spines and would bite (Breckenridge 1944). Some Minnesotans still believe the Mudpuppy is a dangerous animal.

Eastern Newt

Notophthalmus viridescens

Description

The Eastern Newt is a small salamander with a total length ranging from 6.5 to 14 centimeters (2½ to 5½ inches) (Conant and Collins 1991). Adults are olive green with a row of reddish spots on each side. The ventral surface is yellowish with scattered black dots. Aquatic adults have a vertically flattened and finned tail, which assists in swimming. The rear legs are larger than the front legs. Aquatic forms have a smooth skin. Males can be distinguished by their enlarged tail fins and swollen cloacas during the breeding season.

The juvenile, terrestrial phase (eft) is smaller than the adult, with a length of 4 to 8 centimeters (1½ to 3 inches). Individuals are reddish brown with a lighter belly. Efts found south and east of Minnesota tend to be bright orange. Eft skin is dry and granular.

Distribution

The Eastern Newt is found throughout most of the eastern United States, west to eastern Texas in the south and to Minnesota in the north. In Minnesota, the known range is spotty. There are scattered

Eastern Newt, adult

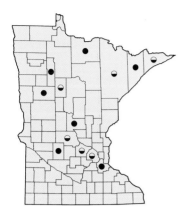

populations in the upper Mississippi River drainage. They appear to be more common in the northern counties.

Habitat

Eastern Newts are found in temporary and permanent lakes, streams, and wetlands adjacent to woodlands. Most of Minnesota's records are from small, clear-flowing streams. They can be found in coniferous and deciduous forests where there is an understory with numerous logs and abundant leaf litter.

Life History

Efts are encountered on land in summer and fall, especially during rainy or overcast days with high humidity. The juvenile stage may last four to seven years or be nonexistent (Breckenridge 1944; Gill

Eastern Newt, eft

1978). In Minnesota, it appears that the eft stage may be short (i.e., one or two years), but better documentation is needed.

Aquatic adults can be found in streams and ponds year-round. In the fall they migrate to deeper ponds because shallow ponds become oxygen deficient in the winter (Pfingsten and Downs 1989). Adults overwinter on land, as do the efts, if conditions are right (Healy 1974). During the summer, sedentary adults rarely move from pond to pond, but efts will wander wherever there is adequate habitat (Healy 1975).

Aquatic adults eat various aquatic insect larvae, amphibian eggs and larvae, and fingernail clams. Efts eat terrestrial insects, small crustaceans, and worms.

Adult Eastern Newts breed in the spring in fish-free streams and ponds. In Minnesota, breeding probably occurs in early May. After congregating at breeding sites, Eastern Newts conduct a courtship dance during which the male fans the female with his tail (Verrell 1982). The male deposits a spermatophore on the bottom of the pool, and the female then positions her cloaca over the spermatophore to pick it up. Two to three days later the female lays six to ten eggs (Pfingsten and Downs 1989). The female may breed up to 30 times over the course of the breeding season (Gill 1978). Eggs hatch in two to four weeks depending on the temperature of the water.

The larvae spend the summer in the natal pond feeding on small aquatic insects and growing to a length of 4 centimeters (1½ inches). They are preyed on by other salamander larvae, adult newts, and large aquatic insects. By late summer, larvae usually transform into terrestrial efts, or they may skip the eft phase and transform directly into aquatic adults.

The skin of an eft is toxic and makes most predators ill if they attempt to eat them (Bishop 1941). The eft's orange red coloration serves as a warning signal to potential predators. Efts are often active during the day and wander boldly across the forest floor, protected by their warning coloration.

Remarks

The subspecies of the Eastern Newt found in Minnesota is the Central Newt, *Notophthalmus viridescens louisianensis* (Conant and Collins 1991).

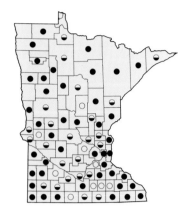

American Toad

Bufo americanus

Description

The American Toad is the common toad of Minnesota. Body color is normally brown but can range from dark brown to tan and rarely is red or green. Variable white and black splotches occur on the back. The majority of the black spots on the back have one or two "warts" in each spot. The belly is white with gray and black flecking, especially on the throat. The oval parotoid glands are separated from the cranial crest or attached by a narrow spur. Males have a single round vocal sac. American Toads' snout-vent length ranges from 5 to 9 centimeters (2 to 3½ inches) (Conant and Collins 1991).

The warts on the femur are larger than those found on the tibia. This characteristic distinguishes the American Toad from Woodhouse's Toad, which has similar-sized warts on the femur and tibia. The parotoid glands and cranial crests are normally fused in Woodhouse's Toad, but this characteristic is variable.

Toad tadpoles are small and dark colored. They reach a length of 2.5 centimeters (1 inch). The body color is gray black with clear

American Toad, adult, Goodhue County, Minnesota

tail fins. The fins do not extend onto the body and are rounded at the tip. The three species of toads in Minnesota have very similar tadpoles, which are impossible to identify without close examination.

Distribution

American Toads are found east of the Great Plains and north of the Gulf of Mexico coastal plain. The northern limit is Hudson Bay in Quebec and Ontario. In Minnesota, the American Toad is found statewide. The western border of the state is the approximate western edge of the toad's national range.

American Toad, red phase, Goodhue County, Minnesota

Habitat

American Toads are found in many different habitats in Minnesota. They are found in the bogs and coniferous forests of the north (Karns 1984, 1992a) and throughout the wooded areas of central and southern Minnesota. Prairies provide good habitat in the southwest part of the state, but the prairies of the Red River valley lack American Toads. Ewert (1969) described the American Toad as a woodland toad and the Great Plains Toad as a prairie toad. This distinction may be true on the northwestern Minnesota prairies, but American Toads are regularly found on Minnesota's west-central and southwestern prairies (Moriarty 1988).

Life History

American Toads overwinter by burrowing into well-drained, preferably sandy soils. Winter dormancy normally begins in early October, but toads have been seen as late as 24 October. They burrow deep enough to stay below the frost line (Ewert 1969; Tester et al. 1965), which varies from approximately 12 to 58 centimeters deep (5 to 23 inches). Burrow depths are adjusted as the frost line shifts. When conditions are extremely dry during the summer, shallow burrows are used for estivation.

American Toads emerge from winter dormancy in late April. Movements to breeding pools occur several weeks later, from early May to mid-June. Toads have a moderate fidelity to breeding sites (Ewert 1969), which include ponds, lakes, rivers, and swamps. Breeding congregations are normally large, and dozens of amplexing pairs of toads can commonly be seen floating near the edges of ponds. During the breeding season, male toads, like many male anurans, attempt to amplex with anything that swims by, including other male toads or frogs.

Postbreeding movements have been recorded up to 1,000 meters (3,300 feet), but most are much shorter (Ewert 1969). These movements are nocturnal with peaks of activity on warm, wet evenings. American Toads tend to rest at the ground's surface or under litter during the day. Movements back to overwintering areas in the fall tend to be diurnal because of cool temperatures in the evenings.

The male's call is a high-pitched, rapid trill that lasts 20 to 30 seconds. The trill is a single note with little variation in pitch. Calling begins at dusk but may continue throughout the day if it is cloudy or raining.

Females lay 4,000 to 20,000 eggs (Collins 1982). Eggs hatch in two to eight days depending on the water temperature. Warmer temperatures speed up the development of the eggs. Tadpoles school and look like a large black mass moving around through the shallows of ponds or streams. They generally metamorphose into toadlets in late July but are capable of speeding up metamorphosis if they are trapped in drying pools. Toadlets are less than 1 centimeter (½ inch) in length when they transform.

American Toad, albino, LeSueur County, Minnesota

American Toads feed on a variety of terrestrial insects and worms. Feeding activity is nocturnal except during rainy weather. Toads stalk their prey for short distances. They use their tongues to capture prey, and then they use their front legs to stuff the prey into their mouth. American Toads are eaten by a variety of birds, but their primary predators are snakes, especially hognose snakes that feed almost exclusively on toads.

American Toads defend themselves from predators by inflating their bodies to look larger and to prevent being swallowed. If the bluff fails and the attack continues, the toads tuck their heads down and present their parotoid glands. The glands secrete a bitter-tasting toxin that can make the attacker sick (DeGraaff 1991). Toads may also urinate on their attacker. This action seems to be the best defense when picked up by humans!

Remarks

The Eastern American Toad (*Bufo americanus americanus*) is the subspecies found in Minnesota (Conant and Collins 1991). The common myth of toads transmitting warts to humans has no basis in fact. Warts in humans are caused by a virus. The "warts" on toads are skin glands. An albino American Toad was collected in LeSueur County in 1992. This is the first record of an albino American Toad from Minnesota.

Great Plains Toad

Bufo cognatus

Description

The Great Plains Toad has distinctive large, dark spots with light edges on its back, and each spot has a number of small warts. Background color may be gray brown to green. The belly is a uniform white or ivory with no black flecking. Males may have a dark throat (Smith 1978). The male's vocal sac is oblong and extends beyond the snout when inflated. The cranial crests are reduced and form a V between the eyes. Great Plains Toads' snout-vent length ranges from 5 to 9 centimeters (2 to 3½ inches), which is similar in size to the American Toad. The oval parotoid glands are not as prominent as those of the American Toad and Canadian Toad.

Great Plains Toad tadpoles are very similar in appearance to American Toad tadpoles (see the American Toad species account for a detailed description).

Distribution

The distribution of the Great Plains Toad is similar to its common name. It is found in the Great Plains of North America from Montana to Minnesota and south into Mexico and the Colorado River drainage. In Minnesota the species is found along the western border of the state from Marshall County south to Rock County. The eastern edge of the range is in Nicollet County.

Great Plains Toad, adult

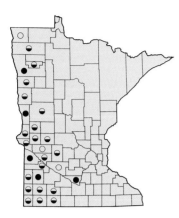

Habitat

Great Plains Toads inhabit prairies. In Minnesota they use tallgrass prairies and nonnative grasslands. They are rarely found in woodlands (Ewert 1969). The toads select high, dry ground for overwintering sites. They burrow deeper than American Toads, up to 100 centimeters (40 inches) (Ewert 1969).

Life History

The Great Plains Toad is the most fossorial of Minnesota's toads. This characteristic is an adaptation to living in dry grassland habitats. This toad is also a very rapid burrower (Ewert 1969). Emergence and breeding are triggered by early summer thunderstorms. Without waiting for other individuals to emerge, the toads move immediately to the breeding pools. In areas of little water, calling sites may be limited and ephemeral. Such opportunistic behavior may provide a competitive advantage to early toads, who secure the best calling sites. Breeding takes place anytime between mid-May and mid-July (Breckenridge 1944). Females lay up to 20,000 eggs per year (Collins 1982). Tadpoles take approximately six weeks to transform (Breckenridge 1944).

After breeding, their movements to feeding sites range from 300 to 1,300 meters (1,000 to 4,000 feet). Daily movements are approximately 30 meters (100 feet) (Ewert 1969). Great Plains Toads estivate in the summer during dry, hot weather. If weather conditions are not favorable, it is common for this toad to remain underground through winter without coming out of estivation.

The mating call of the Great Plains Toad is harsh with a pulsating mechanical quality, in contrast to the steady musical trill of the American Toad (Breckenridge 1944). Individual calls last from 20 to 50 seconds (Conant and Collins 1991).

Great Plains Toads feed on terrestrial insects. Beetles and ants have been reported as prey items (Collins 1982). Hammerson (1982) reports that this toad is an effective predator on agricultural pests such as cutworms, moths, and flies. The predators of Great Plains Toads are similar to those of American Toads.

Remarks

Breckenridge (1944) reported that no toads were seen in the western prairies in the early 1930s, but when it rained in 1937, Great Plains Toads emerged in great numbers. Great Plains Toads were not found on the prairies during 1988 (Moriarty 1988), which was the second year of a drought.

Canadian Toad

Bufo hemiophrys

Description

The distinguishing feature of the Canadian Toad is a large boss between the eyes. The boss is a raised bump formed by the fusion of the cranial crests. The body color is different shades of brown with variable patterns of white and black. The dominant spots are black, with one or two warts per spot. The belly is white with gray

Canadian Toad, adult, Clay County, Minnesota

and black flecking, especially on the throat. Males have a single round vocal sac. Canadian Toads' snout-vent length ranges in size from 5 to 9 centimeters (2 to 3½ inches) (Conant and Collins 1991). When Canadian Toads first transform, their snout-vent length is less than 1 centimeter (½ inch), and they look identical to American Toads. The cranial boss is the only characteristic that separates the appearance of these two species.

Canadian Toad tadpoles are very similar in appearance to American Toad tadpoles (see the American Toad species account for a detailed description).

Distribution

The range of the Canadian Toad in the United States is northwest Minnesota and North Dakota. In Canada they are found on the

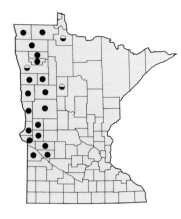

prairies of Manitoba and Saskatchewan. In Minnesota they are found from the Minnesota River in Lac Qui Parle County north through the Red River valley.

Habitat

Canadian Toads are found in the same habitats as American Toads, ranging from woodlands to wetlands. They are not found in the interior of vast expanses of prairie (Ewert 1969). They overwinter on upland sites approximately 25 meters (80 feet) from wetlands.

During the summer, adult toads are found in proximity to water. They are the most aquatic of Minnesota's toads (Breckenridge and Tester 1961).

Life History

The overwintering habits of Canadian Toads differ from American Toads. Canadian Toads overwinter communally, whereas American Toads overwinter individually. They congregate in Mima mounds, which are small earth mounds 3 to 12 meters (9 to 39 feet) in diameter and 1 meter (3 feet) high (Breckenridge and Tester 1961). These mounds, thought to be caused by gopher activity, have coarse weedy vegetation and loose soils compared to the surrounding prairie. Tester and Breckenridge (1964) found that 99% of the toads were in Mima mounds, with an average of 950 toads per mound, whereas less than 1% of the toads were in the surrounding uplands. Like other toads, they burrow during the winter to stay just below the frost line (Tester 1981; Tester and Breckenridge 1964).

The breeding habits of Canadian Toads are similar to those of American Toads. Males have a similar call, except that the trill length is shorter (2 to 8.5 seconds; Preston 1982). Eggs hatch in several days. The tadpoles metamorphose in late June and early July.

Remarks

Some researchers (Cook 1983; Preston 1982) feel that Canadian Toads and American Toads are subspecies because of the presence of an intergradation zone in Manitoba and Ontario, Canada, where successful breeding occurs between the two species. Green (1983), however, treats them as separate species that sometimes hybridize when their ranges overlap.

Northern Cricket Frog

Acris crepitans

Description

Northern Cricket Frogs are small frogs with a snout-vent length that ranges from 2 to 3.8 centimeters (⅝ to 1½ inches). They are slightly larger than *Pseudacris* species. Skin color is brown ranging to gray, with variable green blotches. Darker-colored warts are also present. Most Northern Cricket Frogs have a green or dark brown triangle between the eyes and a lighter middorsal stripe. They lack enlarged toe pads but do have terminal disks on their toes. Hind feet are webbed. The sexes are similar, but males may develop gray spotting on their vocal pouch.

Northern Cricket Frog tadpoles are the only tadpoles in Minnesota with a black-tipped tail. This tail makes them easy to distinguish from other tadpoles of their size. They reach a length of 3.5 centimeters (1½ inches).

Distribution

Northern Cricket Frogs are found in the central and southeastern United States. The western limit of the range extends from Nebraska south to Texas. They are absent from the Appalachian Mountains and Atlantic coastal plain.

Northern Cricket Frogs have been recorded from the southeastern and southwestern corners of Minnesota. The only recent records are from Houston County (Nehl 1981; Whitford 1991). Northern Cricket Frogs have been declining over much of the northern part of their range (Mossman and Hine 1985).

Northern Cricket Frog, adult

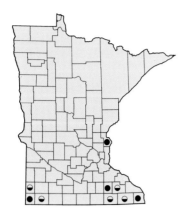

Habitat

Northern Cricket Frogs are often found along the shorelines of sluggish streams and ponds. They prefer muddy shorelines with abundant emergent vegetation where the water's edge is in an unshaded open area. Vogt (1981) found them using stock ponds on farms in southern Wisconsin.

The overwintering habits of Northern Cricket Frogs are poorly known. In Ohio (Walker 1946), they were found up to 30 centimeters (12 inches) below the soil surface adjacent to streams and ponds.

Life History

Northern Cricket Frogs emerge from winter dormancy in late April. They are one of the last frogs to breed in Minnesota, breeding from late May into July along with Green Frogs and Bullfrogs. Breeding choruses are stimulated by rain. The male's call is a glick, glick, glick sound similar to the clicking of ball bearings. Identification by call can be difficult because Virginia Rails, which are found in many of the same habitats, make a similar sound. Northern Cricket Frogs normally call in choruses of more than one male. Females lay up to 200 eggs in clumps of 10 to 15 each. In Wisconsin, Vogt (1981) found clumps of eggs attached to vegetation in flowing water.

Five to ten weeks after hatching, the tadpoles metamorphose into adults in early August. Young frogs stay active into late September, whereas the adults become inactive in August (Johnson and Christiansen 1976). These small frogs feed on tiny insects, eating enough to fill their stomachs three times a day (Johnson and Christiansen 1976).

Northern Cricket Frogs stay near water throughout the summer (Vogt 1981) but will travel overland during dry weather (Fitch 1958a). They escape predators by using their remarkable jumping skills. A cricket frog can jump up to 1 meter (3 feet) in a single leap (Vogt 1981).

Remarks

Northern Cricket Frogs are currently listed by the Minnesota Department of Natural Resources as a special concern species (Coffin and Pfannmuller 1988). This species should probably be elevated to threatened or endangered status. A 1990-91 survey for the Nongame Wildlife Program reported a suspected call from Houston County, but the frog was not located (Whitford 1991).

The subspecies in Minnesota is Blanchard's Cricket Frog, *Acris crepitans blanchardi* (Conant and Collins 1991).

Cope's Gray Treefrog

Hyla chrysoscelis

Description

Cope's Gray Treefrog is a medium-sized treefrog with an average snout-vent length of 3.5 centimeters (1½ inches). Their snout-vent length ranges from 3 to 5 centimeters (1¼ to 2 inches) (Conant and Collins 1991). The toe pads are well developed and easily visible. The skin is smooth (Vogt 1981). Skin color changes from gray to green depending on temperature and habitat. Green coloration normally occurs in warmer temperatures and when the treefrogs

are on green vegetation. During the breeding season, adults tend to be green without any blotches. When the frogs are gray, large dark blotches are visible on the back. Unlike those of Gray Treefrogs, these blotches are not bordered by black (Vogt 1981). The insides of the thighs and shanks are yellow. The Gray Treefrog (*Hyla versicolor*) is slightly larger with an average snout-vent length of 4.3 centimeters (1¾ inches). The two frogs were thought to be the same species until 1968 (Ralin 1968).

Tadpoles are high finned, with the top fin extending onto the upper body. The tail is mottled with black. The fin may have an

*Cope's Gray Treefrog, adult,
Rice County, Minnesota*

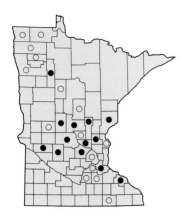

orange or red tinge. A mature tadpole will reach 3.5 centimeters (1½ inches).

Distribution

The overall distribution of Cope's Gray Treefrog is thought to be the same as the Gray Treefrog. They range east of the Great Plains from a line through eastern North Dakota to central Texas to the Atlantic.

In Minnesota, recent records show Cope's Gray Treefrog in the central third of the state. Records before 1968 may be included with those of the Gray Treefrog. Additional field work is needed to delineate the full extent of their range.

Habitat

Cope's Gray Treefrogs are associated with prairie edges and oak savannahs (Vogt 1981). They are not found in forest interiors, but they do frequent woodland edges, where they overlap with Gray Treefrogs.

Life History

The life history of Cope's Gray Treefrog is similar to the Gray Treefrog. Both species spend their winter in a partially frozen state under leaf litter, rocks, or logs (Schmid 1982). After emerging in mid- to late April, they spend time feeding in the uplands. They head to the breeding ponds in mid-May and breed through June.

At the breeding ponds, the males call from surrounding trees and emergent vegetation during the day or early evening. The calling perches of Cope's Gray Treefrogs range up to 3 meters (10 feet) above pond level in trees (Vogt 1981). The male's call is a fast metallic trill, compared to the Gray Treefrog's slower more musical trill. Cope's Gray Treefrogs breed in deeper water than chorus frogs (Walker 1946). They lay up to 2,000 eggs singly or in small clusters. The tadpoles transform in eight to ten weeks.

Young frogs leave the pond in mid-July to join the adults that are feeding in the shrubs and trees. During dry periods, both juveniles and adults will estivate in hollow logs.

Remarks

See Remarks under Gray Treefrog. A "blue" Cope's Gray Treefrog was collected in Wright County in 1990 (Moriarty, personal observation). The frog was normal in every respect except for being light blue rather than green.

Gray Treefrog

Hyla versicolor

Description

The Gray Treefrog is the largest treefrog in Minnesota, with a snout-vent length that ranges from 3 to 5 centimeters (1¼ to 2 inches). Individuals are gray with dark blotches, and the blotches have black borders. The skin color can change to green, except for the black borders, which always remain visible in adults. Like those of Cope's Gray Treefrog, the inner surfaces of the thighs and shanks are bright yellow. Gray Treefrogs have large toe pads, which enable them to be very good climbers. They have rough skin, whereas Cope's Gray Treefrogs have smooth skin.

Gray Treefrog, adult, Goodhue County, Minnesota

Gray Treefrog tadpoles are very similar in appearance to Cope's Gray Treefrog tadpoles (see the Cope's Gray Treefrog species account for a detailed description).

Distribution

Gray Treefrogs are found from the Great Plains east to the Atlantic coast, except for northern Maine and southern Florida. In Minnesota they are found statewide except for the southwest corner.

Habitat

Gray Treefrogs are found in a wide range of woodland habitats, both deciduous and coniferous. They use marshes and bogs asso-

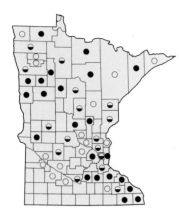

ciated with woodlands. They are not found on prairies, but they do use floodplain forests in the prairie region.

Life History

Gray Treefrogs overwinter under leaf litter, rocks, or logs in a manner similar to Cope's Gray Treefrogs. Their unusual overwintering strategy was first documented in Minnesota (Schmid 1982). Glycerol is accumulated in their body fluids during the fall when the temperature begins to cool. This process protects the cells from rupturing when the frog partially freezes. When the frog begins to freeze, the liver converts the glycerol into glucose. Glucose is then circulated to the major organs so that ice crystals will not form in the organ tissues. Ice forms in the body cavity around the organs and in between the muscle cells. Up to 65% of the total body water is frozen (Storey and Storey 1990). Schmid (1982) found that the frogs can be cooled down to -7.2° C (19° F) for weeks and survive.

After emerging, Gray Treefrogs spend time feeding in the uplands. They move to the breeding ponds in mid-May and breed through June. Males call from perches as high as 10 meters (30 feet) up in surrounding trees during the day or early evening (Vogt 1981). Any treefrog calling from above 3 meters (10 feet) is a Gray Treefrog because Cope's Gray Treefrog apparently does not call from above that height (Vogt 1981). The call, a melodic trill, is slower than the Cope's fast metallic trill. The trill rate is affected by the ambient temperature at the breeding pond, the trill rate being faster in warmer

Gray Treefrog, adults,
Clearwater County, Minnesota

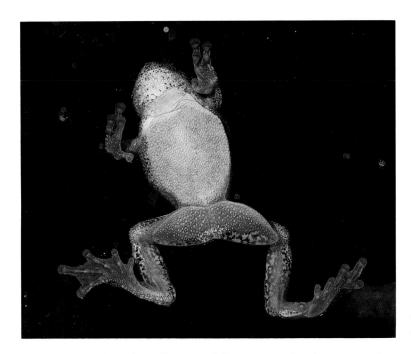

Gray Treefrog, adult underside,
Goodhue County, Minnesota

temperatures, but the trill rates of the two species do not overlap (Jaslow and Vogt 1977). Females lay up to 2,000 eggs singly or in small clusters. The tadpoles transform in eight to ten weeks.

Young frogs leave the pond to join the adults in late July or early August, feeding in the shrubs and trees, sometimes as high as 10 meters (30 feet) above the ground. Gray Treefrogs feed on a variety of insects, but beetles and caterpillars comprise the majority of their diet (Vogt 1981). During the day, Gray Treefrogs spend their time under loose bark, in tree cavities, or in bird nest boxes (McComb and Noble 1981).

Remarks

Before 1968 (Ralin 1968), the Gray Treefrog and Cope's Gray Treefrog were considered to be the same species. The Gray Treefrog is a tetraploid (twice the normal number of pairs of chromosomes), and Cope's Gray Treefrog is a diploid (normal number of chromosomes). Cope's Gray Treefrog has 24 chromosomes, and the Gray Treefrog has 48. Thus, absolute identification can only be made by karyotype (chromosome) analysis.

A long history of taxonomic confusion makes it difficult to analyze distribution and habitat information before 1968. Early publications (Breckenridge 1944; Wright and Wright 1949) combined information, and thus the life history differences are difficult to determine. Jaslow and Vogt (1977) demonstrated that Cope's Gray Treefrog is a prairie-associated species and the Gray Treefrog is a forest-associated species.

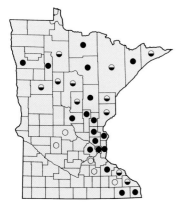

Spring Peeper

Pseudacris crucifer

Description

Spring Peepers are among the smallest frogs in Minnesota. Their snout-vent length ranges from 1.9 to 3.2 centimeters (¾ to 1¼ inches). Skin color varies from light brown to gray and dark brown. Individuals are sometimes a bright bronze color. Temperature affects the color of the frog. Colder frogs are dark, and warmer frogs are light in color. The Spring Peeper has a distinctive X on its back, thus its scientific name *crucifer*, which is Latin for crossbearer. The belly is light tan with no markings. The toe pads are reduced but distinct.

Spring Peeper tadpoles are small, with an average total length of 3 centimeters (1⅛ inches). Tail fins are medium in height. Fins are heavily mottled but have a clear band adjacent to the tail muscle.

Distribution

Spring Peeper, adult, Goodhue County, Minnesota

Spring Peepers are found throughout the eastern United States east of the Great Plains and south of James Bay, Canada (51° N latitude). In Minnesota, Spring Peepers are found in the nonprairie counties.

Habitat

Spring Peepers are normally found in woodlands, both deciduous and coniferous, where they spend most of their time near wetlands. Prairie wetlands are used when they are adjacent to woodlands. Spring Peepers are usually absent from urban areas because the uplands surrounding wetlands have been intensively developed.

Life History

Spring Peepers normally emerge in early April about the time the ground thaws. They overwinter on land under leaf litter. Like the bodies of Gray Treefrogs and Wood Frogs, up to 65% of the Spring Peeper's body freezes during the winter months (Schmid 1982).

Spring Peepers start breeding in April soon after emergence and continue through May. They initiate calling near the end of the Wood Frog's breeding season. Their call is a high-pitched peep or ping, which can be heard emanating from low vegetation in wetlands. Large choruses sound like sleigh bells and can be deafening when heard up close. Eggs are laid singly (Walker 1946) or in small clusters that are attached to submerged vegetation. Tadpoles take 12 to 14 weeks to transform after hatching (Wright 1914).

Spring Peepers feed on small insects and invertebrates, as do Minnesota's other small frogs. Most feeding is done while hunting in low vegetation (McAlister 1963).

Remarks

There is only one subspecies of Spring Peeper in Minnesota, the Northern Spring Peeper (*Pseudacris crucifer crucifer*) (Conant and Collins 1991). The Spring Peeper had been placed in the genus *Hyla* until 1986 (Hedges 1986).

Populations of Spring Peepers have been declining in Wisconsin over the last ten years. (Michael Mossman, personal communication). Populations in Minnesota have not been monitored.

Spring Peepers have all but disappeared from the Twin Cities area because of urbanization. Hennepin Parks' biologists attempted to reintroduce them into some of the parks in the mid-1980s (Donna Compton, personal communication). Because of the drought from 1987 to 1989, the success of this relocation experiment was very limited.

Western Chorus Frog

Pseudacris triseriata

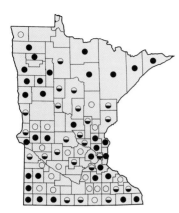

Description

Western Chorus Frogs, with a maximum snout-vent length of 3.2 centimeters (1¼ inches), are similar in size to the Spring Peepers. Females are slightly larger than males. Their body shape is slender with a pointed head. Skin color is variable and ranges from light brown to shades of red, gray, or green. The Western Chorus Frog has three, sometimes broken, longitudinal stripes on its back. The belly is tan with no markings. Color morphs of these frogs have been studied by Hoppe (1981). He reported that the brown phase is predominant in the warmer prairie areas of Minnesota and that a higher proportion of red and green morphs are found in the forested, cooler parts of the state. Toe pads are greatly reduced and are difficult to see with the naked eye. The toes are partially webbed.

Western Chorus Frog tadpoles lack the mottling found in other hylid tadpoles. They are small, with a maximum length of 3 centimeters (1⅛ inches). The tail fins are clear with the dorsal fin extending onto the body.

Distribution

Western Chorus Frogs are found in the central United States and Canada. They range from the Rocky Mountains east to the Atlantic, with the exception of the northeastern United States, the Appalachian Mountains, the southeast coastal plain, and west Texas. Their range extends north into the Northwest Territories and central Ontario. In Minnesota they are found statewide.

Habitat

Western Chorus Frogs require temporary or permanent waters without fish populations. These wetlands are found in many moist habitats in Minnesota. Western Chorus Frogs venture into the uplands for a short distance, normally remaining within 100 meters (109 yards) of the breeding pond (Kramer 1974). This species is tolerant of urbanization and can be found in wetlands surrounded by development. Individuals apparently overwinter under rocks and logs adjacent to the water's edge (Vogt 1981).

Life History

Western Chorus Frogs are among the first frogs to emerge in the spring. They emerge from late March through early April. Breeding activity begins immediately and continues into early May. They are commonly found in or heard calling from grassy wetlands. Their call is a clicking sound similar to the sound made when running one's thumb down the teeth of a comb. The speed of the one-to-two-second call varies with temperature, speeding up as the temperature becomes warmer. When approached, Western Chorus Frogs abruptly stop calling and will not resume for some time. The cessation of calling by one frog usually results in the shutting down of the entire chorus.

When they breed, Western Chorus Frogs lay small groups of eggs (5 to 20) attached to submerged vegetation. Smith (1934)

Western Chorus Frog, adult, Jackson County, Minnesota

found egg masses with up to 75 eggs. Individual females may lay hundreds of eggs over the course of the breeding season (Pettus and Angleton 1967). The eggs hatch quickly, how quickly depending on the water temperature. Tadpoles transform in eight to ten weeks (Breckenridge 1944).

Western Chorus Frogs feed on small prey items, such as emerging aquatic insects, beetles, and other small insects. Whitaker (1971) found that they feed mainly on ants and spiders.

Remarks

Wisconsin frog and toad surveys have reported an annual 3% decline of Western Chorus Frogs (Michael Mossman, personal communication). If this rate of decline continues, it could lead to the disappearance of Western Chorus Frogs from much of Wisconsin. Monitoring of Western Chorus Frog populations should also be initiated in Minnesota.

Conant and Collins (1991) list two subspecies of Western Chorus Frogs in Minnesota. *Pseudacris triseriata triseriata* is found throughout the southern two-thirds of the state and intergrades with *P. t. maculata* (Boreal Chorus Frog) in the northern third of the state. Platz (1989) concluded that the two subspecies were actually two separate species based on the study of specimens from South Dakota south into Kansas. There have been no studies to determine the status of the two subspecies in Minnesota.

Bullfrog

Rana catesbeiana

Description

The Bullfrog is the largest frog in Minnesota. The green skin color of the Bullfrog varies in shade depending on the frog's size and the air temperature. Lighter shades of skin color are found in smaller frogs or during warm temperatures. Adults, especially males, are sometimes a mottled green and brown. Newly transformed frogs are spotted. The belly is white with a gray to yellow wash, especially under the chin, and is sometimes mottled with brown. Individuals can reach a snout-vent length of 20.3 centimeters (8 inches) (Conant and Collins 1991).

Bullfrogs lack a dorsolateral ridge. The webbing on the hind foot is complete except for the end of the fourth toe. Males have large, convex tympanic membranes that are larger than their eyes, whereas females have flat tympanic membranes the same size as their eyes.

Bullfrog tadpoles are the largest tadpoles in the state. They are green with dark mottling. Black spots are scattered over the upper body and tail. A mature tadpole can reach 12 centimeters (4¾ inches). The body length to tail ratio is 1:1.5.

*Bullfrog, adult male,
Houston County, Minnesota*

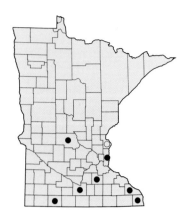

Distribution

The Bullfrog is native to the region east of the Rocky Mountains, except the northern Plains. It has been introduced throughout the western United States and can now be found in nearly every state.

In Minnesota, the natural distribution of the Bullfrog is limited to the extreme southeastern corner from Winona south along the Mississippi River backwaters. There are introduced populations in Blue Earth, Chisago, Jackson, Stearns, and Washington counties.

Habitat

Bullfrogs are rarely found far from the edge of permanent bodies of water, including rivers, lakes, and ponds. They use areas with thick emergent vegetation and require open access to water. Bull-

Bullfrog, adult female,
Houston County, Minnesota

frogs are commonly found along the sloughs and backwaters of the Mississippi River in Houston County. Adults and tadpoles overwinter underwater in lakes and rivers that are sufficiently deep to avoid oxygen depletion.

Life History

Bullfrogs breed later than other frogs in Minnesota. They emerge from winter dormancy in early May and feed before breeding. Males start calling the well-known deep baritone "jug-a-rum" in June and continue into mid-July. They establish territories along the shore of a lake or river and defend it from other males. Females lay up to 20,000 eggs (Johnson 1987) in a large surface film. The tadpoles take two to three years of growing before they metamorphose (Wright 1920), the longest time of any Minnesota frog. The activity season in Minnesota is not long enough for full development of the tadpoles in one or two summers. The young frogs then take from two to five years to become sexually mature (DeGraaf and Rudis 1983). Growth and maturation are slower at colder temperatures.

Bullfrogs have small home ranges, the radius varying from 0.6 to 11.3 meters (2 to 37 feet) with an average of 2.6 meters (8 feet) (Bury and Whelan 1984). Their main defense is to leap away from shore in a series of quick jumps over the water surface (Vogt 1981). If caught, they may give a distress call that is suggestive of a cat scream.

Bullfrogs eat anything that can fit into their mouths. Their diet is primarily insects but includes earthworms, frogs, small turtles, snakes, bats, mice, and ducklings (Bury and Whelan 1984). Bullfrogs in turn are preyed on by humans, raccoons, mink, and large fish.

Remarks

The Bullfrog in Minnesota is listed by the state as special concern because of its restricted natural distribution (Coffin and Pfannmuller 1988). Bullfrogs are a game species in Minnesota and are hunted for their legs, which are considered a delicacy. Collection is regulated by the Minnesota Department of Natural Resources' Section of Fisheries through the use of hunting seasons and bag limits.

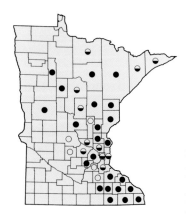

Green Frog

Rana clamitans

Description

Green Frogs are medium-sized frogs with skin color that ranges from green to brown. Young frogs generally have a blotched skin pattern. The upper lip of the Green Frog is a lighter and brighter green than the head. The belly is white, and adult males usually have a yellow throat. The dorsolateral fold may be reduced and less obvious in large adult males. The tympanum is proportionally larger in male Green Frogs than in females. Green Frogs range in snout-vent length from 6 to 9 centimeters (2⅜ to 3½ inches); however, some individuals can exceed 10.8 centimeters (4¼ inches) (Conant and Collins 1991). The webbing on the Green Frog's hind feet is incomplete, only extending to the second digit of the longest toe, unlike the webbing of the Bullfrog, which is complete. Special attention is needed for correct identification where Green Frogs and Mink Frogs are found together in Minnesota. Mink Frogs give off a rotten-onion odor when their skin is scratched, whereas Green Frogs do not.

Tadpoles of Green Frogs are 7.4 to 10 centimeters (3 to 4 inches) in total length with a body to tail length ratio of 1:1.8. A few dark marks are present on the body, in contrast to the tail and tail fin, which are strongly mottled.

Distribution

Green Frogs are found east of the Great Plains from the Gulf of Mexico north to central Ontario and Quebec. In Minnesota, they are found in the eastern half of the state.

Habitat

Green Frogs occur in wetlands with permanent water and emergent vegetation including rivers, streams, and their associated backwaters (Fleming 1976). Lakes and ponds with shallow margins and springs and seeps with permanent water are also used. Green Frogs require aquatic sites that do not freeze solid and that maintain enough oxygen for overwintering tadpoles and adults.

Life History

Green Frogs emerge from winter dormancy in late April (Walker 1946). They breed from late May to mid-August in the same area as they overwinter (Breckenridge 1944). Males call with a single "plunk," a sound similar to that of a plucked, out-of-tune banjo string. They defend a territory that ranges from 12 to 21 square meters (14⅓ to 25 square yards) (Hamilton 1948). Females lay up to 4,000 eggs per year in large floating masses. Tadpoles metamorphose late in the season if they are from early eggs (Vogt 1981). Most tadpoles overwinter and transform throughout the following summer. Newly metamorphosed frogs are terrestrial and spend their first summer on land (Vogt 1981), thus reducing competition for food resources with adults. Young frogs mature in their second year after metamorphosis (Wells 1977).

Adult Green Frogs have an average home range of 61 square meters (73 square yards), but they can range up to 200 square meters (240 square yards) (Hamilton 1948). These frogs are highly aquatic and rarely venture from water after their first summer. In

Green Frog, adult male,
Lake County, Minnesota

northern Minnesota, they regularly occur in association with Mink Frogs. Green Frogs are found along the water's edge, whereas Mink Frogs prefer floating vegetation in deeper water. This partitioning of habitat keeps the two species from competing for the same food resources (Fleming 1976).

When disturbed, Green Frogs dive from shore into the water and swim to the bottom to elude predators. Large fish (e.g., bass and northern pike) and Northern Water Snakes regularly feed on them.

*Green Frog, juvenile albino,
Pine County, Minnesota
(Photo by John Moriarty)*

Green Frogs prey on an assortment of insects and occasionally on frogs, crayfish, and small fish.

Remarks

There are two subspecies of the Green Frog; the one found in Minnesota is *Rana clamitans melanota* (Conant and Collins 1991).

Minnesota has a population of Green Frogs in Pine County with a high percentage of albino tadpoles. No albino adults have been reported. Several tadpoles were raised in captivity until metamorphosis, but the transformed frogs did not survive (Moriarty, personal observation). Normal tadpoles from the same pond transformed and survived.

Pickerel Frog

Rana palustris

Description

Pickerel Frogs are small tan ranids with two distinctive parallel rows of dark brown squarish spots on their back and a bright yellow or orange coloring in the groin area. Males have vocal sacs on either side of the head, which are evident when they call, and they develop swollen thumbs during the breeding season. The snout-vent length of Pickerel Frogs ranges from 4.5 to 8 centimeters (1¾ to 3¼ inches). They are smaller than the similar looking Northern Leopard Frogs. Northern Leopard Frogs may have a light yellow wash in the groin area, but the spots on their backs are roundish and randomly distributed.

Pickerel Frog tadpoles have a low dorsal fin and a wide ventral fin. The body has scattered mottling, which becomes heavier on the tail. Their total length ranges from 4.8 to 5.5 centimeters (1⅞ to 2⅛ inches), and the body to tail length ratio is 1:1.7.

Pickerel Frog, adult,
Houston County, Minnesota

Distribution

Pickerel Frogs are found throughout the eastern United States and the southern Great Plains with the exception of most of Illinois and the extreme southeastern United States. They are restricted to the southeast corner of Minnesota.

Habitat

Pickerel Frogs are found along the edges of small ponds, mid-sized rivers, and spring-fed streams, in both wooded and open areas. During the summer, they venture into wet meadows, especially those adjacent to streams. They rarely venture far into uplands, as Northern Leopard Frogs do; however, Pickerel Frogs were found on bluff prairies in Houston County at least 500 meters (547 yards) from water (Oldfield, personal observation). Pickerel Frogs overwinter in streams and ponds. In the southern United States, they overwinter in caves, sometimes in crevices in the cave ceiling (Moriarty, personal observation).

Life History

Emergence occurs in late April, and the breeding season begins in May and early June. Males call with a soft, low-pitched snore during the day as well as at night. Because they regularly call while totally submerged, their voice has limited carrying capacity (Barbour 1971). Females lay 200 to 3,000 eggs and attach them to vegetation and twigs (Wright and Wright 1949). The eggs usually hatch in two weeks (DeGraaff and Rudis 1983). Tadpoles metamorphose in 80 to 100 days, but they may overwinter as tadpoles if breeding occurs late in the season.

The diet of Pickerel Frogs consists of terrestrial arthropods and insects, including beetles and grasshoppers that venture too close to the water's edge.

Pickerel Frogs generally stay close to water year-round. Their proximity to water is advantageous for escaping predators. Another defense mechanism is toxic skin secretions. Pickerel Frogs are very distasteful to predators, and their toxic secretions can kill other amphibians, including other Pickerel Frogs, that are placed together in the same container.

Remarks

The state of Minnesota currently lists Pickerel Frogs as a special concern species because of their restricted range (Coffin and Pfannmuller 1988).

Northern Leopard Frog

Rana pipiens

Description

The Northern Leopard Frog is familiar to most Minnesotans. Skin color is green or brown with two or three rows of irregular-sized dark spots on the back. Dorsolateral ridges are prominent. The legs have dark bars, and the belly is white. Occasionally there is a light yellow wash on the undersides of the legs. Juvenile coloration is similar to that of adults. The snout-vent length of this medium-

Northern Leopard Frog, adult, Goodhue County, Minnesota

sized frog ranges from 5 to 9 centimeters (2 to 3½ inches) with a record of 11.1 centimeters (4⅜ inches) (Conant and Collins 1991). Males have paired vocal pouches and develop swollen thumbs during the breeding season.

In addition to the normal color pattern, there are two variants of the Northern Leopard Frog in Minnesota, the Burnsi and Kandiyohi forms. Burnsi frogs lack spots although the legs may be barred in some individuals. Kandiyohi frogs have extra black pigment between spots. These two variants were originally described as separate species (Weed 1922), but later work revealed that they were

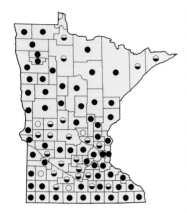

both *Rana pipiens,* differing from normal Northern Leopard Frogs by a single gene (Breckenridge 1944). Even with intensive field work, only two or three Kandiyohi morphs have been found per year (Hoppe and McKinnell 1989, 1991a). The Burnsi phase frogs are more prevalent and can be found in bait shops from time to time.

Tadpoles of Northern Leopard Frogs have a dark back, a cream belly, and a tail that is lighter in color than the body. They range in size from 4.5 to 8.4 centimeters (1¾ to 3⁵⁄₁₆ inches) and have a body to tail ratio of 1:1.5. They are similar to Green Frog tadpoles but darker.

Distribution

In the United States, Northern Leopard Frogs are found from the Great Basin east through the north-central United States into New England. In Canada they extend from Nova Scotia to the Northwest Territories. Northern Leopard Frogs are found statewide in Minnesota. They are the only amphibian with records from every county. The Burnsi form occurs more commonly in the east-central part of the state, whereas the Kandiyohi form occurs in west-central Minnesota (Hoppe and McKinnell 1991a, b).

Habitat

Northern Leopard Frogs use a wide range of habitats, but they are most abundant in wet meadows and open fields adjacent to ponds and lakes. They prefer meadows with grasses 15 to 30 centimeters (6 to 12 inches) tall. The grasses are sufficiently tall to provide cover for hiding but not so tall as to interfere with their movements. Insects, a valuable food source, are common and accessible in these areas (Merrell 1977). Northern Leopard Frogs may travel up to 1.5 kilometers (0.9 mile) from water if there is adequate moisture and humidity in the grassy cover. Overwintering occurs in the water, where they may be found in the aquatic vegetation of ponds and streams. Large congregations of Northern Leopard Frogs have been found under the ice at the inflows to ponds, where currents provide adequate oxygen.

Life History

Individuals become active as water temperatures begin to rise in the spring. By the time of spring thaw, Northern Leopard Frogs are moving overland to breeding ponds. In the spring, overland movements occur more often during the day, since evening temperatures are too cool (Merrell 1977). On rainy nights in early fall, large migrations of Northern Leopard Frogs can been seen crossing Minnesota's roads. They may travel approximately 100 meters (109 yards) each night from mid-September to the end of October before overwintering in ponds and streams (Dole 1965).

Male Northern Leopard Frogs begin calling when water temperatures are above 20° C (68° F) and after they reach the breeding ponds in late April. The call is a low snore mixed with resonant grunts and squeaks. At the peak of the breeding season, males attempt amplexus with other males or anything else that is in the way including floating beer cans (Merrell 1977). Females are never abundant in the breeding ponds because they only stay long enough to lay their eggs (Merrell 1970). Females may lay up to 6,500 eggs; in Minnesota, Merrell (1965) has reported a range of 2,000 to 5,000. Eggs are laid in globular masses, often concentrated in one area of the pond. Tadpoles metamorphose in approximately three months after the eggs are laid, but they may not metamorphose the first year if breeding is late or the summer is cool. Juveniles leave the water and head to grassy areas to feed on terrestrial insects, but they remain closer to the water than adults do.

Northern Leopard Frog, burnsi, *Chisago County, Minnesota*

Adults feed primarily on insects and occasionally on small frogs, worms, or snails. They take only prey that is moving (Merrell 1977). Predators that feed on Northern Leopard Frogs include herons, raccoons, snakes, and owls. Humans use large numbers of these frogs for fishing bait. Additionally, cars and mowers kill untold numbers.

Remarks

Until recently the leopard frog was thought to be a single, wide-ranging species found throughout the United States excluding the West Coast (Conant 1958). In the 1970s, the leopard frog complex was split into four species. Today, the Southern Leopard Frog (*Rana utricularia*), Plains Leopard Frog (*Rana blairi*), and Rio Grande Frog (*Rana berlandieri*) are recognized as different species and have a combined range from Texas to Nebraska and east to Florida and New Jersey.

Northern Leopard Frog, kandiyohi, *Roberts County, South Dakota*

Northern Leopard Frogs are regulated by the Minnesota Department of Natural Resources' Section of Fisheries. A fishing license is required for collecting. Approximately 1,450 kilograms (3,200 pounds; over 50,000 frogs) were sold for nonbait purposes, mainly to biological supply houses, in 1989 (Roy Johannes, personal communication). Large numbers of frogs are captured and used for fishing bait, but the DNR does not keep records.

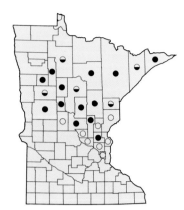

Mink Frog

Rana septentrionalis

Description

Mink Frogs are frequently seen sitting on lily pads in lakes and ponds in northern Minnesota. Skin color is green with brown mottling on the dorsal surface, and the belly color ranges from white to light yellow with gray mottling. The sides of the head and lips are bright green. Dorsolateral ridges vary in prominence among individuals, ranging from very prominent to faint. A distinguishing characteristic of the Mink Frog is a skin odor similar to the smell of rotten onions, which is given off when the frog's back is scratched. The size of a male's tympanum is larger than its eye, whereas that of a female's is equal to or smaller than her eye. The snout-vent length

Mink Frog, adult,
Itasca County, Minnesota

of this small to medium-sized frog ranges from 5 to 7 centimeters (2 to 2¾ inches). Females tend to be larger than males (Hedeen 1970).

Mink Frogs appear similar to Green Frogs but can be distinguished upon close examination. If the rotten-onion skin odor is not evident, then a hind foot should be examined. The webbing on the hind feet of Mink Frogs extends all the way to the tip of the fifth toe; the webbing only goes to the second digit on Green Frogs.

Mink Frog tadpoles are brilliant green or yellowish green with dark black spots and a reddish tail fin (Vogt 1981). They are 2.5 to 3.5 centimeters (1 to 1⅜ inches) in length and are similar in shape to Green Frog tadpoles.

Distribution

The Mink Frog is found along the northern edge of the United States from Minnesota to northern New England and adjacent Canada. The species is found in the northern half of Minnesota including the northeast.

Habitat

Ponds, lakes, and slow-moving rivers throughout the forested areas of the state are the primary habitats utilized by Mink Frogs. Individuals are often seen sitting on water lilies or other emergent vegetation, including floating sphagnum borders of bogs. Mink Frogs spend the winter underwater in ponds, streams, and bogs.

Life History

Mink Frogs emerge late from winter dormancy. Males begin their calling in late May, and the breeding season extends from late June into early August. Males float in the water while making a "knock-knock-knock" vocalization. The eggs are laid in a globular mass that contains 500 to 4,000 eggs. Vogt (1981) reports that eggs are readily laid in water 1 meter (3 feet) deep or deeper. Tadpoles metamorphose in one year, but some may take two years (Hedeen 1970).

The Mink Frog is the most aquatic frog in Minnesota (Schmid 1965). Hedeen (1970) found that during the summer individuals rested with only their eyes and nose out of the water. In contrast Green Frogs remain near the shore (Fleming 1976). Mink Frogs move out on land on humid nights or during rain. When they are sitting on water lilies, they can easily be approached from canoes (Oldfield, personal observation).

Insects and their larvae comprise the bulk of the Mink Frog's diet, although the frogs will take minnows and other aquatic invertebrates (Hedeen 1970). Predators that feed on other frogs, such as raccoons, skunks, and garter snakes, also feed on Mink Frogs. Their musky odor may discourage some predators.

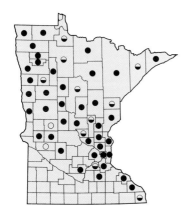

Wood Frog

Rana sylvatica

Description

The Wood Frog sports a distinctive black face mask. Skin color ranges from light tan to dark brown, and a pinkish tinge is sometimes present. Solid or dashed dark brown lines may follow along the prominent dorsolateral folds. Some individuals from northern and western Minnesota have a narrow white middorsal stripe. The belly is white and lacks markings. They are small to medium-sized frogs with a snout-vent length that ranges from 5 to 7 centimeters (2 to 2¾ inches) snout-vent length; adult females are slightly larger than adult males. The male's vocal sacs are paired and evident during the breeding season, even when deflated (Fishbeck 1968).

Wood Frog tadpoles have a greenish brown body without distinct markings, although the rounded tail fins have faint mottling. The tadpoles are 4.2 to 4.8 centimeters (1⅝ to 1⅞ inches) long, and the body to tail ratio is 1:1.8.

Distribution

*Wood Frog, adult,
Wabasha County, Minnesota*

Wood Frogs are found in the northeast and north-central United States, ranging south to Georgia and Tennessee in the Appalachian

Wood Frog, adult and eggs,
Wabasha County, Minnesota

Mountains. They are found across most of Canada west to Alaska and north of the Arctic Circle. They are found farther north than any other frog species in the Western Hemisphere. In Minnesota, Wood Frogs are found statewide except for the southwestern corner. Their distribution is spotty in the southeastern counties.

Habitat

Wood Frogs are found in moist forests, both deciduous and coniferous. In prairie areas they may be found in bottomland forests along rivers. Marshes or small ponds (permanent or temporary) are required for breeding sites. In Itasca State Park, Fishbeck (1968) found juvenile Wood Frogs living in sphagnum moss, which provides good cover for escape from predators. Winter is spent partially frozen under leaf litter on the woodland floor (Schmid 1982).

Life History

Wood Frogs are one of the earliest frogs to breed in Minnesota, starting as soon as the ice disappears from small ponds in late March or early April. In some years breeding is postponed up to a week because of a cold spell or snow (Fishbeck 1968). Flooded alder stands or meadows with standing water are regularly used for egg laying during the short breeding season, which begins and ends in less than two weeks.

At breeding ponds males call while floating on the water's surface, vocalizing during the day or night. The call is a ducklike quacking, and a chorus of frogs sounds similar to a group of feeding mallards. Large globular masses of eggs (500 to 800) may be attached to vegetation or left floating on the water's surface. Fifty to 100 egg masses are usually clustered at one end of the pond in a small area. Karns (1984) found deposition sites with over 400 egg masses in Koochiching County peatlands. Studies by Waldman (1982) indicate that these large black floating egg mats have higher temperatures than the surrounding water, thus providing a warmer environment for egg development. Eggs hatch in 14 to 20 days depending on the water temperature. Tadpoles metamorphose after six to nine weeks, and the young frogs move into the woods. Summer activity is dependent upon weather. During dry periods, Wood Frogs spend long inactive periods in leaf litter or under logs.

When Wood Frogs are active and feeding, their diet is varied but primarily consists of flies and beetles (Vogt 1981). Wood Frogs are preyed on by garter snakes, birds, and raccoons. Vogt (1981) found mink feeding on individuals at breeding ponds.

Remarks

Wood Frogs are the most common amphibians in the peatlands of northern Minnesota, and this species demonstrates a high tolerance for acidic waters (Karns 1992a). Wood Frogs breed successfully in peatland waters with a pH as low as 4.5 (Karns 1992b). This ability to withstand acidic conditions may allow Wood Frogs to survive in areas with increased acid precipitation and runoff.

REPTILES

CLASS REPTILIA

Of all the living and extinct animals, dinosaurs have captured the imagination of humans more than any other group. Highly successful, dinosaurs ruled during the Age of Reptiles that lasted for at least 200 million years. The earliest known reptile fossil is 315 million years old, and the last known "thunder lizards" perished 65 million years ago. Reptiles have continued to the present day with 6,500 known living species. Four orders of reptiles are found on the earth today. Order Rhynchocephalia contains one species, the Tuatara, found on several New Zealand islands. It is the sole survivor of a large group of primitive reptiles. Twenty-two species of the order Crocodilia (crocodilians) are found throughout the world, primarily in the tropics and subtropics. Order Testudines (turtles and tortoises) includes 245 species of distinctive reptiles with a protective shell. Order Squamata (lizards and snakes) is divided into three suborders. Worm lizards of the suborder Amphisbaenia are represented by 140 species and are found in the warmer regions of the world. Lacertilia (lizards), the largest suborder, comprises 3,750 species worldwide. Finally, a relatively modern group of reptiles, the snakes of suborder Serpentes, also has a worldwide

*Timber Rattlesnake,
reptile skin, Goodhue County,
Minnesota*

distribution. This group is made up of 2,390 species. Reptiles found in Minnesota include 9 turtles, 3 lizards, and 17 snakes.

Turtles have an upper shell (carapace) and a lower shell (plastron) connected at the sides by a bridge that allows the occupant to withdraw its head, legs, and tail inside for protection. Softshells have pliable shells in contrast to the rigid bony structure of other species. Turtles have claws on their toes and lack teeth. Most lizards have four legs and claws on their toes, although some species lack limbs. The tails of many lizard species are easily broken off when grasped by a predator, and the shortened tail is generally capable of regrowing. Lizards have eyelids and ear openings on the sides of their heads. Snakes are legless. They lack ear openings and have forked tongues. Instead of eyelids, snakes have a clear scale called a spectacle covering the eye. A segmented rattle is found on the end of the tail of our native rattlesnakes.

The most distinguishing feature of reptiles is their skin, which is comprised of scales or plates. In comparison to the skin of amphibians, the skin of reptiles markedly retards water loss and provides greater protection against abrasion. Reptiles are less dependent upon water; thus many species have been able to adapt well to dry terrestrial habitats.

Brightly colored skin pigments can be found in many species. Skin color plays an important role in attracting mates, eluding predators, and capturing prey. Several species of lizards are capable of remarkable changes in skin color. To make room for growth and to replace old skin with new, reptiles periodically shed their skin. Starting at the nose, snakes crawl out of their old skin as it turns inside out. Lizards shed in patches, and most turtles periodically lose the outer covering of their scutes. Young and growing animals shed more frequently than adults.

Reptiles do not undergo a transformation as do amphibians. A newborn reptile is a miniature replica of its parents and generally closely resembles them. Reptiles breath air with lungs throughout life. Some aquatic forms are capable of extracting small amounts of dissolved oxygen from water through special membranes located in their throat and cloaca. By supplementing oxygen needs with absorption, these species are capable of being submerged in water for prolonged periods.

With only a few exceptions, reptile reproduction is bisexual with both sexes contributing genetic material to the next generation. Courtship and breeding behaviors can be simple or elaborate, and they vary greatly from species to species. In some cases these courtship activities are instrumental in preventing interspecies breeding. Rep-

Painted Turtles, basking,
Goodhue County, Minnesota

tiles begin life as a result of internal fertilization. Females of several species have the capacity to store live sperm in their reproductive tracts, and egg fertilization occurs several months after breeding. Male lizards and snakes have paired copulatory organs called

Painted Turtle, depositing eggs, Goodhue County, Minnesota

Common Garter Snakes, courting behavior, Goodhue County, Minnesota

hemipenes; during copulation, however, only one of the organs is used. (See the individual species accounts for more detailed descriptions of reproductive behavior.)

The shelled amniote egg was an important evolutionary step for reptiles because it broke their tie to water for egg development and allowed them to reproduce in terrestrial environments. Many reptile species lay eggs; however, a number of lizards and snakes give birth to fully developed young. Eggs are generally laid by the female in

moist soil or humus and are abandoned for development. Several species of reptiles demonstrate egg tending and provide primitive
parental care to their young. Female skinks found in Minnesota
brood their egg clutch until the young hatch. Newborn rattlesnakes
stay with their mother for a period of 10 to 14 days after birth.

Gopher Snakes, hatching,
Anoka County, Minnesota

Many reptiles have a highly developed sense of smell, which is used
primarily to procure food and locate mates. Lizards and snakes use
their tongues to "taste" the environment. Their tongues relay small
particles of their surroundings to a pair of Jacobson's organs, located
in the back of the mouth, for sensory analysis. Sight is well developed in many species. Aquatic turtles depend upon visual cues to
detect approaching predators while they bask. Reptilian vocalizations
are rare, and their sense of hearing is poorly developed. Snakes are
totally deaf, but they are remarkably sensitive to vibrations. Pit vipers
possess a highly developed pair of infrared-sensitive facial pits. The
pits are capable of detecting very small changes in temperature (e.g.,
the snake can tell when a warm-blooded prey animal comes within
striking distance).

Food requirements vary among reptilian species. Turtles may
be herbivorous, carnivorous, or omnivorous. Hatchlings of Minnesota's turtle species are carnivorous, but they may begin eating vegetation as they mature. A large percentage of lizards are carnivorous,

Gopher Snake, feeding,
Goodhue County, Minnesota

and all snakes and crocodilians are carnivorous. Snakes consume their prey whole, and they are capable of swallowing food items larger than their head because of elastic articulations in their jaws. Three methods of securing prey are used by snakes in Minnesota. The seize-and-swallow method is used by such species as the Racer and garter snakes. Constrictors such as the Gopher Snake and Fox

Wood Turtle, feeding

Snake grasp the animal in their mouth and constrict it with body coils. Death of the prey is due to suffocation. Rattlesnakes use venom to immobilize their prey before they swallow it.

Some reptilian species mature in less than 12 months, whereas others require as many as 20 years to reach adulthood. The longevity of some species of turtles and tortoises is known to exceed 100 years, although 15 to 20 years is average for most turtles and large snakes. The life span of small snakes and the majority of lizards does not exceed 10 years.

REPTILE FAMILIES NATIVE TO MINNESOTA

Family Trionychidae—Softshells

Softshells comprise a relatively small family of turtles with only 22 species in 6 genera. They are found across Asia, Africa, and North America. Softshells have a distinctive flattened shape, a long snorkel-like nose, and expansive webbing on their feet. Leathery skin covers their carapace and plastron. Softshell turtles are highly aquatic and are fast, agile swimmers. They are also capable of surprising bursts of speed on land.

Of the three species of softshell turtles found in the continental United States, two, the Smooth Softshell and the Spiny Softshell, are found in Minnesota. Both species are at home in major river systems and are occasionally found in large ponds and reservoirs. They are frequently observed on riverbanks and on downed trees at the water's edge.

Family Chelydridae—Snapping Turtles

Only two species are assigned to this turtle family, both of which occur in the United States. Snapping turtles have massive heads, small X-shaped plastrons, and a long tail armed with a crest of bony plates. These turtles are highly aquatic and are seldom seen on land except during periods of nesting.

The largest turtle in Minnesota and the sole representative of Chelydridae is the Snapping Turtle. It is found in almost any body of permanent water in the state.

Family Emydidae—Pond and River Turtles

Emydidae is the largest family of turtles with 31 genera and 85 species. Excluding Australia they are found worldwide in tropical and temperate regions. Many members of the family are highly aquatic and spend much of their time in or close to water. These small to medium-sized turtles have a well-developed carapace and plastron with a broad bridge connecting the upper and lower shells on each side. There is some degree of webbing between the toes to aid swimming activities. Many species also exhibit elaborate skin patterns in bright colors of yellow, red, or green.

Minnesota is home to six species of pond and river turtles. Included in the list are the Painted Turtle, the Wood Turtle, Blanding's Turtle, the Common Map Turtle, the Ouachita Map Turtle, and the False Map Turtle.

Family Teiidae—Racerunners and Whiptails

Teiidae is a large family of 227 species and 39 genera of New World lizards with the vast majority of species in South America. They are built for speed with well-developed legs, a pointed head, and a long, thin tail. Small granular scales on the back contrast with large rectangular belly scales. Their tongue is long and deeply forked like that of snakes. The smallest teiid is 7.6 centimeters (3 inches) long, and the largest exceeds 122 centimeters (48 inches). Racerunners and whiptails are diurnal, terrestrial, and oviparous. Several species of teiids are unisexual and reproduce by parthenogenesis.

Excluding several introduced forms in southern Florida, there are 15 species of racerunners and whiptails native to the United States. All species belong to the genus *Cnemidophorus*. One teiid ranges into Minnesota, the Six-lined Racerunner.

Family Scincidae—Skinks

Scincidae is the third largest lizard family with nearly 1,275 species worldwide. Representatives of 85 genera are found on every continent except Antarctica, and they are especially abundant in the tropics of Southeast Asia. The United States has 14 species belonging to 3 genera.

A typical skink has numerous shiny, smooth scales covering a sausage-shaped body and tail. The tail readily breaks off when grasped by a predator, and the wriggling tail segment serves as a decoy while the skink runs for safety. These diurnal lizards are chiefly terrestrial and customarily feed on small invertebrates. Virtually all New World species lay eggs, and females typically guard the egg clutch until hatching.

Minnesota has two species of skinks, both belonging to the genus *Eumeces*. The Prairie Skink is relatively common across the state, but the Five-lined Skink is found only in selected localities.

Family Colubridae—Colubrid Snakes

Colubridae is the largest family of snakes and contains 65% of all snakes in the world. Over 1,550 species are known worldwide, and representatives are found on every continent except Antarctica. The

United States has 92 representatives of this interesting and diverse group of snakes.

Fifteen of Minnesota's 17 snake species belong to this family. They range in size from the small Ringneck Snake and Redbelly Snake to the large Gopher snake and Rat Snake. They may be stout-bodied, such as the Eastern Hognose and Western Hognose Snakes, or slender and sleek, such as the Racer and the Smooth Green Snake. Some species are live-bearers, whereas others lay eggs. A few species produce a very mild toxin to help immobilize prey, but none are dangerous to humans. Other Minnesota colubrids include the Fox Snake, the Milk Snake, the Northern Water Snake, the Brown Snake, the Plains Garter Snake, the Common Garter Snake, and the Lined Snake.

Family Viperidae—Vipers and Pit Vipers

Of the 187 species of venomous vipers found worldwide, approximately 75% are pit vipers belonging to the subfamily Crotalinae. Pit vipers have unique, highly sophisticated, heat-sensitive facial pits located on each side of the head between the eye and the nostril. These pits allow the snakes to locate warm-blooded prey in total darkness. All pit vipers have vertical pupils. They have stout bodies, narrow necks, broad heads, and a pair of hollow, retractable fangs on the front of the upper jaw. The United States is home to 17 species of pit vipers, 15 of which are members of 2 genera of rattlesnakes. Although many species of snakes (venomous and nonvenomous) vibrate their tails when alarmed, only rattlesnakes have a segmented rattle on the end of their tail that produces a distinctive sonorous buzz. Rattles may have evolved as a warning device to prevent large herbivores from stepping on the snakes.

The rattlesnakes are the only snakes with elliptical pupils that are native to Minnesota. Pit vipers found in Minnesota are the Timber Rattlesnake and the extremely rare Massasauga. These snakes are dangerous to humans and should be avoided or observed from a safe distance. When hiking in southeastern Minnesota where rattlesnakes may be encountered, people should wear substantial footwear and watch where they place their hands. In the unlikely event that a venomous snake bite occurs, the bite victim should be kept calm and should be taken directly to the nearest hospital. Nearly all first-aid measures for snake bites are either ineffective or potentially dangerous and should be avoided. Additional information concerning field first aid for venomous snake bites is available in a current Red Cross manual. At the hospital the attending physician should confer with the Minnesota Poison Control Center if he or she is unfamiliar with modern treatment methods.

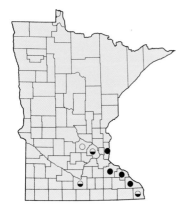

Smooth Softshell

Apalone mutica

Description

The Smooth Softshell is a medium-sized turtle with delicate-appearing features and a pancake-shaped shell. The completely smooth, keelless carapace is leatherlike and flexible, lacking the hard plate-like scutes common to the majority of turtles. The head has a long, tubular snout, and the feet are paddlelike with extensive webbing. Adult males and juveniles have a brown or grayish tan carapace with numerous, scattered small dark brown dots or dashes. The carapace of adult females is tan or brown with irregular dark brown blotches and patches. The plastron of the Smooth Softshell is unmarked white or light gray, and the underlying bones are visible as darker areas of gray. Dorsal coloration of the limbs, tail, head, and neck is similar to that of the carapace. A black-bordered cream or orange line extends from each eye back onto the turtle's neck. The carapace of hatchlings is light brown with a scattering of small dark dots and dashes.

Smooth Softshell, adult male, Wabasha County, Minnesota

Males have thick tails with the cloacal opening well beyond the edge of the carapace near the tail tip. Females have a less robust tail with the cloacal opening close to the carapace edge. Males are smaller with a carapace length of 11.5 to 17.8 centimeters (4½ to 7 inches), whereas females range from 16.5 to 35.6 centimeters (6½ to 14 inches; Conant and Collins 1991).

The Spiny Softshell is the only turtle species in Minnesota that is easily confused with the Smooth Softshell. Ordinarily, a positive identification is possible after the turtle is in hand. In contrast to the carapace of the Smooth Softshell, the carapace of the Spiny Softshell may feel like sandpaper. Spines and bumps are present along the front edge of the Spiny Softshell's carapace; the front edge of the Smooth Softshell's carapace is smooth. The Spiny Softshell also has a lateral projection on the nasal septum that extends into the nasal opening. The nasal septum of the Smooth Softshell lacks lateral projections.

Distribution

The Smooth Softshell is found across the central United States ranging from western Pennsylvania to southern North Dakota and south to eastern New Mexico and the Florida panhandle. The turtle's range follows along major river systems including the Mississippi, Missouri, Ohio, Arkansas, and Alabama. The Smooth Softshell is infrequently reported in Minnesota, with records primarily confined to the Mississippi and St. Croix rivers. Wright County is as far north as they have been found in the state. There is a single specimen from the Minnesota River in Blue Earth County.

Habitat

In Minnesota this species is found only in large rivers with moderate to fast currents. It prefers sand or mud bottoms; dense aquatic vegetation and rocky bottoms are avoided. The winter is spent burrowed in the mud on the river bottom to avoid freezing temperatures (Collins 1982).

Life History

Smooth Softshells become active in early to mid-May (Vogt 1981), when they can be seen basking on sandbars close to the water's edge. They spend large amounts of time buried in the sand in shallow water periodically using their long necks and snouts as snorkels. They are also capable of obtaining absorbed oxygen from the water through membranes lining their pharynx and cloaca, thereby allowing them to remain submerged for extended periods of time (Cahn 1937).

The diet of this highly carnivorous turtle includes fish, frogs, tadpoles, mudpuppies, crayfish, aquatic insects, snails, bivalves, and worms (Ernst and Barbour 1972). Plummer and Farrar (1981) demonstrated that female turtles in Kansas obtain most of their food from deep water, whereas the males hunt in shallow water. Smooth softshells obtain much of their food as they prowl through the water probing with their long necks and noses, but they may also wait in ambush while buried. Highly aquatic, Smooth Softshells are fully capable of chasing down and catching fish.

Breeding most likely occurs in May and June in Minnesota. According to Ernst and Barbour (1972), females mature at seven years of age at a carapace length of 17 to 22 centimeters (6¾ to 8¾ inches), and males become sexually active at a carapace length of 11 to 12.5 centimeters (4¼ to 5 inches). Males actively seek out females by swimming around and investigating other turtles. The receptive female is mounted from behind, and copulation takes place in the water.

Nesting occurs in June and early July on sandbars and riverbanks in full sunlight (Vogt 1981). The female uses her hind feet to dig an egg cavity generally within 18 meters (60 feet) of the water. Females are easily frightened by intruders and may abandon the nesting procedure if disturbed. Clutches normally consist of 15 to 25 eggs, although the range is 4 to 33 (Ernst and Barbour 1972). Eggs resemble Ping-Pong balls with a diameter of 2.0 to 2.3 centimeters (¾ to ⅞ inch) and have thick, hard white shells. After 8 to 12 weeks of development within the eggs, the hatchlings tear through the shells using their front claws. They are equipped with an egg tooth (caruncle) but make less use of it than other turtle species do.

Hatchling Smooth Softshells are nearly circular in shape and average 4.1 centimeters (1⅝ inches) in carapace length (Ernst and Barbour 1972). The hatchling comes from the egg with a turned up snout and a spherical-shaped shell; after a short period, its shell flattens out. The caruncle falls off in seven to ten days.

Wariness and speed comprise the basic self-defense plan of Smooth Softshells. They dive in the water and bury themselves in the river bottom at the slightest hint of danger. If surprised on land, they can outdistance a human on level terrain (Ernst and Barbour 1972). Adult turtles have few natural enemies, but hatchlings succumb to large fish, turtles, snakes, wading birds, and small mammals. Skunks, raccoons, and crows excavate the nests and eat the eggs.

Remarks

The classification of softshell turtles was changed in 1987 (Meylan 1987), and the scientific name of the Smooth Softshell was changed

from *Trionyx muticus* to *Apalone mutica*. Breckenridge (1944) used the name brown soft-shelled turtle (*Amyda mutica*) to describe this species. According to Conant and Collins (1991), the subspecies of Smooth Softshell found in Minnesota is the Midland Smooth Softshell (*Apalone mutica mutica*).

Smooth Softshell, hatchling, Washington County, Minnesota

Although Smooth Softshells may feed on small game fish, it is doubtful that this species does any significant damage to fish populations (Ernst and Barbour 1972). Smooth Softshells are timid and rarely scratch or bite when handled, whereas Spiny Softshells tend to be much more aggressive.

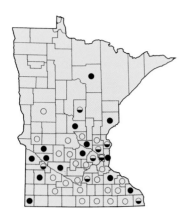

Spiny Softshell

Apalone spinifera

Description

The Spiny Softshell is a medium to large turtle with a flattened profile, pointed snout, and a leathery shell lacking bony plates. The front edge of the oval-shaped carapace has numerous spines or projections in mature turtles. Dorsal coloration of the shell and appendages ranges from olive green to tan with dark brown or black markings. The carapace of males and immature females is adorned with prominent ocelli (eyelike spots) and a dark line running along the shell margin. Adult females have blotches of light and dark creating a camouflage pattern that makes the ocelli and margin line

Spiny Softshell, adult male, Goodhue County, Minnesota

less obvious. The upper surfaces of the legs and neck are decorated with numerous black blotches and bold lines. The feet have extensive webbing between the toes. A yellow stripe with a black border begins at the nostril, divides into two stripes on top of the snout, and continues through the eyes and down the neck on each side. The nasal septum has a ridge projecting laterally into both nasal openings. Typically, the hingeless white plastron shows dark underlying bones. Juvenile turtles resemble adult males in shape and coloration, but their carapaces remain smooth until they mature.

Adult males are significantly smaller than females. Males are 12.5 to 23.5 centimeters (5 to 9¼ inches) in carapace length, whereas females are 18 to 45.7 centimeters (7 to 18 inches; Conant and Collins 1991). The largest Spiny Softshell specimen from Minnesota, which is in the James Ford Bell Museum of Natural History, is a female with a carapace length of 47 centimeters (18½ inches). Males have longer, thicker tails with the cloacal opening very close to the tail tip. The dorsal surface of the male's carapace has a rough sandpaper texture.

In contrast to the Spiny Softshell, the adult Smooth Softshell's carapace is smooth along the front edge. Additionally, the nasal septum of the Spiny Softshell has a transverse ridge (not found in the Smooth Softshell) that projects into the nasal openings.

Distribution

The Spiny Softshell ranges from western New York to central Minnesota and then south to Texas and extreme northern Florida. Disjunct populations are found in eastern New York, Vermont, and New Jersey. This turtle is also found in Montana and along the Colorado and Rio Grande rivers in several southwestern states. In Minnesota the distribution of the Spiny Softshell follows major river drainages in the central and southern portions of the state. Individuals have also been located in several northern counties in mid-sized rivers and lakes.

Habitat

The Spiny Softshell is primarily a river turtle in Minnesota, but it is also found in large lakes and impoundments. Mud or sand bottoms with gravel, or sandbars and beaches are important habitat requirements. This species avoids aquatic conditions with rocky bottoms or abundant emergent vegetation. Spiny Softshells overwinter underwater, buried in sand or mud bottoms (Ernst and Barbour 1972).

Life History

Emerging from winter dormancy on warm days during late April and May, this highly aquatic turtle spends considerable time on banks, sandbars, or fallen trees basking at the river's edge. Time in the water is spent foraging, floating with the current, or buried on the bottom in shallow water. When the turtle is concealed under mud or sand, its long neck and nose periodically serve as a snorkel. The vascular lining of the pharynx and cloaca aids in respiration by

Spiny Softshell, hatchlings, Winona County, Minnesota

absorbing dissolved oxygen from the water, allowing individuals to remain submerged for up to five hours at room temperature (Dunson 1960).

The carnivorous Spiny Softshell actively searches for food or lies buried waiting to ambush prey. Studies indicate that this turtle feeds primarily on invertebrates including crayfish and aquatic insects. Mollusks, fish, frogs, tadpoles, earthworms, and carrion are also eaten (Ernst and Barbour 1972).

In Minnesota courtship and mating are primarily springtime events followed by egg laying in June and early July. The female Spiny Softshell selects an open sandy or gravelly area close to the water to lay her eggs. She excavates an egg cavity to a depth of 10 to 25 centimeters (4 to 10 inches). As she digs, her hind feet spray sand over the top of her carapace. Breckenridge (1960) reported that a female in Minnesota dug a nest in 15 minutes, deposited 17 eggs in 6 minutes, and covered the eggs in 5 minutes. Females often abandon the nesting process and scramble for the water if disturbed.

The spherical, brittle eggs are white and measure 2.8 to 3.2 centimeters (1 to 1¼ inches) in diameter. Clutch size ranges from 4 to 32 eggs, but a typical size is 15 to 20. Females may nest two times each season (Ernst and Barbour 1972), but this behavior has not been documented in Minnesota. Hatchlings leave the eggs in late August or early September with curled noses and rounded carapaces. Several hours after hatching, the carapace flattens out to a length of 3.2 to 3.8 centimeters (1¼ to 1½ inches). Overwintering in the nest has been reported in Indiana (Minton 1972).

Breckenridge (1955) published growth rate data from Minnesota Spiny Softshells. He reported that a 10-year-old female had a carapace length of 25 centimeters (9⅞ inches); a 15-year-old, 30 centimeters (11¾ inches); a 20-year-old, 33 centimeters (13 inches); a 30-year old, 38 centimeters (15 inches); and a 53-year-old, 43 centimeters (17 inches). A ten-year-old male was 16 centimeters (6¼ inches); and a 15-year-old, 17 centimeters (6¾ inches).

Spiny Softshells are extremely wary and quickly seek the safety of water if disturbed. When captured, they are exceptionally pugnacious. Swift strikes by the long neck, successive attempts to bite with the sharp beak, and rapid raking actions of the clawed feet make large individuals difficult to handle. The best control is obtained by firmly gripping the base of the hind legs while holding the turtle well away from one's body.

Nests of Spiny Softshells are destroyed by raccoons and skunks. Hatchlings fall prey to fish, larger turtles, wading birds, and carnivorous mammals. Large adults have few natural predators, although human activities can have an adverse impact on populations.

Remarks

Taxonomy changes of softshell turtles by Meylan (1987) resulted in a change of name for the Spiny Softshell from *Trionyx spiniferus* to *Apalone spinifera*. Breckenridge (1944) used the name *Amyda spinifera*. Two subspecies of the Spiny Softshell occur in Minnesota (Conant and Collins 1991). The Mississippi and St. Croix river valleys are the zone of intergradation between the eastern Spiny Softshell (*A. s. spinifera*) and the western Spiny Softshell (*A. s. hartwegi*). The eastern subspecies has large black-bordered ocelli on the carapace, whereas the western variety has small dots and eyespots.

Spiny Softshells are taken for food by turtle trappers in Minnesota, but the extent of harvest is unknown as they are seldom sold commercially. These turtles are frequently referred to as "leatherbacks" or "pancake turtles." They have lived more than 25 years in captivity (Behler and King 1979).

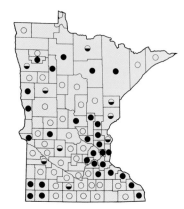

Snapping Turtle

Chelydra serpentina

Description

Minnesota's largest turtle is well known for its ill disposition and aggressive attitude. The Snapping Turtle is equipped with a massive carapace and a large head with powerful jaws. The carapace has three longitudinal keels, which wear down and become smooth in old adults. Serrations are apparent on the back edge of the dorsal shell. The tail is longer than the carapace and has a dorsal row of sawtooth projections. The carapace, which is often covered with mud or algae, is brown, olive, or black. Normally there is a pattern of radiating lines on each scute in young turtles. The small, X-shaped plastron is light yellow or tan and provides little protection for the underside of the turtle. The dorsal surfaces of the limbs and head are gray or brown with varying amounts of mottling. The upper and lower jaws of the mouth are pale yellow with vertical black lines. Tubercles are present on the long neck. Snapping Turtles have well-developed limbs with strong claws.

Snapping Turtle, adult female, St. Louis County, Minnesota

Male Snapping Turtles reach larger sizes than females, and their tails are proportionally longer. In contrast to that of the female, the cloacal opening of the male is posterior to the carapace margin. Hatchling Snapping Turtles are dark brown to black and bear small white flecks on their undersides.

Snapping Turtle, plastron, Goodhue County, Minnesota

Straight-line measurement of the carapace of adult Snapping Turtles ranges from 20.3 to 36 centimeters (8 to 14 inches), and the average adult weighs 4.5 to 16 kilograms (10 to 35 pounds; Conant and Collins 1991). The largest known Minnesota individual was a male snagged by a fisherman in the Popple River in Itasca County during the summer of 1986 (Gerholdt and Oldfield 1987). "Minnesota Fats" had a carapace length of 49.4 centimeters (19½ inches) and weighed 29.6 kilograms (65 pounds).

Distribution

The range of the Snapping Turtle is from Maine and adjacent Canada west to Montana and south to New Mexico and southern Florida. This species is found across the entire United States east of the Rocky Mountains. The Snapping Turtle has a statewide distribution in Minnesota.

Habitat

Snapping Turtles make a home in almost any type of permanent freshwater body including ponds, lakes, marshes, rivers, creeks, and backwater sloughs. Larger populations of Snapping Turtles are found in water bodies with mud bottoms and abundant aquatic vegetation.

These turtles often congregate in large numbers to overwinter below the ice in muskrat tunnels, streams, and holes in riverbanks (Vogt 1981). They bury themselves in decaying vegetation and mud while waiting out freezing weather. On occasion, Snapping Turtles have been seen slowly moving through the water under the ice during midwinter (Ernst and Barbour 1972).

Life History

Snapping Turtles become active with the onset of warm weather in late April or May and can be seen basking with other turtle species. They bask less frequently during the summer because they are intolerant of high temperatures and rapidly lose body water by evaporation (Ernst and Barbour 1972).

Snapping Turtles are highly aquatic. They either lie on the bottom in shallow water, extending their long necks just far enough to project their nostrils above the water for air, or they float beneath the water surface with nostrils and eyes exposed. During the day they frequently hide beneath submerged logs, rocks, and debris. When night arrives, they become active and crawl along the bottom in search of food. Overland migration of adults occasionally occurs during wet springs (Oldfield, personal observation). If their pond dries up during summer, they are forced to make an overland trek in search of water.

The omnivorous Snapping Turtle is not a finicky eater. It eats insects, crayfish, clams, snails, earthworms, leeches, freshwater sponges, fish, fish eggs, frogs, toads, tadpoles, amphibian eggs, salamanders, snakes, small turtles, birds, small mammals, carrion, and various types of aquatic plants (Ernst and Barbour 1972). An unusual event was reported in Minnesota in which a Snapping Turtle killed an adult Trumpeter Swan. The submerged turtle grasped the neck of the feeding swan in its mouth, and the bird drowned while attempting to escape (Moriarty 1990). Snapping Turtles must feed while submerged because water pressure is essential for swallowing. Small food items are swallowed whole, but larger ones are held with their mouth and torn apart with their front claws. Adult turtles tend to wait in ambush for prey, whereas young Snapping Turtles are more likely to search for food.

Snapping Turtles are sexually mature at five to seven years of age at a carapace length of 20 centimeters (7⅞ inches). Mating occurs during chance encounters any time from April to October. Legler (1955) described underwater courtship activity between a pair in which they faced each other on the bottom and made sideward sweeps of their necks in sequences of ten at intervals of ten seconds. Actual mating takes place when the male mounts the female and forcibly grips her carapace with his claws while he bites at her head and neck. Copulation is achieved when he curls his tail under hers, inserting his penis into her cloacal opening. Female Snapping Turtles are known to retain viable sperm for several years (Collins 1982).

Egg laying takes place during June in Minnesota. Females often make lengthy trips away from water to seek suitable open areas for nesting. Sandy riverbanks, fields, road embankments, and lawns are commonly chosen. The greatest incidence of nesting activity occurs in early morning or late evening when temperatures are greater than 15.5° C (60° F) and there is a light rain (Hammer 1969). The nest is dug entirely with the female's hind legs to a depth of 10 to 17.8 centimeters (4 to 7 inches). At one-minute intervals she deposits 20 to 30 eggs (up to 83), guiding them into the cavity with her hind legs. The white eggs have a tough, leathery shell and are shaped like Ping-Pong balls with a diameter of 2.3 to 3.3 centimeters (⅞ to 1¼ inches). After covering the nest, she returns to the water. Egg development takes 50 to 125 days depending on the weather, but most eggs hatch in approximately 55 days. Laboratory incubation of Minnesota Snapping Turtle eggs produced 50% males and 50% females at 28° C (82.4° F); lower temperatures, however, produced predominantly males whereas higher produced mostly females (Jeff Lang, personal communication). Young Snapping Turtles must exit the nest in the fall because they are unlikely to survive nest temperatures during winter in Minnesota (Lang, personal communication). Hatchlings have a carapace length of 2.6 to 3.1 centimeters (1 to 1¼ inches).

A Snapping Turtle pulled from its watery home or cornered on land lives up to its name by repeatedly lunging and striking with its mouth agape. It is capable of delivering a painful and damaging bite, and care should be exercised when handling one. To carry one, it is best to securely grasp the turtle's hind legs near the shell and hold the turtle at a safe distance from one's legs. Suspending a large Snapping Turtle by its tail can cause serious damage to the turtle's spinal cord. Typically, agitated turtles emit a strong pungent odor. While in the water, they seem more intent on crawling or swimming away than on standing their ground.

Adult Snapping Turtles have few predators other than humans and their automobiles, but natural predation of eggs and young is remarkably high. Raccoons, skunks, fox, and opossum dig up nests and eat freshly laid eggs. Nest destruction rates in some areas approach 90% (Oldfield, personal observation). Hatchlings and immature turtles fall prey to crows, herons, bitterns, Bullfrogs, snakes, and large predatory fish.

Remarks

Chelydra serpentina serpentina, or the Common Snapping Turtle, is the subspecies of Snapping Turtle found in Minnesota (Conant and Collins 1991). "Snapper" is a widespread nickname.

Significant numbers of Snapping Turtles are harvested each year in Minnesota for human consumption. During the winter, commercial turtle hunters locate overwintering congregations by probing through the ice with long poles. The turtles are pulled up through the ice with a sharp hook on the end of the pole. Nesting females are captured on land during the month of June, and baited turtle traps are commonly used during warmer months. A study by the Minnesota Pollution Control Agency in 1982 showed that Snapping Turtles from the Mississippi River in the southeastern part of the state contained high levels of toxic PCBs.

The Minnesota Department of Natural Resources gives special concern status to the Snapping Turtle primarily because of harvesting pressures. Harvesting is substantial and unregulated, although licensing is required (Coffin and Pfannmuller 1988). A recent study conducted in Ontario, Canada (Obbaard 1985), indicates that Snapping Turtles are a species that cannot sustain continual harvesting pressures. Vulnerable females should be provided protection during the nesting season by closing the harvest season during May and June.

Painted Turtle

Chrysemys picta

Description

The well-known, small to medium-sized Painted Turtle is appropriately named for the colorful design on its plastron and marginal scutes. Its oval carapace is smooth, flattened, and unkeeled. The upper shell is dark olive to black with a netlike pattern of faint lines. The reddish color on the edge of the carapace continues onto the ventral surface of the marginal scales, interrupted by patterns of black and yellow. The large plastron is heavily bridged to the carapace and has a ground color of pale orange or red with an elaborate

Painted Turtle, adult male, Goodhue County, Minnesota

design of black, gray, tan, and yellow. The head, legs, and tail are dark olive or black with conspicuous yellow or red lines. Generally, a bold yellow streak is present behind each eye. The upper jaw is notched.

Mature male Painted Turtles are smaller than females, and they have a more oblong-shaped carapace, elongated foreclaws, and a longer tail with the vent beyond the carapace edge. Hatchling Painted Turtles have a circular carapace with a weak keel. Their coloration and markings are similar to those of adults, although colors found on the plastron tend to be more vivid in young turtles. The caruncle (egg tooth) drops off by the fifth day (Vogt 1981).

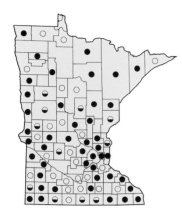

Adult Painted Turtles have a carapace length of 9 to 18 centimeters (3½ to 7 inches; Conant and Collins 1991). The largest reported Minnesota individual was a female from Murray County with a carapace length of 21.5 centimeters (8½ inches).

Distribution

Painted Turtles are found from Maine south to northern Georgia and west to the eastern border of Texas. The northern border of their range runs west through southern Canada and the northern United States to Washington and Oregon. Scattered, disjunct populations are found in several southwestern states. This species is the only conspicuous basking turtle in many northern states (Conant and Collins 1991). In Minnesota the Painted Turtle has a statewide distribution, although it is less common in the lakes of the northeastern part of the state.

Painted Turtle, plastron, Lake County, Minnesota

Painted Turtle, stained plastron, Wabasha County, Minnesota

Habitat

Permanent bodies of water, such as ponds, lakes, marshes, sloughs, and creeks, with soft bottoms, aquatic vegetation, and ample basking sites are the preferred habitat of the Painted Turtle (Ernst and Barbour 1972). Individuals are also found in the state's larger rivers and in lakes with rocky shores, but the turtles do not attain high populations in these localities. Overwintering occurs in water and mud under the ice. Large numbers may group together behind submerged logs or rocks. Preston (1982) observed individuals resting on the bottom of a shallow ice-covered pond in British Columbia.

Life History

The cold-tolerant Painted Turtle can be seen basking on logs as early as mid-April on warm sunny days. They remain active until late October. After spending the night under water, these diurnal reptiles alternate periods of basking, which usually last two hours, with periods of foraging for food (Ernst and Barbour 1972). They frequently share basking sites with other turtles and can often be seen stacked two or three high.

Adult Painted Turtles are omnivorous, and they obtain food by foraging in the water along the bottom and through surface vegetation. According to Vogt (1981), approximately 60% of their diet is animal matter (snails, crayfish, insects, fish carrion, and tadpoles), and the remainder is plant material (algae, cattail, and duckweed). The turtles actively pursue most animal prey, but occasionally they wait in ambush. Hatchling and juvenile Painted Turtles are carnivorous.

Painted Turtles reach sexual maturity at four to six years of age, and there is evidence that maturity is associated with size rather than age (Ernst and Barbour 1972). The majority of courtship and mating takes place in shallow water during May and early June. A male follows a female, overtakes her, and positions himself in front of and facing her. He uses his long front claws to gently stroke her head and neck. She usually reacts by stroking his front legs with her foreclaws. At the conclusion of the courting behavior, she sinks to the bottom. The male mounts her carapace grasping the edges with his claws and curls his tail under hers to achieve copulation (Collins 1982).

Egg laying begins in late May and may extend well into July, but the majority of the nesting takes place during June in Minnesota. Gravid turtles seek out open areas (south-facing hillsides, sand beaches, railroad rights-of-way, road shoulders, etc.) with loose soil or sand to dig flask-shaped egg chambers with their hind legs. Generally 8 to 9 (2 to 20) white, elliptical eggs with leathery shells comprise a clutch. Average egg size is 3.2 centimeters by 1.9 centimeters (1¼ by ¾ inches; Vogt 1981). Studies by Moll (1973) in Wisconsin showed that two-thirds of female Painted Turtles in Wisconsin laid two clutches per year. Jeff Lang (personal communication) reported that double clutching occurs in northern Minnesota as well and that the sex of the hatchling is determined by nest temperatures. Laboratory temperatures above 29° C (84.2° F) produced mostly females whereas lower temperatures resulted in high numbers of males.

Hatching begins in late August after 72 to 80 days of development within the egg, but the young turtles frequently stay in the nest until the next spring. Woolverton (1961) studied Painted Turtle nests in northern Minnesota. He found live hatchlings in a nest on 25 October that had been constructed by a female turtle on 25 June. Hatchlings emerged from the nest the following June after surviving temperatures of -11° C (12.2° F).

Large numbers of Painted Turtle nests are destroyed by raccoons, skunks, opossum, foxes, and thirteen-lined ground squirrels. Hatchlings and juvenile turtles fall prey to mink, crows, larger turtles, garter snakes, Northern Water Snakes, Bullfrogs, and predatory fish. Thousands are killed each year by automobiles.

Remarks

Of the four recognized subspecies of Painted Turtles, only the Western Painted Turtle (*Chrysemys picta bellii*) is found in Minnesota (Conant and Collins 1991). A common misnomer for this species is "mud turtle."

Large numbers of Painted Turtles from Mississippi River backwaters and ponds in the Weaver Dunes area in Wabasha County have dark rust-brown plastrons. Similar individuals are occasionally found in other areas of the state. This coloration is presumably due to absorption of chemicals from the water (Vogt 1981). The original color returns after the turtle sheds its scutes.

Painted Turtles are the most prevalent turtle species in Minnesota, and some ponds are virtually teeming with them. A Michigan population studied by Gibbons (1968b) showed a sex ratio of 1:1 and an estimated population of 94 per hectare (38 per acre). He found that only 2% of the eggs developed into juveniles that became part of the adult population. Painted Turtles are commercially collected in Minnesota for biological supply companies.

Longevity is thought to exceed 40 years in the wild (Gibbons 1968a), but the longest reported captivity period is 16 years (Bowler 1977).

Wood Turtle

Clemmys insculpta

Description

The Wood Turtle, an attractive turtle with a distinctive, sculptured shell, is rare in Minnesota. Each large scute on its broad, rugged carapace is shaped like a low pyramid formed by a stack of concentric growth rings. The back edge of the upper shell is flattened and serrated. The turtle's carapace ranges from light tan to rich dark brown. Some individuals may have prominent yellow lines on each scute arranged in a sunburst pattern. The hingeless plastron is yellow with large black blotches located laterally on the scutes. The underside of the marginals is similarly patterned. The dorsal surfaces of the extremities are dark brown with occasional yellow flecking. The skin covering the soft body parts near the shell, the lower surface of the neck, and the undersides of the legs and tail is yellow. The iris of the Wood Turtle's eye is rich brown with a thin yellow inner margin. In rare individuals the entire eye color is yellow (Oldfield, personal observation).

Adult male Wood Turtles are somewhat larger than females. When a male and female are comparable in size, the head of the

Wood Turtle, adult female, Goodhue County, Minnesota

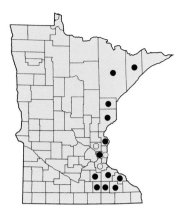

male is significantly larger than that of the female. Unlike the female, the male has a concave plastron, a long, thick tail, and large plate-like scales on his forelegs. Hatchlings have a greenish gray, unkeeled, circular shell that is nearly flat. The hatchling's tail is almost as long as its carapace. Young turtles lack the yellow coloration of adults.

Adult Wood Turtles have a carapace length ranging from 14 to 20 centimeters (5½ to 8 inches; Conant and Collins 1991). The largest known Wood Turtle from Minnesota was a male from St. Louis County with a length of 25 centimeters (9⅞ inches) and a weight of 1,860 grams (4.1 pounds; Dick Buech, personal communication).

Distribution

Wood Turtles are found from the northeastern United States, from northern Virginia to Maine, extending westward through parts of southern Canada, Michigan, and Wisconsin into eastern Minnesota and northeastern Iowa. Records for Wood Turtles come from 15 eastern Minnesota counties, where they are associated with mid-sized rivers flowing through forested areas. The species is uncommon in the state even in areas of suitable habitat.

Habitat

The Wood Turtle's primary habitat in Minnesota includes a river with a fairly narrow floodplain and distinct rises to uplands. Much of the floodplain and most of the uplands are wooded. Ewert (1985) speculates that appropriate habitat extends no farther than 366 meters (400 yards) inland from the home river. In northern Minnesota Wood Turtles with radio transmitters generally stayed within 100 meters (109 yards) of the river (Dick Buech, personal communication). Wood Turtles share habitat with Snapping Turtles, Painted Turtles, Common Map Turtles, and Spiny Softshells. Individual Wood Turtles overwinter in the water beneath the ice in bank undercuts and near log jams.

Life History

Wood Turtles become active by late April and begin basking along riverbanks on warm days. Diurnal in their habits, Wood Turtles are the most terrestrial of Minnesota turtles. Individuals from the western part of the species' range, including Minnesota, remain closer to water than their eastern counterparts (Harding and Bloomer 1979).

According to Ewert (1985), Wood Turtles obtain nearly all of their food on land. This omnivorous turtle generally refuses fish; it eats various succulent forbs, willow leaves, dandelions, strawberries, raspberries, blueberries, mushrooms, earthworms, slugs, and a variety of insects. Occasionally, carrion is taken; Farrell and Graham (1991) reported a male eating a dead fish. Kaufmann (1989) reported an interesting foraging behavior in Wood Turtles—they "stomp" for worms. Turtles were observed to rock back and forth from side to side and alternately stomp the soil with their front feet. The vibrations caused by this "stomping" induced earthworms to surface. Emerging worms were seized and eaten by the turtles.

The Wood Turtle is a late-maturing species and produces one clutch of eggs per year. Farrell and Graham (1991) reported that the turtles reach sexual maturity at approximately 14 years; however, Brooks et al. (1992) indicated that maturity may be closer to

Wood Turtle, hatchling twins, Goodhue County, Minnesota

17 or 18 years in more northern locations. Courtship and mating occur primarily in the spring, but fall activity has been observed. The male and female approach each other slowly with necks extended and heads held high. As they come closer, they suddenly lower their heads and swing them from side to side (Carr 1952). The male then climbs astride the female and clamps his claws around the edge of her carapace. He bites at her head and aggressively thumps his plastron against her carapace. Courtship takes place in shallow water, and the pair may remain in copulation for one to two hours (Harding and Bloomer 1979).

Nesting activity occurs on sandbars, riverbanks, open hillsides, and abandoned railroad grades during late May and much of June. Females leave the water in late afternoon to find a nesting site. Sometimes the female digs a shallow body form with her front legs before digging the egg chamber with her rear legs (Farrell and Graham 1991). She deposits a clutch of 4 to 12 (typically 7 to 9) off-white, elliptical eggs with leathery shells averaging 3.2 by 2.3 centimeters (1¼ by ⅞ inches). Once the eggs are deposited, she uses her rear legs to fill the cavity with sand, and then she tamps the nesting site with her plastron. The entire procedure may take three hours or longer (Pallas 1960).

Egg development takes 58 to 71 days depending upon weather. Young emerge from the nest in late August or September. Hatchling Wood Turtles have a carapace length of 2.8 to 3.8 centimeters (1⅛ to 1½ inches).

Large numbers of Wood Turtle nests are destroyed by mammalian predators such as raccoons, skunks, and fox. The young fall prey to these predators as well as to large birds and carnivorous fish. Adult turtles probably have few enemies; it is not unusual, however, to find wild individuals with amputated toes and tails (Oldfield, personal observation). When a raccoon encounters a Wood Turtle away from the water, it could conceivably inflict such damage while attempting to eat the turtle.

Remarks

Most Wood Turtles are mild mannered. Newly captured turtles seldom, if ever, attempt to bite. Typically, they emerge from their protective shell after a short period. A captive was reported to live 58 years (Oliver 1955). Wood Turtles are capable of a vocalization similar to the sound produced by a muted teakettle. Male turtles are known to emit this sound during courtship (Pope 1939).

The Wood Turtle was once marketed for human food, especially in the eastern part of its range (Harding and Bloomer 1979). In the past, this species has also been extensively collected for the pet trade and biological supply houses. Nearly all states with Wood Turtles have passed legislation to protect this unique and diminishing reptile. Populations in Minnesota are not large. Wood Turtles are classified as threatened in Minnesota and are protected by the Minnesota Department of Natural Resources (Coffin and Pfannmuller 1988).

Blanding's Turtle

Emydoidea blandingii

Description

A bright yellow chin and a helmet-shaped profile are characteristic of this marsh inhabitant. The Blanding's Turtle is a medium to large turtle with a black or dark blue dome-shaped carapace with muted yellow spots and bars. The large yellow plastron is hinged across the anterior third enabling individuals to pull the front edge of the lower shell firmly up against the carapace to provide additional protection. Large dark brown to black blotches are present on the lateral edge of each plastral scute. The head and appendages are dark brown or blue gray with small dots of light brown or yellow. A distinctive

field mark is the bright yellow chin and neck. This species of turtle has an unusually long neck and a large rounded head with protruding eyes. A notch in the upper jaw creates the impression that the turtle is "smiling."

Blanding's Turtle, adult female, Wabasha County, Minnesota

Mature males are significantly larger than females. The male's tail is longer, its cloacal opening is beyond the edge of the carapace, and its plastron is concave. Hatchlings have a dark brown or gray

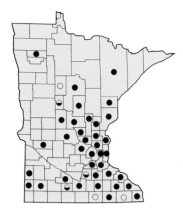

carapace with a moderate keel. Their plastron has a large, central dark blotch, and the hinge is undeveloped. A hatchling's tail is proportionately longer than an adult's tail. Juvenile Blanding's Turtles are similar in coloration to adults, but the light spots and markings are more conspicuous.

The average adult Blanding's Turtle ranges from 12.5 to 18 centimeters (5 to 7 inches) in straight-line upper shell length (Conant and Collins 1991). The largest recorded specimen from Minnesota was a male from Sherburne County with a carapace length of 27 centimeters (10⅝ inches).

Distribution

The Blanding's Turtle is known from southern Ontario and the Great Lakes states westward to western Nebraska. It is found as far south as central Illinois. Scattered populations are located in several New England states. The Blanding's turtle has a substantial

Blanding's Turtle, hatchling, Wabasha County, Minnesota

range within Minnesota excluding the northeastern corner of the state. It is found in areas of suitable habitat across much of the state, but large populations are known from only a few localities.

Habitat

Blanding's Turtles favor open areas. Shallow, slow-moving waters with mud bottoms and abundant aquatic vegetation are preferred. Extensive marshes bordering rivers provide excellent habitat (Vogt

1981). In Minnesota, Blanding's Turtles are primarily marsh and pond inhabitants and are frequently found in association with Snapping Turtles and Painted Turtles. They are also found in bogs in east-central Minnesota and in small stream complexes in the southwest region of the state (Moriarty 1986). Blanding's Turtles achieve protection from freezing temperatures by overwintering in the muddy bottoms of marshes and ponds.

Life History

Individuals emerge from overwintering and begin basking in early April on warm, sunny days. These cold-tolerant turtles have been observed swimming beneath winter ice (Ernst and Barbour 1972). Blanding's Turtles are chiefly diurnal, and they spend large amounts of time basking on muskrat houses, logs, banks, and dikes. Between periods of basking, they forage for food along the bottoms of ponds or marshes.

When it comes to food, Blanding's Turtles are not picky. They eat crayfish, frogs, snails, fish, insects, tadpoles, earthworms, slugs, grubs, and occasionally succulent vegetation and berries. Lagler (1940) reported that 56.6% of their diet in Michigan was crustaceans. As a rule, aquatic turtles cannot swallow food out of water, but the Blanding's Turtle is an exception.

Courtship in Blanding's Turtles has most frequently been observed during the months of April and May, but courting has been reported in other months. Vogt (1981) described courtship and mating in Wisconsin. The ambitious male swims about seeking a female. When a female is found, he approaches her from behind, positions himself on top of her carapace, and begins biting at her head and front limbs. With his neck fully extended, he swings his neck from side to side in front of the female's head. When she becomes submissive, copulation takes place.

Nesting occurs during the first two weeks of June in Minnesota. Females are most active late in the afternoon and at dusk. Hundreds can be seen crossing roads, fields and prairie at Weaver Dunes in Wabasha County during movements to and from nesting localities at the peak of the season. After crawling up to 1.6 kilometers (1 mile) and going through the laborious process of depositing the eggs, females may hide near a bush and return to the marsh the next evening (Oldfield personal observation).

A nest is dug entirely by the female's hind feet in an open sandy area. The size of the egg clutch is reported to be 6 to 15; most females, however, deposit 8 to 10 elliptical white eggs with pliable shells that average 3.8 by 2.4 centimeters (1½ by 1 inches; Vogt 1981). During the growth of the turtle embryo, the egg develops thin calcium plaques that make the eggshell brittle. After a development period of approximately two months, hatchlings leave the nest in September with an average carapace length of 3.1 centimeters (1¼ inches). Often, they must make a long overland trek to find water.

Blanding's Turtles are mild-mannered and do not attempt to bite. If molested or threatened, they simply pull into the shell and wait for danger to pass.

Nests and young of Blanding's Turtles fall victim to raccoons, skunks, and predatory birds. Draining of marshes and swamps destroys the habitat of this inoffensive species. A major threat to adults is the automobile. Despite the placement of turtle-crossing signs along a stretch of highway near the town of Weaver, numerous females are killed during the nesting migration. The majority of the killing appears to be intentional. Turtles can easily be seen, and the traffic is light on the highway.

Remarks

The entire plastron of the Blanding's Turtle may be stained dark reddish brown, which obscures the normal pattern. This staining is evident in populations of turtles found along the lower Mississippi River drainage. Normal coloration returns when the scutes are shed. An adult albino female was reported from Washington County during the summer of 1992.

This turtle was named after William Blanding, an early naturalist from Philadelphia. A nesting female from Chisago County with carved initials on her plastron was determined to be at least 75 years old (Brecke and Moriarty 1989). The Blanding's turtle is classified as threatened in Minnesota and is given total protection (Coffin and Pfannmuller 1988).

Common Map Turtle

Graptemys geographica

Description

The Common Map Turtle has a low vertebral keel and a strongly serrated margin on the posterior edge of its carapace. The upper shell is olive green to brown and has thin yellow lines that produce a reticulate pattern that is especially evident on the marginal scutes. Recently shed turtles reveal large dark brown to black blotches scattered randomly over the carapace. The large plastron is either light yellow or cream, and it generally has indistinct dark smudges along the seams. The olive or brown skin of the head, neck, legs, and tail is embellished with numerous greenish yellow to bright yellow lines forming a pattern similar to the contour lines of topographic maps. Marginal undersides are similarly marked with swirling light lines against a dark background. An isolated oval or triangular-shaped, light green to yellow spot is located posterior and dorsal to each eye.

Males of this species are markedly smaller than females. The male has a stronger keel, pronounced shell markings, a long, thick tail, and

Common Map Turtle,
adult female,
Houston County, Minnesota

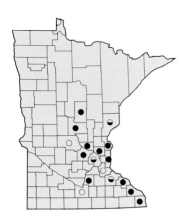

long claws on his front feet. The female Common Map Turtle has a large, massive head and a broad, unmarked upper lip. Hatchling and juvenile Common Map Turtles have a brightly marked carapace, a pronounced plastral pattern, and a strongly defined keel (Ernst and Barbour 1972).

Adult females have a carapace length of 18 to 27.3 centimeters (7 to 10¾ inches), whereas males have a carapace length of 9 to 15.9 centimeters (3½ to 6¼ inches; Conant and Collins 1991).

Common Map Turtles are easily confused with Ouachita Map Turtles and False Map Turtles. The Common Map Turtle has an isolated "eyespot" behind and above each eye. Behind the eye of the False Map Turtle is either a yellow bar or crescent, whereas the Ouachita Map Turtle has numerous bold yellow spots on its face. Adult female Common Map Turtles have proportionally larger heads than adult females of the other two *Graptemys* species.

Distribution

The Common Map Turtle is a reptile of the north and central river drainages of the eastern United States. Populations are found from Vermont and adjacent Canada west to Minnesota and Kansas and south to Arkansas and central Alabama. New York, New Jersey, Maryland, and Pennsylvania harbor isolated populations. The Minnesota distribution of this turtle follows the Mississippi, Minnesota, and St. Croix rivers and their tributaries from the southeastern corner of the state into the central region.

Habitat

Highly aquatic, Common Map Turtles are found in large and mid-sized rivers. They require soft bottoms and ample basking sites surrounded by open water. Backwater sloughs and oxbows within a river's floodplain seem to provide ideal habitat. These turtles overwinter in groups under the ice behind log and rock piles. They also find protection from freezing temperatures in muskrat and beaver channels (Vogt 1981).

Life History

After leaving overwintering sites, Common Map Turtles begin basking on logs, fallen trees, and mud banks during April and early May. On sunny days they spend considerable time basking, often beginning at 8:00 or 9:00 in the morning (Evermann and Clark 1916). They are gregarious baskers—as many as 50 to 60 turtles may be stacked two and three high on a single log. The slightest hint of danger causes them all to plunge into the water. At night, they sleep on the bottom adjacent to submerged logs (Vogt 1981).

The large crushing jaws of female Common Map Turtles are an adaptation for eating freshwater clams, snails, and crayfish. Males eat aquatic insect larvae and small mollusks. Other food items recorded for Common Map Turtles include fish carrion and aquatic plants (Ernst and Barbour 1972). When foraging for food, these turtles prowl along the river bottom searching through aquatic vegetation.

Spring is the principal mating season, although courting pairs have been observed in the fall (Evermann and Clark 1916). Males actively pursue the larger females during courtship activity. Minnesota females begin nesting in early June, and the egg-laying season extends into early July. It is possible that females deposit two clutches

*Common Map Turtle,
adult head, Houston County,
Minnesota*

of 10 to 20 eggs each season, although this has not been confirmed in Minnesota. Gravid females leave the water and often travel a considerable distance to find an open site to dig their nests (Carr 1952). Common Map Turtles prefer to nest on overcast days with light rain; however, they also nest during the early morning on sunny days. Females may make several trial excavations before laying eggs. If an intruder happens along while a female is nesting, she pulls in her head and waits for the danger to pass. Eggs are white with leathery shells and are approximately 3.5 centimeters (1⅜ inches) long and 2.2 centimeters (⅞ inch) wide.

Hatchlings may emerge in early September or overwinter to leave the nest in May or June of the following year (Vogt 1981). Laboratory experiments demonstrated that the sex of a hatchling is determined by the temperature at which the eggs develop rather than by sex chromosomes. Eggs incubated at 30.5° C (86.9° F) produced mostly females, whereas those incubated at 25° C (77° F) resulted in a high percentage of males (Bull and Vogt 1979). Hatchlings average 3.2 centimeters (1¼ inches) in carapace length (Johnson 1987).

Self-defense for this species includes wariness and prompt use of the water as a refuge. Females caught away from water pull into their shell and may attempt to bite if agitated.

Common Map Turtle nests are destroyed by raccoon, skunk, and fox; hatchling turtles must avoid a host of birds, fish, and mammals to survive. Many adults from the Mississippi River near Red Wing have amputated toes, missing feet, and damaged shells indicating that they have been attacked by predators (Oldfield, personal observation). Environmental pollution and habitat destruction are the greatest threats to their existence.

Remarks

According to Ernst and Barbour (1972), the flesh of the Common Map Turtle is palatable, but the difficulty in capturing them in any great numbers precludes commercial use. These turtles are often used as targets by thoughtless shooters. "Turtle plunking" is a cruel and wasteful practice.

Ouachita Map Turtle

Graptemys ouachitensis

Description

One of three map turtles native to Minnesota, the Ouachita Map Turtle has a boldly marked face. This member of the genus *Graptemys* has a prominent medial keel with blunt projections on the second, third, and fourth vertebrals, and the rear of the carapace is markedly serrated. The oval-shaped upper shell is dark olive, brown, or gray, and each scute has at least one black smudge marking on its posterior

edge. Young individuals may display a pattern of yellow or orange interconnected circles, but old adults are often quite dark with little discernable pattern. The light yellow plastron is often tinted with orange, and there are black irregular-shaped markings along the seams of the scutes. A dark swirling pattern is noticeable on the bridge and the lower surface of the marginals. Skin coloration is dark green to black with a network of fine yellow lines on the neck, legs, and tail. Behind each eye is a large rectangular or oval yellow blotch. Occasionally, this postorbital marking is continuous with

Ouachita Map Turtle, adult male, Goodhue County, Minnesota

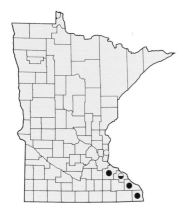

another prominent spot that occurs just above the angle of the jaw. Located directly below the eye on the mandible is another yellow spot. Additionally, an unpaired spot occurs in the center of the lower jaw just below the mouth. Most turtles have yellow eyes, but occasionally individuals are found with striking white irises (Oldfield, personal observation).

The adult female Ouachita Map Turtle is considerably larger than the male, a characteristic shared with other members of the genus *Graptemys*. According to Vogt (1981), adult females have a carapace length of 12 to 26 centimeters (4¾ to 10¼ inches), and males have a carapace length of 9 to 16 centimeters (3½ to 6¼ inches). Male turtles have elongated toenails on their front feet and a long, well-muscled tail with the cloacal opening beyond the edge of the carapace.

The markings of males and juveniles are bolder with proportionately larger spots and brighter colors than found in adult females. The vertebral keels of males and young turtles are prominently elevated with black-tipped projections. Hatchlings are olive green or brown with pale circular lines on their carapace, and the plastral pattern is significantly less extensive when compared to the plastron of hatchling False Map Turtles.

It is difficult to distinguish between this species and the other two Minnesota map turtles without seeing head markings. If the turtle is not in hand, careful stalking of basking turtles with a spotting scope is required to make the determination. False Map Turtles

Ouachita Map Turtle, adult head, Goodhue County, Minnesota

have an "eyebrow" mark, and Common Map Turtles have an isolated postorbital spot, in contrast to the multiple face markings of the Ouachita Map Turtle.

Distribution

The Ouachita Map Turtle ranges from Minnesota and Wisconsin south to Louisiana through the states of the Mississippi River basin. In Minnesota this species is found in association with the Mississippi River in four southeastern counties.

Habitat

Ouachita Map Turtles are big-river turtles and are found in areas of relatively strong currents, abundant aquatic vegetation, and ample basking sites away from the shoreline. Vogt (1981) reported that he found them overwintering behind wing dams in the Mississippi River along with Common Map Turtles and False Map Turtles.

Life History

Seasonal and daily activities of Ouachita Map Turtles are similar to those of False Map Turtles, which are close relatives. They become active in early May and seek overwintering sites in early October. Diurnal, these turtles spend great amounts of time basking, often stacked two and three high, with other turtles of the same or different species. Basking sites are located on logs and muskrat houses in open water.

Vogt (1981) reported on the feeding habits of Ouachita Map Turtles. He indicated that females often feed at the water's surface, consuming vegetation and available insects. Vegetation (pondweed, duckweed, eelgrass, mana grass, arrowhead, and algae) makes up 40% of their diet, and aquatic insect larvae (caddisfly, mayfly, and damselfly) make up another 44%. Males are primarily carnivorous and forage below the surface.

Courtship probably occurs in the spring and fall, although observations in the field have not been recorded. The male recognizes a female of his species by her head markings and cloacal scents (Vogt 1980). The male swims around to face the female, placing his nose against hers while he drums her ears and neck with his long claws. The number of strokes per drumming bout averages 5.2 and appears to be species specific (Vogt 1993). Copulation occurs after the male mounts the female's carapace.

Ouachita Map Turtles nest on sandbars and beaches during June and July within 100 meters (109 yards) of water. Generally, two clutches of 8 to 17 white elliptical eggs with leathery shells are laid during the nesting season. Eggs average 3.4 centimeters (1⅓ inches) by 2.2 centimeters (⅞ inch). Hatchlings emerge in September from early clutches and the following spring from late clutches. The average carapace length at hatching is 3 centimeters (1⅛ inches).

Sex in this species is determined by the temperature at which the eggs develop and not by sex chromosomes. Eggs incubated at 25° C (77° F) in the laboratory hatched into males, whereas those incubated at 30.5° C (87° F) became females (Bull and Vogt 1979).

Like other species of map turtles, the Ouachita Map Turtle is extremely wary and shy. The turtles rely on the water not only as a home but also as a sanctuary from potential predators.

Ouachita Map Turtle nests and hatchlings are subject to the same list of predators as other Minnesota turtles. Decapitated adult females were found on nesting beaches along the Mississippi River (Oldfield, personal observation). Raccoons, weasels, or mink were probably responsible for these deaths.

Remarks

Vogt (1980, 1993) compiled sufficient data to demonstrate that the Ouachita Map Turtle is a sympatric species of the False Map Turtle. The subspecies of Ouachita Map Turtle found in Minnesota is *Graptemys ouachitensis ouachitensis*.

Since this turtle prefers an aquatic habitat and is extremely wary, few Minnesotans ever see the boldly decorated face of the Ouachita Map Turtle up close.

False Map Turtle

Graptemys pseudogeographica

Description

The False Map Turtle is a medium-sized turtle of Minnesota's rivers with a conspicuous vertebral keel and a single "eyebrow" mark behind each eye. Ground coloration of the carapace ranges from light olive to dark brown, and there are one or more large, black smudged blotches on each scute. Some individuals display a net-like pattern of faint yellow or orange lines on the upper shell. The vertebral keel is formed by black-tipped, blunt projections on the second, third, and fourth scutes down the center of the back. The posterior edge of the oval carapace is serrated. Ventral coloration is light yellow or cream with dark concentric swirls along the seams and underneath the marginals. The bridge is also marked with dark bars and swirls. Plastral coloration fades to a yellow brown mottling in adult females. Skin of the appendages, neck, and head is dark olive, dark brown, or black with numerous narrow yellow lines. Behind each orbit is a distinct yellow crescent or bar, which may occasionally be divided.

False Map Turtle, adult male, Goodhue County, Minnesota

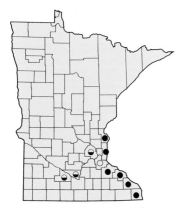

The hatchling's carapace is bright olive green with numerous yellow lines and a black-tipped keel. At least 75% of the plastron is covered with interconnecting dark green or black swirls.

In comparison to adult females, the smaller males have a longer tail, longer front toenails, and a more pronounced vertebral keel. Adult females are 12 to 27.7 centimeters (4¾ to 10⅞ inches) in carapace length, and males are 9 to 15 centimeters (3½ to 5⅞ inches; Vogt 1993).

Making positive identification of the three species of map turtles requires a close-up view of head and neck markings (see the accounts of the Common Map Turtle and the Ouachita Map Turtle for comparisons).

Distribution

False Map Turtles are found along the Mississippi River and its major tributaries through the heartland of the United States from extreme southern North Dakota, Minnesota, and Wisconsin to

False Map Turtle, adult head, Goodhue County, Minnesota

Texas and Louisiana. Records exist of False Map Turtles from counties bordering the St. Croix, Minnesota, and Mississippi rivers in southeast and south-central Minnesota.

Habitat

In Minnesota, False Map Turtles are found in large rivers and the associated sloughs and oxbows of these rivers. Soft bottoms, basking sites away from shore, and abundant aquatic vegetation are required. According to Vogt (1981), these turtles overwinter behind logs

and rocks on the river bottom. He found them piled up with other map turtle species behind wing dams along the Mississippi River.

False Map Turtle,
adult male and female,
Goodhue County, Minnesota

Life History

False Map Turtles leave overwintering areas in late April or early May and remain active until October. The turtles spend a tremendous amount of time basking with other turtles on muskrat houses, stumps, and logs. At night they sleep on submerged logs on the river bottom.

False Map Turtles swim through the water, feeding anywhere from the bottom to the surface; 41.5% of their diet is plant material, 22.5% is insects, 15.7% is mollusks, 10% is fish, and 9.5% is unidentified matter (Vogt 1981). Lacking broad crushing jaws like those found in adult female Common Map Turtles, this species seldom feeds on clams or snails.

False Map Turtles court and mate in the spring and fall. Swimming to face the female, the male drums her head and neck with his long front toenails. The number of strokes per drumming bout averages 10.3, twice the number of strokes performed by courting male Ouachita Map Turtles. Many females lay two egg clutches per season, and egg laying occurs in late May, June, or early July on open sandbars and beaches near the water. A nest about 14 centimeters (5½ inches) deep is dug using her hind feet. Clutch size is usually 12 to 16 eggs with as many as 22. The elliptical eggs have pliable shells and average 2.2 by 3.4 centimeters (⅞ by 1⅜ inches). After covering the nest and packing the soil, the female returns to the water.

Egg development requires 60 to 75 days, and young emerge in September or the following spring. The sex of False Map Turtles is determined by temperature: eggs maintained at 25° C (77° F) produced predominantly males, whereas eggs maintained at 35° C (95° F) produced females (Vogt 1980). Hatchling False Map Turtles are circular shaped and average 3.3 centimeters (1¼ inches) in carapace length.

False Map Turtles are no different than other map turtles in temperament. They are extremely wary and difficult to approach when they are basking. If a female is surprised while away from water on her nesting mission, she pulls into her shell to wait out the danger.

A host of carnivorous vertebrates destroy nests. Adults have few predators, but they have to contend with polluted waterways and habitat changes brought on by humans.

Remarks

The subspecies of False Map Turtle found in Minnesota is *Graptemys pseudogeographica pseudogeographica*. The Ouachita Map Turtle, once considered a subspecies of the False Map Turtle, has been elevated to full species status (Vogt 1993).

A False Map Turtle lived 21.5 years at the Philadelphia Zoological Garden (Ernst and Barbour 1972). This species is occasionally taken for human food, but because of the difficulty of capturing it in worthwhile numbers, there is little commercial interest.

Six-lined Racerunner

Cnemidophorus sexlineatus

Description

The Six-lined Racerunner is an appropriate name for this speedy lizard, since it is capable of running and winning a race with a would-be human captor. An indefinite tan middorsal stripe originating at the base of the head is flanked on each side by three distinct yellow or yellowish green stripes that extend to the base of the tail. The top of the head, the dorsal surface of the legs, and the tail are light

Six-lined Racerunner, adult male, Houston County, Minnesota

brown. The area on the back between the stripes is dark brown. The belly of females and juveniles is light gray or white, and the belly of adult males is bluish. During the breeding season males develop a light blue coloration on their chin and lips, and they have a brilliant lime green wash along the sides of their head and the anterior third of their body. The tails of hatchlings and juvenile Six-lined Racerunners are light blue, and the body stripes extend onto the tail for about a third of its length.

The Six-lined Racerunner reaches a total length of 24 centimeters (9½ inches) and has a snout-vent length of 6 to 8 centimeters (2⅓ to 3⅛ inches; Vogt 1981).

In contrast to skinks, members of the genus *Cnemidophorus* have pointed noses, large scales on top of their heads, and rectangular belly plates.

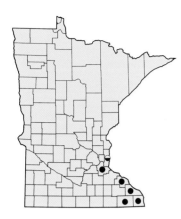

Distribution

The Six-lined Racerunner ranges across the southeastern two-thirds of the United States with a northern extension along the Mississippi River valley into Minnesota and Wisconsin. Records and sightings in Minnesota are spotty. Six southeastern counties have confirmed locality records.

Habitat

In Minnesota, Six-lined Racerunners are found in open sandy or gravelly areas with sparse ground vegetation. Prairies on south-facing hills and sand outwashes in river floodplains are preferred, but populations are also encountered along rock and cinder fills of railroad tracks and dikes along the Mississippi River. These lizards are often found in colonies of sizable populations. Overwintering and estivation take place in underground burrows. These refuges are ordinarily self-excavated in loose soil.

Life History

The Six-lined Racerunner is the least cold tolerant of all Minnesota reptiles. Adults emerge from overwintering in mid-May, and by late August they have retired for the season. Hatchlings remain active and continue feeding into September to increase body fat stores (Vogt 1981).

Fitch (1958b) found that on warm, sunny days Six-lined Racerunners are active from 8:00 A.M. until 3:00 P.M. with an optimal air temperature of 34° C (93° F). Adults have been found active at an air temperature of 22° C (72° F) on steep bluff prairies in Winona County in mid-May (Oldfield and Dan Keyler, personal observation). They may seek shelter under vegetation or underground for brief periods during the hottest part of the day. On cool days they remain

Six-lined Racerunner, juvenile

in burrows or hidden under ground cover. Vogt (1981) determined that individuals maintain home ranges of 160 square meters (191 square yards) in Wisconsin, although Fitch (1958a) estimated home ranges to be 1,000 square meters (1,196 square yards or 0.25 acre) in eastern Kansas. Territorial behavior has not been observed with this species.

Six-lined Racerunners pursue and consume a variety of arthropod prey including grasshoppers, crickets, katydids, moths, beetles, bugs, ants, spiders, and flies. Before swallowing large grasshoppers, the lizard grasps and holds the prey in its jaws while scraping it against the ground to tear off the long rear legs. A keen sense of smell and good eyesight are used to find and follow quarry.

Courtship and breeding occur during late May and early June, shortly after the lizards emerge from their winter retreat. The male courts the female by displaying his vivid coloration. If the female is receptive, she allows him to grasp the skin on the back of her neck with his jaws while he positions his tail under hers to achieve copulation.

Clutches of one to six eggs are laid in a burrow dug by the female at a depth of 10 centimeters (3⅞ inches) in loose sand during mid-June. Egg tending does not occur. In Missouri and farther south, older females normally lay two clutches each season (Johnson 1987). The white eggs with thin, leathery shells average 1.6 by 0.9 centimeters (⅝ by ⅜ inch) and normally take two months to hatch (Johnson 1987). Hatchlings have a total length of 5 centimeters (2 inches).

Six-lined Racerunners depend upon speed for self-defense. They move with nervous, short spurts when foraging, and at the slightest hint of danger they quickly accelerate to speeds of 29 kilometers per hour (18 miles per hour; Vogt 1981). The first glimpse of these lizards is generally a blurred streak as they make a dash to hide in ground vegetation or a burrow. They may lose their tail to predators, but it is not as fragile as a skink's tail, and most Six-lined Racerunners encountered in the wild still possess their original tail. It is unusual for these lizards to bite when captured.

Natural predators include birds of prey, small mammals, and snakes. Racers are significant predators because they have the speed to pursue and capture racerunners. Milk Snakes feed on Six-lined Racerunners when the lizards are less active in their burrows.

Remarks

The Prairie Racerunner, *Cnemidophorus sexlineatus viridis,* is the subspecies found in Minnesota (Conant and Collins 1991). Two colorful and fitting nicknames for these lizards are "fieldstreaks" and "sandlappers."

Five-lined Skink

Eumeces fasciatus

Description

The Five-lined Skink is a small, robust lizard with smooth, shiny scales and relatively small legs. Coloration varies with age and breeding condition, but the lizard gets its name from the five yellowish stripes that extend longitudinally along the back and sides. The mid-dorsal stripe forks at the neck forming a narrow V across the top of the head. The black or dark brown background coloration of juvenile and young adults creates a distinct five-lined pattern that markedly contrasts with the bright metallic-blue tail. Mature females retain a lined pattern on a lighter background, whereas mature males become a uniform gray or light brown. Tails of adult males are generally gray, and those of females tend to be blue gray. The nose, lips, cheeks, and throat of a male in breeding condition are bright orange red.

The total length of the Five-lined Skink ranges from 12.5 to 21.5 centimeters (5 to 8½ inches), and the maximum snout-vent length is 8.6 centimeters (3⅜ inches; Conant and Collins 1991).

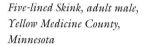

Five-lined Skink, adult male, Yellow Medicine County, Minnesota

The Five-lined Skink is very similar in appearance to the Prairie Skink; a close look is needed to make the distinction. The Prairie Skink has dark brown bands along its sides and broad tan stripes down its back. In contrast to the Five-lined Skink, the Six-lined

Racerunner has dull, rough scales rather than shiny, smooth ones, and it has large rectangular belly plates instead of the small, uniform abdominal scales of skinks.

Five-lined Skink, adult female, Yellow Medicine County, Minnesota

Distribution

The Five-lined Skink ranges across the eastern half of the United States excluding the extreme northeastern states and southern Florida. This species has an unusual, patchy distribution in Minnesota. Breckenridge (1944) reported records from Redwood and Yellow Medicine counties along the Minnesota River. Further field work confirmed the earlier localities and documented additional records in Renville, Fillmore, and Houston counties (Lang 1982a; Moriarty 1986). In 1992, Five-lined Skinks were confirmed as residents of Chisago County. These scattered Minnesota localities appear to be disjunct from the primary range.

Habitat

The habitat for the Five-lined Skink is generally described as humid woodlands and wooded lots with decaying leaf litter, stumps, and logs (Conant and Collins 1991). In Minnesota, however, the species is found on or near granite outcrops in the dissected terrain of the Minnesota River valley (Lang 1982a). This species is found in southeastern Minnesota in association with limestone outcrops and bluff prairies in proximity to deciduous forest. Five-lined Skinks retreat to depths of 1.5 to 3 meters (5 to 10 feet) in rock fissures and cracks below the frost line to survive Minnesota winters (Lang 1982a).

Life History

In Minnesota the diurnal Five-lined Skink becomes active in early May at air temperatures of 15.5° to 32° C (60° to 90° F). After a flurry of activity in late spring and early summer, this species becomes increasingly difficult to find before it retreats to overwintering sites by September. This lizard is secretive and remains under protective cover much of the time. It can be found under rocks and ground debris such as cardboard, sheets of corrugated metal, tar paper, and cloth (Lang 1982a). Although on occasion the lizards climb into low shrubs to bask or forage, they are primarily terrestrial. According to Fitch (1954), their home territory has a diameter of 9 to 27.5 meters (30 to 90 feet).

These lizards feed on small invertebrates such as crickets, locusts, beetles, insect larvae, caterpillars, grasshoppers, moths, and snails. The predominant food for Five-lined Skinks in Minnesota is roaches and spiders, and they lap droplets of dew from vegetation for their water needs (Lang 1982a).

Breeding activity peaks during the third and fourth weeks of May in Minnesota. Five-lined Skinks emerging from their second overwintering are sexually mature. Males aggressively defend territories against intruders, and these interactions occasionally result in fighting. Males locate females by sight and scent. Upon finding a receptive mate, the male grasps the skin behind her head with his mouth while curling his tail under hers to achieve copulation. About a month later, the gravid female excavates a small chamber under a rock or within decaying vegetation and deposits 5 to 13 (average of 9) pliable, white eggs. She stays with the eggs until they hatch, guarding against predators and keeping the nest free of spoiled eggs by eating them. The eggs require 30 to 60 days to hatch. Hatchlings vary from 5.1 to 6.4 centimeters (2 to 2½ inches) in total length (Conant and Collins 1991).

If a predator encounters a Five-lined Skink and grasps its tail, the tail readily disjoints, leaving a wriggling decoy while the skink makes a dash for safety. When frightened and cornered, a Five-lined Skink can break off its own tail by pushing it against a firm surface. Very little blood is lost. The tail regenerates over time, but the replacement appendage is never as long or colorful as the original.

Five-lined Skinks inevitably attempt to bite a human captor, but ordinarily their small teeth cannot penetrate skin. Natural predators of this species include snakes, hawks, and small mammals such as shrews, raccoons, skunks, and opossums.

Five-lined Skink, juvenile, Houston County, Minnesota

Remarks

The bright blue tail of young Five-lined Skinks is the basis for names such as "blue-tailed skink" and "blue devil."

In Minnesota the Five-lined Skink is classified as endangered and is currently the only reptile so classified in the state. The primary reason for this status is the widely scattered and disjunct populations (Coffin and Pfannmuller 1988). Due to fire suppression in the Minnesota River valley, the encroachment of red cedar has substantially reduced available habitat for this species (Lang 1982a).

Prairie Skink

Eumeces septentrionalis

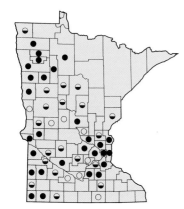

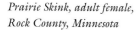

Description

Of the three lizard species found in Minnesota, the Prairie Skink is the most widespread. This medium-sized skink has small legs and a body that is cylindrical in cross section. Body scales are smooth and shiny. Three wide light tan stripes separated by two narrow dark lines run longitudinally from the head onto the tail. Additionally, three black or dark brown stripes are found on each side separated by two narrow white stripes. Coloration of the tail is essentially the same as the body, although the stripes become less defined toward the tip. The abdomen is unmarked gray or tan, and the lizard's legs are light brown. During the breeding season, adult males have bright orange throats, lips, and chins. Hatchling Prairie Skinks are black with seven thin yellowish stripes and a brilliant metallic-blue tail.

Prairie Skinks range in total length from 13.3 to 22.4 centimeters (5¼ to 8¾ inches). The maximum body length is 9 centimeters (3½ inches; Conant and Collins 1991).

The two species of Minnesota skinks are frequently confused. Prairie Skinks, in contrast to Five-lined Skinks, lack an inverted V

Prairie Skink, adult female, Rock County, Minnesota

on top of their heads. Prairie Skinks have wide light brown stripes down their backs and wide dark brown stripes on their sides, whereas Five-lined Skinks have narrow light-colored stripes along their backs and sides.

Distribution

The Prairie Skink is found in a north to south band from Minnesota and western Wisconsin to eastern Texas. An isolated population is found in southern Manitoba. With the exception of the northeast and the bluff lands in the southeast, the Prairie Skink is found in suitable habitat across the state of Minnesota.

Habitat

Open grassy areas in association with pine barrens and oak savannas with loose sandy soil and scattered rocks are ideal habitat for Prairie Skinks. They are also found on gravely glacial outwashes and extensive rock outcrops if there is sufficient vegetation to provide cover and insect food. Vogt (1981) indicates that they frequently live on sandbanks along creeks and rivers. Prairie Skinks overwinter below the frost line in self-constructed burrows at depths of 0.3 to 1.4 meters (1 to 4½ feet), either singly or in small groups (Breckenridge 1943).

Life History

Prairie Skinks typically begin their activity in early May. They remain active through September, but adults become difficult to find late in the season. Highly secretive, this species spends much of the day under rocks and other ground cover (Collins 1982). They remain underground when air temperatures are not suitable for activity.

Prairie Skinks principally feed on small arthropods including crickets, grasshoppers, treehoppers, leafhoppers, beetles, caterpillars, and spiders. They occasionally consume the young of their own kind (Breckenridge 1943).

Courtship has not been reported in Minnesota, but ordinarily the breeding season is the last half of May, when males sport their bright breeding colors. The female digs a nest under a rock or log and lays 5 to 13 eggs (average of 9) in late June or early July. The eggs are dirty white in color and have soft leathery shells. The average egg size at the time of laying is 0.8 by 1.3 centimeters (⁵⁄₁₆ by ½ inch), and the egg increases to 1.1 by 1.9 centimeters (⁷⁄₁₆ by ¾ inch) just before hatching (Breckenridge 1943). The egg development period ranges from 40 to 52 days depending on the weather. The female skink guards and tends the eggs until they hatch, and she provides two to three days of maternal care to the hatchlings before they leave the nest (Somma 1987). Young Prairie Skinks grow rapidly and are ready to begin breeding during their third season or when they are just shy of two years of age (Breckenridge 1943).

Like the Five-lined Skink and many other lizard species, this reptile uses an easily disjointed tail to help baffle predators. The tail regrows, but it never attains its original length or color. This species generally attempts to bite when handled, but its small mouth and teeth are unlikely to break the skin of a human hand.

Natural predators include marsh hawks, barred owls, kestrels, shrikes, striped ground squirrels, and raccoons (Vogt 1981). Prairie Skinks impaled on barbed wire by loggerhead shrikes have been found in Clay County (Bonnie Brooks-Erpelding, personal communication). The Western Hognose Snake may be an important predator of the Prairie Skink in Minnesota where the two species share the same habitat (John Meltzer, personal communication).

Remarks

According to Conant and Collins (1991), the subspecies of Prairie Skink found in Minnesota is the Northern Prairie Skink (*Eumeces septentrionalis septentrionalis*). In the past this species was referred to as the Black-banded skink (Breckenridge 1943).

Racer

Coluber constrictor

Description

A slender body built for speed, prominent eyes, and an alert attitude are key characteristics of the Racer. The dorsal color of adults is solid slate blue or light brown. The throat and neck are usually bright yellow. The yellow throat grades into a light gray or smoky white abdomen. The Racer has a divided anal plate and smooth body scales. Adult males have longer tails than females; up to 27% of their total length may be tail. Racer hatchlings and juveniles differ markedly from adults until their third summer. Young snakes have reddish brown or black dorsal blotches on a gray background, and their white ventral surface is covered with numerous small reddish brown spots.

The total length of adults ranges from 90 to 152 centimeters (36 to 60 inches; Conant and Collins 1991). According to Breckenridge (1944), the largest specimen recorded in Minnesota was found in Houston County with a length of 140 centimeters (55 inches).

No other species of snake in Minnesota is likely to be confused with an adult Racer, with the possible exception of the Smooth

Racer, adult female,
Goodhue County, Minnesota

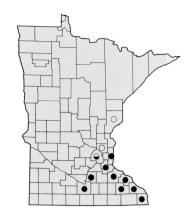

Racer, juvenile,
Winona County, Minnesota

Green Snake. The brilliant color of the Smooth Green Snake fades after death to a bluish gray, but a Racer the size of an adult Smooth Green Snake still has a blotched juvenile pattern. Juvenile Racers can be confused with the young of several species, but the only other Minnesota species with smooth scales and a blotched pattern is the Milk Snake. Milk Snakes have a single anal plate in contrast to the divided plate of the Racer.

Distribution

The Racer has a broad distribution in the United States. It is found from southern Maine to Florida and west to the Pacific Coast. However, large gaps occur in its range in the Southwest and the Upper Midwest including northern Minnesota and the eastern Dakotas. In Minnesota, Racers are found as far north as Pine County and as far west as LeSueur County, but their distribution is primarily restricted to counties in the southeastern corner of the state.

Habitat

Individuals live in a variety of open dry habitats such as brushy areas along the edges of deciduous woodlands, grass prairies, bluff prairies, and old fields. Because these snakes primarily hunt by sight, they avoid areas of dense vegetation. Racers overwinter in mammal burrows, rock crevices, gravel banks, stone walls, and abandoned wells. They may share these winter homes with other Racers, Timber Rattlesnakes, Rat Snakes, Gopher Snakes, and Common Garter Snakes.

Life History

Racers become active on warm days during the last half of April, and they bask for several days near their overwintering site before leaving to forage for food. They are active, fast moving, and diurnal, and they are frequently found basking in bushes and shrubs. Racers have a wide tolerance to air temperatures, and they are often out when other snake species are under cover. According to Fitch (1963a), they may be active at temperatures of 15.5° to 32° C (60° to 90° F). They have large home ranges of 9.7 to 10.5 hectares (24 to 26 acres; Fitch 1963a).

Racers are opportunistic feeders consuming a large variety of food items. They eat small mammals, birds, reptiles, amphibians, and large insects. Prey items also include snails, spiders, and bird eggs. In Minnesota, Six-lined Racerunners are an important food source where available.

While hunting, the Racer holds its head 15 to 20 centimeters (6 to 8 inches) above the ground to gain elevation and to get a better view of its surroundings. The snake makes a quick dash to catch and seize prey when it is spotted. The Racer is not a constrictor as the scientific name indicates; however, it uses its body to press struggling prey to the ground. The snake repeatedly bites and chews on the prey item until it is sufficiently subdued and then swallows it whole.

Details on Racer reproduction in Minnesota are scanty, but field studies by Fitch (1963a) in Kansas provide considerable information. Mating generally takes place during May and early June. The male trails the female by scent and initiates courting by moving alongside her with a jerking motion. After the female becomes passive, the male places his tail under hers to achieve copulation. In late June or early July the female lays a clutch of 8 to 21 eggs under logs, in rotting stumps, or inside mammal burrows. One clutch per year is normal. The cream-colored eggs are elliptical in shape with a leathery shell, and they average 3.0 by 2.0 centimeters (1³⁄₁₆ by ¾ inches). Eggs hatch in 43 to 65 days depending upon ambient temperatures. Hatchling Racers emerge from the nest in late August or early September at a total length of 20 to 35 centimeters (8 to 14 inches). They reach reproductive maturity within two to three years (Fitch 1963).

Racers primarily rely on flight for self-defense, but they will defend themselves. When surprised they make a dash for cover at high speed; they have been clocked at 6.5 kilometers per hour (4 miles per hour; Vogt 1981). If cornered, Racers rapidly vibrate their tail and readily strike at the adversary.

Natural enemies include hawks, crows, fox, raccoons, and skunks, but human activities take the largest toll. Automobiles kill countless individuals each year to say nothing of the losses resulting from habitat destruction.

Remarks

Authorities recognize several subspecies of Racer across the United States. The various subspecies are primarily differentiated by body color including blue, brown, black, gray, tan, and mottled. The Eastern Yellowbelly Racer (*Coluber constrictor flaviventris*) is the subspecies found in Minnesota (Collins 1990). The Racer is given special concern status by the Minnesota Department of Natural Resources.

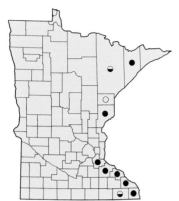

Ringneck Snake

Diadophis punctatus

Description

The Ringneck Snake is a small, shiny blue-black or gray-black snake with a conspicuous yellow or orange ring around its neck. The light yellow or bright orange belly is in marked contrast to its dark back. The orange may grade into brick red under the tail. The bright abdominal color is accented with many small black spots, although they may be absent in individuals from northern Minnesota. Ringneck Snakes have smooth dorsal scales and a divided anal plate.

The total length of the Ringneck Snake ranges from 25.4 to 38 centimeters (10 to 15 inches; Conant and Collins 1991). Adult females are generally larger than males.

Redbelly and Brown Snakes are similar in size and dorsal coloration, but they have keeled body scales, lack a brightly colored necklace, and have unspotted bellies.

Distribution

The Ringneck Snake has an extensive continental range. It is found from Maine to Minnesota and south to Florida, Texas, and Arizona; it is also found in the Pacific coastal states. In Minnesota, this species is encountered in scattered populations, primarily in eastern counties.

Habitat

In southeastern Minnesota, the Ringneck Snake prefers south or west-facing hillsides. They can be found under rocks in forested areas or on steep bluff prairies. Distribution within apparently suitable habitat is spotty—populations may be found on one hill but be absent on a nearby hill. In northern Minnesota, they are occasionally found under rocks, logs, or bark in damp deciduous forests. Abundant ground cover is a critical requirement of this species. Rock crevices and mammal burrows below the frost line are used for overwintering. During the hot part of summer they estivate in similar locations.

Life History

In Minnesota the activity season for Ringneck Snakes begins in April and ends in October. They are extremely secretive and rarely bask, depending upon warm soil under shallow rocks to thermoregulate.

Under the cover of darkness they forage for earthworms, slugs, sow bugs, grubs, and spiders. Small salamanders, frogs, lizards, and snakes are used as food where available (Ernst and Barbour 1989). The most probable salamander prey in Minnesota are the Blue-spotted and Redback Salamanders. Ringneck Snakes rely heavily on their sense of smell to locate food, and they are powerful constrictors once the prey animal is seized.

Courtship and mating occur during the spring and fall when individuals are gregarious. They are sexually mature in two or three years. Females lay eggs during early summer in moist sand under bark or rocks. Rotting logs and decaying tree stumps are also used as nesting sites. Clutch size varies from 2 to 10 eggs with the average being 4. Eggs average 1.3 by 2.8 centimeters (½ by 1 inch) and have thin, leathery shells with a bumpy texture. Forty to 60 days of development within the egg are required; however, Peterson (1956) reported a female that gave birth to six live young. Communal nesting has been reported, and as many as 55 eggs have been found in one nest (Blanchard 1936). Hatchlings are 8.5 to 11.5 centimeters (3⅜ to 4½ inches) long.

Individuals rarely attempt to bite when handled, but they will writhe and discharge a foul-smelling musk. When threatened by a predator, they will corkscrew their tail exposing the brightly col-

Ringneck Snake, adult, Goodhue County, Minnesota

Ringneck Snake, edwardsii *subspecies*

ored underside while they keep their head hidden under body coils. Death feigning has been reported and was witnessed on one occasion (Oldfield and Jim Gerholdt, personal observation). Ringneck Snakes serve as food for larger snakes, such as Racers and Milk Snakes, as well as for hawks, owls, and small mammals.

Remarks

Two subspecies of Ringneck Snakes occur in Minnesota. The Prairie Ringneck (*Diadophis punctatus arnyi*) is found in the southeastern counties. The belly is brightly colored with numerous black spots. The Northern Ringneck (*D. p. edwardsii*) is found in Pine County and north. The northern form has a paler abdomen with meager or no spotting.

This inoffensive little snake has been nicknamed the "corkscrew snake" because of its habit of tail coiling when alarmed.

Rat Snake

Elaphe obsoleta

Description

The adult Rat Snake is a large, impressive constrictor with a white chin and throat and weakly keeled dorsal scales. A pattern of mid-dorsal blotches is generally discernible. The skin of the back and sides, especially on the anterior third of the snake, shows small flecks of red, orange, or white. The belly is dark gray or brown with indistinct darker specks or checkerboard blotches. The cross-sectional shape of the Rat Snake's body is very similar to a loaf of bread, with vertical sides, a rounded top, and a flat bottom. Rat Snakes have a divided anal plate. Young Rat Snakes are distinctly different from adults. They have a gray ground color with a bold pattern of dark blotches down the length of the body. A dark band runs from the eye to the corner of the mouth. The ventral surface of a juvenile shows a checkerboard pattern of dark brown or black on a light background. After two years juvenile coloration begins changing to that of the adult.

The average length of an adult is 107 to 183 centimeters (42 to 72 inches; Conant and Collins 1991).

Rat Snake, adult

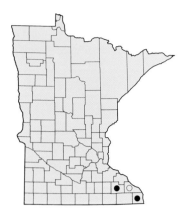

Young Rat Snakes are easily confused with the young of several other Minnesota snakes. Juvenile Racers and Milk Snakes also have a blotched pattern, but they have nonkeeled scales. Hatchling Gopher Snakes have strongly keeled scales, a pointed nose, and a single anal plate. The most reliable way to distinguish a juvenile Rat Snake from a Fox Snake is to count ventral scales. Rat Snakes have 221 or more ventral scales, whereas Fox Snakes have 216 or less.

Distribution

The Rat Snake has a broad distribution across the eastern United States, extending from southern New England south to the Florida Keys and west to Texas and extreme southeastern Minnesota. This species is extremely rare in Minnesota. Only four documented individuals have been reported over a span of 50 years. Counties of record include Houston, Winona, and Olmsted. It is unlikely that this species has ever been common in Minnesota.

Habitat

The Rat Snake is a woodland species making its home in rocky, timbered upland, wooded valleys, and forests on the backside of south-facing bluffs. According to Vogt (1981), Rat Snakes in Wisconsin are found in moist, wooded east and north slopes near bluffs along rivers. Known records indicate that the only suitable Rat Snake habitat in Minnesota occurs in the extreme southeastern counties, where forested hills are dissected by rivers and streams. Rat Snakes overwinter in deep, rocky crevices below the frost line. They very likely share dens with Racers, Gopher Snakes, and Timber Rattlesnakes.

Life History

Emergence from winter dormancy occurs in late April and May. After several days of basking on rocks, the diurnal snakes move into adjacent woodlands, where they are often found 6 to 12 meters (19½ to 39 feet) off the ground in oak and hickory trees (Vogt 1981). They regularly take refuge in cavities of hollow trees. By early October the snakes return to overwintering dens.

Approximately two-thirds of a Rat Snake's diet consists of small mammals such as mice, chipmunks, squirrels, rabbits, and shrews (Fitch 1963b). Birds, bird eggs, and nestlings are also significant food sources. Large prey is seized in the mouth and quickly suffocated by constriction. Small prey may be grabbed and swallowed alive. Juvenile Rat Snakes eat amphibians, lizards, and invertebrates (Johnson 1987).

Nothing is known about Rat Snake reproduction in Minnesota. Mating probably occurs in May and early June. A clutch of 6 to 30

Rat Snake, juvenile

eggs (10 to 14 average) is laid in hollow logs, stumps, or sawdust piles during June or early July (Johnson 1987). The white, leathery eggs are 3.5 to 5.5 centimeters (1⅜ to 2⅛ inches) long and 1.6 to 3.0 centimeters (⅝ to 1⅛ inches) wide. Eggs generally adhere to each other in the nest (Ernst and Barbour 1989). Hatchlings emerge after 60 to 75 days, and they are 28 to 41 centimeters (11 to 16 inches) long.

Rat Snakes freeze when danger threatens, and they rely upon their cryptic coloration to avoid detection. If cornered, they vibrate their tails, elevate their heads, and strike repeatedly. A large snake can deliver a respectable bite. Besides humans and their automobiles, adult Rat Snakes have few enemies other than hawks. Young Rat Snakes are eaten by carnivorous mammals, birds of prey, and other species of snakes.

Remarks

Of the several recognized subspecies of the Rat Snake, only the Black Rat Snake (*Elaphe obsoleta obsoleta*) is found in Minnesota (Conant and Collins 1991). A common nickname for this species is the "pilot blacksnake." This misnomer is derived from unfounded folklore that claims that this species of snake leads rattlesnakes away from danger or back to their dens in the fall.

It is unfortunate that so little is known of this impressive serpent in Minnesota. Suitable climatic conditions and lack of appropriate habitat apparently restrict this species within our state. The Rat Snake has been given special concern status by the Minnesota Department of Natural Resources (Coffin and Pfannmuller 1988).

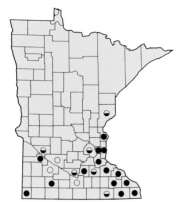

Fox Snake

Elaphe vulpina

Description

The mature Fox Snake is a medium to large snake with an unmarked head and a blotched dorsal pattern. The head, with a rounded nose, is solid brown or reddish brown. There are 34 to 43 large reddish brown, dark brown, or black middorsal blotches and a row of alternating smaller blotches along each side of the body. The dorsal ground color is sooty brown or tan. The belly of the Fox Snake is pale yellow with numerous brown or black rectangular blotches. This stout-bodied snake has weakly keeled scales and a divided anal plate. Young Fox Snakes have a lighter ground color, and the dor-

Fox Snake, adult, Goodhue County, Minnesota

sal blotches are bordered with black. They also have a dark bar across the top of the head connecting the eyes, as well as a bar from the eye to the corner of the mouth on each side of the head.

The average adult Fox Snake is 91 to 137 centimeters (36 to 54 inches) long (Conant and Collins 1991). A large individual found in Goodhue County had a total length of 155 centimeters (61 inches).

Fox Snakes are frequently confused with several other Minnesota species. Gopher Snakes have a boldly marked, pointed head and a

Fox Snake, juvenile,
Goodhue County, Minnesota

single anal plate. Milk Snakes have a single anal plate, and their scales lack keels. Rattlesnakes have a rattle on the end of their tail and a distinctly shaped head with vertical pupils. Juvenile Fox Snakes are easily confused with the young of several other Minnesota species (see the Rat Snake species account for an explanation of confusing juvenile snakes).

Distribution

The range of the Fox Snake is limited to the north-central United States and extreme southern Ontario. It is found from eastern Michigan across Wisconsin to eastern Nebraska and south to Illinois and northern Missouri. In Minnesota, the range of the Fox Snake covers the southern half of the state with Pine County having the northernmost record. It is broadly distributed along major river valleys including the Mississippi, Minnesota, St. Croix, and Missouri.

Habitat

Fox Snakes are at home in river bottom forests, upland hardwoods, pine barrens, and prairies. They are rarely found far from rivers or streams. Rock crevices, mammal burrows, and other suitable areas below the frost line serve as overwintering sites. Vogt (1981) found 166 Fox Snakes overwintering in an abandoned well in central Wisconsin. Many of them were totally submerged in the water. A similar situation was found in Minnesota (Jim Gerholdt, personal communication).

Life History

Fox Snakes emerge from winter dormancy during the last two weeks of April. Although primarily diurnal, they are often found crossing highways on warm, rainy evenings. Fox Snakes are very capable climbers but spend considerable time on the ground. They often take cover under logs, boards, or discarded tin.

Prey items include mice, chipmunks, ground squirrels, and other small mammals (Vogt 1981). Birds and bird eggs, either on the ground or in trees, are also taken. Being powerful constrictors, Fox Snakes quickly subdue larger prey by suffocation with their body coils before swallowing. Hatchlings feed on invertebrates, small frogs, and juvenile rodents.

Fox Snakes probably mate during late April and early May. About 30 days later the female finds a desirable nesting site under logs in damp soil, in rotting humus, or in woodlot sawdust piles. She deposits an egg clutch of 8 to 27 eggs (Vogt 1981). The elongated, leathery eggs average 4.5 by 2.8 centimeters (1¾ by 1⅛ inches) and frequently adhere to each other. Communal nesting by several females has been reported (Ernst and Barbour 1989). The egg development period varies from 35 to 78 days depending on ambient temperatures. Hatchlings are 23 to 31 centimeters (9 to 12 inches) in total length.

When surprised by an enemy, a Fox Snake rapidly vibrates its tail and repeatedly strikes from a coiled position attempting to bite the intruder. A freshly captured Fox Snake releases musk from glands at the base of its tail. This musk has an odor similar to that of a red fox, which may be the origin of the snake's common name.

Hawks capture and feed on adult snakes, and juveniles fall prey to carnivorous mammals, birds, and other snakes. The greatest loss of Fox Snakes is due to automobiles and habitat destruction. Moreover, the Fox Snake is sometimes collected for the pet trade.

Remarks

There are two recognized subspecies of Fox Snake. Only the Western Fox Snake (*Elaphe vulpina vulpina*) is found in Minnesota (Conant and Collins 1991).

Unfortunately the Fox Snake is often misidentified. It is often mistaken for a rattlesnake because of its habit of vibrating its tail when alarmed. Its solid-colored reddish-brown head leads to its incorrect identification as a copperhead (a species not found in Minnesota). As a result, Fox Snakes are dispatched as venomous serpents by the uninformed. Additional misnomers applied to the Fox Snake are spotted adder, pine snake, and bullsnake. Because of habitat alteration and collection pressures, the Minnesota Department of Natural Resources classifies the Fox Snake as a special concern species (Coffin and Pfannmuller 1988).

Western Hognose Snake

Heterodon nasicus

Description

The "prairie rooter" is a medium-sized, stout-bodied snake with a shovel-shaped snout used for digging in loose, sandy soil. The flattened, upturned rostrum bears a sharp point and a dorsal ridge. The ground color of this species is tan or buffy gray. A single row of 35 to 40 large, dark brown blotches runs along the back. Two rows of smaller spots are found on each side of the body. The blotches form a fractured ring pattern on the tail. Two oblong, dark brown blotches are located on the back of the neck. A dark bar connects the eyes and extends from each eye to the corner of the mouth on each side of the head. The ventral surface of the snake bears a large, wide black or blue-black stripe that is edged in cream or yellow, and the underside of the tail is black. The dark belly coloration of freshly shed individuals often shows an iridescent sheen. Body scales are keeled, and the divided anal plate is generally a yellowish hue. Males have proportionally longer tails than females. Ground coloration is lighter

Western Hognose Snake, adult, Anoka County, Minnesota

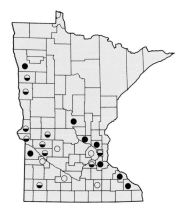

in juveniles, which causes the pattern to be more striking than in adults; otherwise they are similar in appearance.

The length of adults generally falls between 38 and 63.5 centimeters (15 and 25 inches; Conant & Collins 1991). The largest reported individual was a female with a total length of 76 centimeters (30 inches; John Meltzer, personal communication).

The Eastern Hognose Snake, also found in Minnesota, has a less upturned snout, and the underside of its tail is lighter in color than the adjacent belly.

Distribution

The range of the Western Hognose Snake forms a broad band running north and south across the central United States. Commencing in southwest Manitoba and southeast Alberta, the range extends south across the Great Plains into northern Mexico. Disjunct populations are located in Illinois, Missouri, and eastern Texas. In Minnesota, the Western Hognose Snake has a scattered distribution but generally is found along the western edge of the state and across the central section. Several counties in the southeast and southwest have isolated populations.

Habitat

This snake is a prairie animal and prefers open, sandy, or gravelly land. Well-drained, loose loam or sand is needed for the snake's burrowing activities (Platt 1969). River floodplains and sand dunes are used in isolated locales in the southeastern corner of the state. Smith (1961) indicated that Western Hognose Snakes overwinter below the frost line in mammal burrows, but specific information concerning Minnesota wintering sites is unavailable.

Life History

The activity period for this snake extends from early May through late September. Short intervals of estivation may occur during extreme summer conditions (Ernst and Barbour 1989). The Western Hognose Snake is primarily diurnal, concentrating its activity in morning hours and late afternoon and often spending nights in self-excavated burrows. The snake digs in loose soil by thrusting its shovel-like nose side to side while pushing forward.

Western Hognose Snakes consume toads, frogs, salamanders, lizards, small snakes, mice, and shrews. They also eat a variety of eggs including those of turtles, lizards, snakes, and ground-nesting birds (Platt 1969). In Minnesota, Prairie Skinks are an important food source (Breckenridge 1944). The snake locates prey by sight and odor and then rapidly crawls up and seizes it. Struggling prey is held down with a body loop. Enlarged teeth in the back of the upper jaw help to hold and immobilize prey while a toxic saliva is released and chewed into the animal.

Western Hognose Snake reproduction has not been reported on in Minnesota; however, Platt (1969) studied populations in Kansas and discovered that females mature at 20 to 22 months of age with a snout-vent length of 35 to 40 centimeters (14 to 16 inches). Most males mature at one year of age, and they wander widely, searching for odor trails left by females. Mating primarily takes place in the spring, but fall encounters are likely. After a gestation period of approximately 30 days, nest excavation and egg laying take place in July. Eggs are laid singly in a row or in a cluster about 10 centimeters (4 inches) deep in a depression in damp soil. Commonly 8 to 12 eggs form a clutch with the range being 2 to 24. The white or cream eggs are elliptical with smooth, leathery shells, and their average size is 2 by 3.5 centimeters (¾ by 1⅜ inches). Development takes 47 to 75 days, and young hatch from early August through September. It may take a hatchling 40 to 60 hours to leave the egg after first slitting it open (Munro 1949). Hatchling snakes are 14 to 19 centimeters (5½ to 7½ inches) in total length. In captivity young can be highly cannibalistic—they occasionally consume litter mates soon after leaving the egg (John Meltzer, personal communication).

When encountered in the wild, this species attempts to escape by crawling into a hole or burrowing into loose soil. If the snake is cornered, it hides its head under body loops. With further provocation it takes a defensive posture, spreads its neck, hisses, and repeatedly strikes with a closed mouth. If these actions fail to deter the intruder, the snake contorts about, vomits up any recent meal, and flips onto its back with mouth agape and tongue extended. Feces and blood may ooze from the vent. If the snake is turned over, it immediately rolls to its back again. When danger moves on, the snake rights itself from feigning death and crawls off. After a short time in captivity, individuals generally refuse to perform this behavior.

Predators of the Western Hognose Snake include hawks, crows, fox, coyotes, raccoons, and possibly larger snakes. The greatest threat to this species is the continual loss of habitat due to human activities. It is also a desirable pet and is collected for this purpose.

Remarks

There are three recognized subspecies of the Western Hognose Snake. The Plains Hognose Snake (*Heterodon nasicus nasicus*) is the subspecies found in Minnesota (Conant and Collins 1991).

On rare occasions, the bite of the Western Hognose Snake has

*Western Hognose Snake,
death feigning, Anoka County,
Minnesota*

caused a painful envenomation in humans that resulted in swelling and discoloration at the site of the bite (Bragg 1960; Hornfeldt and Keyler 1987). Since the venom is mildly toxic and the snake must chew at some length to introduce the venom, the snake poses no significant danger to humans.

A prairie species, the Western Hognose Snake has lost considerable habitat to agriculture and development. Most of the remaining populations are isolated relicts and are vulnerable to further development. The Minnesota Department of Natural Resources classifies this snake as a special concern species (Coffin and Pfannmuller 1988).

Eastern Hognose Snake

Heterodon platirhinos

Description

The Eastern Hognose Snake is a medium-sized, stout-bodied reptile with a sharply pointed, slightly upturned nose. The rostral plate is flattened underneath and keeled on top. Ground coloration may be gray, yellow brown, or olive brown. Two large dark brown spots adorn the back of the head and resemble "eyespots" when the snake flattens its neck. The rest of the body may be decorated with 20 to 30 large dark brown blotches running down the middle of the back. Lateral to these on each side is a row of small black or dark brown spots. The blotched pattern becomes a ringed design on the tail. Many individuals in Minnesota, especially older adults, have indistinct blotches or lack blotches with the exception of the "eyespots." The belly is a mottled yellowish-brown, dark brown, or gray. The underside of the tail is distinctly lighter colored than the adjacent abdomen. All body scales are keeled, and the anal plate is divided. Young of this species have a distinct blotched dorsal pattern. The ventral surface is black, and the undersides of the neck and tail are yellow or white.

Eastern Hognose Snake, adult, Goodhue County, Minnesota

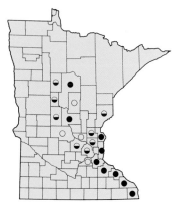

The average length of an adult Eastern Hognose Snake ranges from 51 to 84 centimeters (20 to 33 inches; Conant and Collins 1991). The largest reported from Minnesota was a female from Pine County with a total length of 109 centimeters (43 inches).

The snout of the Eastern Hognose Snake is less upturned than that of the Western Hognose Snake. Another important distinction is that the underside of the tail of the Western species does not markedly differ in color or pattern from its belly. Gopher Snakes have a pointed nose, but they lack the upturned rostrum found in hognose snakes. They also have a single anal plate.

Distribution

The Eastern Hognose Snake ranges across the eastern United States from the southern extreme of New Hampshire south to Florida and west to Texas. This snake reaches the northwestern limit of its distribution in eastern Minnesota. Records of Eastern Hognose Snakes in Minnesota come from central, east-central, and southeastern counties.

Habitat

The habitat of this species consists of river floodplains, open woodlands, grasslands, and old fields. An important component of the habitat is sandy or loamy soil. Sand beaches and adjacent wooded areas along the Mississippi and St. Croix rivers and their tributaries provide these conditions in Minnesota. Individuals overwinter in mammal tunnels or self-dug burrows below the frost line (Platt 1969).

Life History

Eastern Hognose Snakes emerge from overwintering early in the spring and become active by the last half of April. They search for food or mates above ground during morning hours, but much of their time is spent underground. Little is known concerning their home ranges, but Platt (1969) reported movements of 858 meters (938 yards) by males during the breeding season. Reports of Eastern Hognose Snakes swimming are not uncommon. While canoeing the St. Croix River during June, Oldfield witnessed a large adult swimming across from Wisconsin to Minnesota.

Toads are the primary prey of the Eastern Hognose Snake, which has several adaptations for feeding on these amphibians. The modified rostrum enables the snake to search and burrow for hidden toads. Once seized, a struggling toad inflates its body and secretes toxic alkaloids from skin glands. The snake is equipped with elongated teeth in the back of its movable upper jaw, which secures a grip and deflates the toad. The snake's saliva possesses a mild toxin that helps subdue the prey (McKinistry 1978). In addition, this species is apparently immune to toad skin secretions (Huheey 1958). Alternate food items include salamanders, various species of frogs, skinks, small mammals, birds, and arthropods (Wright and Wright 1957).

Sexual maturity occurs at 18 to 21 months of age, and adults are believed to reproduce annually (Platt 1969). Males must actively search for females since they overwinter individually. Courtship and

Eastern Hognose Snake, adult wtih spotted pattern

copulation occur from mid-April through May. Cream-colored, elliptical eggs with thin parchment shells are laid in loose sandy soil or humus in protected areas from late May to early July. Average clutch size is 15 to 25; one Pine County female, however, contained 61 developed eggs (Breckenridge 1944). The size of an egg ranges from 2.1 to 3.9 centimeters (¾ to 1½ inches) by 1.3 to 2.8 centimeters (½ to 1⅛ inches). Egg development takes 50 to 65 days depending on the weather. Ernst and Barbour (1989) reported that young emerge from the egg at a length of 16.8 to 25 centimeters (6⅝ to 9¾ inches).

The Eastern Hognose Snake readily puts on a remarkable show of bluff when threatened. The snake coils its body, spreads its neck, and raises its head like a cobra. It hisses loudly and repeatedly strikes with a closed mouth. If agitated further, it goes into a death-feigning act by contorting its body, gaping its mouth, excreting feces, and rolling onto its back. This performance, however, has a basic flaw. If the snake is turned right side up, it immediately flips on its back again. Once danger passes, the snake rolls over and crawls away. Hatchlings will perform the death-feigning act right out of the egg (Ernst and Barbour 1989).

Predators include birds of prey, small carnivorous mammals, and other species of snakes (Ernst and Barbour 1989). Uninformed humans often kill hognose snakes because of their defensive display. Roadkills and habitat destruction take significant numbers of these interesting serpents.

Remarks

The Eastern Hognose Snake has a long list of nicknames including "blow snake," "hissing adder," "puff adder," "spreadhead," and "sand adder." Generally this species is demanding to maintain in captivity because of the difficulty of obtaining a constant supply of toads. Special concern status is given to the Eastern Hognose Snake in Minnesota (Coffin and Pfannmuller 1988).

Milk Snake

Lampropeltis triangulum

Description

The Milk Snake is a medium-sized snake with a row of large reddish brown to grayish brown saddle blotches down its back. These saddles are bordered in black and alternate with one or two rows of smaller spots along the sides of the body. The dorsal ground color is light gray or light brown, and a light Y- or V-shaped pattern is generally present on the back of the neck. The top of the head is diversely marked, and the chin is a uniform dusty white. The light-colored belly is boldly marked in a checkerboard pattern with an irregular placement of numerous solid black squares. Body scales are smooth, and the anal plate is entire. Hatchling and juvenile snakes are patterned like adults, but the dorsal blotches are often bright red and contrast sharply with a light gray background.

The majority of adult Milk Snakes are 61 to 90 centimeters (24 to 36 inches) long (Conant and Collins 1991). The largest known Minnesota individual, from Goodhue County, was measured at 107 centimeters (42 inches).

Milk Snake, adult,
Wabasha County, Minnesota

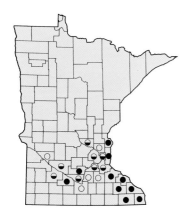

Minnesota snakes that might be confused with Milk Snakes include Fox Snakes, Northern Water Snakes, young Racers, and young Rat Snakes. All of these species, however, have divided anal plates.

Distribution

The range of the Milk Snake, which includes several subspecies, is one of the largest of any North American snake. Its range reaches from southern Maine, south to Florida and west to the Rocky Mountains, virtually spanning the eastern three-fourths of the United States. In Minnesota the Milk Snake is found in the watershed regions of the St. Croix, Mississippi, and Minnesota rivers in the southern third of the state.

Habitat

Minnesota Milk Snakes are primarily found in deciduous wooded valleys and hills often in association with rocky areas near water sources. Woodlots, abandoned rock quarries, and old farmsteads where rodents are common are preferred habitat. Congregations of Milk Snakes are found in rocky upland sites in spring and fall; they often move to lower ground during the summer to hunt. This snake also appears with considerable regularity in small towns, where it is found in basements and around foundations of old homes and buildings. Overwintering sites are in rock outcrops, mammal burrows, cisterns, and foundations of old buildings.

Life History

Milk Snakes emerge from overwintering sites by mid-April. Individuals can be found basking near these sites in early May and again in September (Vogt 1981). Seven adult Milk Snakes were found massed together under one rock in a quarry one May evening (Oldfield, personal observation). Because they are very secretive, the easiest way to find Milk Snakes during late spring and summer is by searching under rocks, logs, boards, and tin. Occasionally they may be found crossing blacktop roads on warm summer nights. By October they return to protected locations to overwinter. John Wilzbacher (personal communication) observed a juvenile crawling on a sidewalk in O. L. Kipp State Park on 20 November at an air temperature of 4.4° C. (40° F).

Milk Snakes are powerful constrictors. They seize prey in their mouth and swiftly wrap body coils around it. Normally, the victim dies of suffocation before being swallowed. About 80% of their food volume consists of small mammals including mice, voles, shrews, and young rats, but Milk Snakes also eat small birds, bird eggs, lizards, lizard eggs, and other snakes (Ernst and Barbour 1989). Williams (1978) reported that small frogs, small fish, earthworms, slugs, and insects are also consumed. According to Vogt (1981), the primary food of hatchling Milk Snakes is the young of other snakes including Ringneck Snakes, Common Garter Snakes, Smooth Green Snakes, Brown Snakes, and Redbelly Snakes.

Courtship and mating take place anytime from emergence through early June. Gestation is 30 to 40 days. During the later half of June, the gravid female selects a site in decaying humus or rotting wood, under rocks, or in mammal burrows to lay 3 to 24 eggs. The average clutch size is 8 to 12, and the white cylindrical eggs are 1.1 to 1.5 centimeters by 2.1 to 3.5 centimeters (⅜ to ½ inch by ⅞ to 1½ inches). By late August or early September, the young snakes leave the eggs to begin life on their own. The total length of newly hatched Milk Snakes ranges from 15 to 25 centimeters (6 to 10 inches).

Milk Snake, adult,
Winona County, Minnesota

When surprised, a Milk Snake coils and rapidly vibrates its tail. Some individuals strike and bite fiercely, and others hide their head under body coils. Hawks, owls, and small carnivorous mammals are predators of the Milk Snake. Automobiles and habitat destruction are responsible for the loss of countless numbers each year.

Remarks

Lampropeltis triangulum triangulum (Eastern Milk Snake) is the only subspecies recognized in Minnesota (Conant and Collins 1991). Occasional individuals are found in southern Minnesota, however, that demonstrate characteristics of the subspecies *L. t. syspila* (Red Milk Snake), which is found in northern Iowa and farther south. The Red Milk Snake has large bright red blotches and a noticeable reduction in lateral spots when compared to the eastern subspecies. The area of intergradation between the two subspecies is broad and probably extends into southeastern Minnesota.

The origin of the name milk snake comes from an erroneous belief that a cow with poor milk production has been recently milked by this serpent. This folklore has no basis in fact. Rodents are plentiful around livestock feeds, and they are the reason Milk Snakes are found in and near barns. Special concern status is given to the Milk Snake by the Minnesota Department of Natural Resources, primarily because of the demand for this species in the pet trade (Coffin and Pfannmuller 1988).

Northern Water Snake

Nerodia sipedon

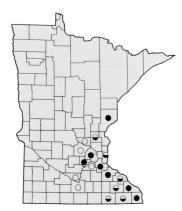

Description

Minnesota's only water snake is the Northern Water Snake. This heavy-bodied aquatic snake possesses a distinct head with a blunt snout. The ground color is reddish brown, tan, or gray. The neck and forepart of the body have dark brown, dark gray, or black bands that are wider than the spaces between them. From midbody toward the tail, these bands break into large squarish dorsal blotches and smaller spots along the sides. The bands and blotches may be outlined with black. Irregular dark markings are found on top of the head, and the chin is off-white. Adult Northern Water Snakes with dry skin are uniform dusky brown or tan with little discernible pattern. When the skin is wet, however, the pattern becomes conspicuous. The cream to yellowish belly has numerous irregularly spaced half-moons with dark borders and reddish brown centers. On occasion, a solid gray or tan individual is found with no dorsal markings and a pale yellowish belly with sparse small black specks. Body scales are strongly keeled, and the anal plate is divided. Juveniles are similarly

Northern Water Snake, adult, Houston County, Minnesota

patterned as adults, but the bands and blotches are more conspicuous because of a lighter ground color.

The adult Northern Water Snake ranges in total length from 61 to 107 centimeters (24 to 42 inches; Conant and Collins 1991).

Two species of snakes that might be confused with the Northern Water Snake because they are frequently found near water are the Fox Snake and the Massasauga. Both of these species, however,

Northern Water Snake, underside, Houston County, Minnesota

have a row of middorsal blotches. In addition, the Fox Snake has a solid-colored head, and the Massasauga has a rattle on the end of its tail. The only other species in Minnesota that has bands across its body is the Timber Rattlesnake, but it has a black tail with a tan rattle.

Distribution

Northern Water Snakes range from southern Maine south to the panhandle of Florida and west to Oklahoma and eastern Colorado. A large section of the southeastern coastal plain is devoid of this species. In Minnesota this snake is found in a band of counties from the extreme southeast northward into Pine County. The distribution of this species follows the Mississippi, Minnesota, and St. Croix rivers and their tributaries.

Habitat

As the common name of this species suggests, it is found in or near water. Almost any body of freshwater including ponds, lakes, rivers, sloughs, creeks, marshes, and bogs provides suitable habitat (Vogt 1981). Sufficient quantities of food, cover, and basking areas in and adjacent to the water are fundamental requirements. Breckenridge (1944) indicated that this species overwinters in upland rock crevices and holes away from water. It may seek shelter in crayfish burrows, muskrat and beaver lodges, earthen dams, and levees (Ernst and Barbour 1989).

Life History

By late April, Northern Water Snakes emerge from their over-wintering sites and remain active until October. They are active both day and night but are primarily diurnal in spring and fall. As many as five or six individuals may pile together basking on rocks, tree roots, and ground vegetation near the water's edge. At the slightest hint of danger, Northern Water Snakes promptly slide into the water and swim off with only their heads above the surface. They have been known to remain totally submerged for over an hour with no ill effects (Ferguson and Thornton 1984).

Northern Water Snakes prefer to eat ectothermic vertebrates, especially fish and amphibians. According to Johnson (1987), up to 95% of their diet consists of small fish such as minnows and darters. Frogs, tadpoles, toads, and salamanders are a significant food source when available. Small mammals, crayfish, snails, slugs, insects, spiders, leeches, earthworms, and other snakes are also taken (Ernst and Barbour 1989). Northern Water Snakes are active hunters—they swiftly pursue prey, which they seize in their mouth and swallow whole.

This species reaches sexual maturity at two to three years of age. Courtship and mating take place in spring after emergence. Several males may simultaneously court a single female, either in the water or on land. The male moves alongside and on top of the female periodically pressing his chin against her back and neck. Once copulation is achieved, they may remain together for several hours (Ernst and Barbour 1989). A single annual litter is produced after a gestation period of approximately 60 days. The developing embryos in the female's uterus are nourished through a placenta (Conway and Fleming 1960). The female gives live birth to an average of 25 (range of 10 to 48) young during August and early September. A large range in litter size has been recorded with 99 being the largest (Slevin 1951). Newborn snakes range in length from 19 to 25 centimeters (7½ to 10 inches).

Northern Water Snakes have a particularly bad disposition. If cornered by an intruder, the snake flattens its head, vibrates its tail, repeatedly strikes, and bites viciously by holding on and chewing.

Although the bite is not dangerous, the wound may bleed excessively because of an anticoagulant component in the snake's saliva. Along with all of these actions, they also spray a foul-smelling fluid from their cloaca.

The Northern Water Snake has many predators including Snapping Turtles, Bullfrogs, hawks, crows, gulls, herons, bitterns, egrets, vultures, raccoons, mink, and large predatory fish. Juvenile snakes are especially vulnerable.

Remarks

Four subspecies of the Northern Water Snake are recognized. *Nerodia sipedon sipedon* (Northern Water Snake) is the subspecies found in Minnesota (Conant and Collins 1991).

Humans frequently kill Northern Water Snakes on sight believing they are dangerous water moccasins. The venomous Cottonmouth (commonly called water moccasin) reaches its northern distributional limit in southern Missouri, several hundred miles from the Minnesota border. Northern Water Snakes are often persecuted by fishermen who believe they remove too many game fish. In actuality, this species reduces competition between fish by feeding on small diseased and injured fish. The snake itself provides food for larger bass and pike, serving as an important link in the natural balance of aquatic ecosystems.

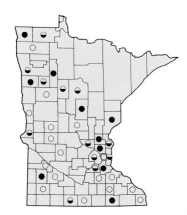

Smooth Green Snake

Opheodrys vernalis

Description

The Smooth Green Snake is a small, beautiful, emerald green colubrid with a slender body and a pristine white or pale yellow abdomen. Infrequently, individuals are light brown or tan instead of green. Their bright red tongue has a black tip. Body scales are smooth, and the anal plate is divided. Hatchlings are olive green.

Smooth Green Snakes reach a length of 36 to 51 centimeters (14 to 20 inches; Vogt 1981).

Shortly after death, the Smooth Green Snake's coloration fades to pale blue, superficially resembling the coloration of the Racer and confusing identification. Racers the size of adult Smooth Green Snakes still bear a juvenile blotched pattern.

Distribution

Smooth Green Snakes are found from southeastern Canada and Maine south to Virginia and west to the Rocky Mountains. The range of this species is broken into numerous isolated populations across the Great Plains. Excluding northeastern Minnesota, records of Smooth Green Snakes are broadly distributed across the state.

Habitat

These snakes are found in prairies and meadows, along the edges of mixed hardwood and pine forests, near the edges of marshes and bogs, and on dry hillsides. They overwinter below the frost line at soil depths greater than 15 centimeters (6 inches). Lang (1969) discovered large numbers of Smooth Green Snakes using abandoned ant mounds as communal overwintering sites with other species including Redbelly, Common Garter, and Plains Garter Snakes.

Life History

The activity season for this species in Minnesota begins in mid-April and extends through September. They are primarily diurnal snakes but are occasionally found crossing roads on warm rainy evenings (Vogt 1981). Smooth Green Snakes climb into shrubs for foraging or basking, but they also spend considerable time on the ground crawling in vegetation and hiding under cover (Johnson 1987).

Smooth Green Snakes consume invertebrates including spiders, slugs, centipedes, millipedes, crickets, grasshoppers, moth and butterfly larvae, and beetles (Ernst and Barbour 1989). They seize prey with their mouths and swallow it whole. They are especially vulnerable to pesticides because of their arthropod diet. Minton (1972) collected two specimens from a sprayed field that died within two weeks.

Mating probably occurs during May, although it has been observed in August (Dymond and Fry 1932). Smooth Green Snakes nest during late July and August, and 3 to 11 eggs is the normal clutch size. Communal nesting is likely given that large numbers of eggs (up to 31) have been found at one site (Cook 1964). Nests are located in mounds of rotting vegetation, decomposing logs, tree hollows, and sawdust piles. Eggs are cylindrical with thin white shells and measure 2.3 by 1.3 centimeters (⅞ by ½ inch). Hatching occurs about a month after egg deposition, and the young snakes are 10 to 15 centimeters (4 to 6 inches) long when they leave the eggs. Egg

development periods as short as four days have been reported, indicating the ability of the female to retain maturing eggs within her body (Vogt 1981). Hatchlings retain residual egg yolk, which allows them to go without feeding for the first two weeks. Young snakes begin foraging for food after they shed their skin the first time.

Smooth Green Snake, adult, Dakota County, Minnesota

The Smooth Green Snake's main line of defense is its cryptic coloration, which makes it very difficult to detect in green vegetation. When threatened, it raises its head, gapes, and strikes, but its small mouth is only capable of inflicting a minor scratch. Predators include birds, mammals, and larger snakes. Habitat destruction and pesticides are significant threats to this species.

Remarks

Conant and Collins (1991) do not list subspecies for this snake. Some people refer to this harmless, inoffensive little serpent as a "grass snake."

Gopher Snake (Bullsnake)

Pituophis catenifer

Description

The Gopher Snake, also known as the Bullsnake, is the longest Minnesota snake, reaching a length of more than 183 centimeters (6 feet). It is a powerful, stout-bodied constrictor with a relatively small head. The yellow head is marked with many black or near black marks including a bold stripe from the eye to the corner of the mouth. There are prominent vertical lines on the upper lip, and the head is pointed with an elongated, protruding rostral plate. Ground color is straw yellow or light brown, and there are 38 to 53 black, dark brown, or reddish brown blotches down the mid-line. The blotched pattern is less obvious near the head but becomes bolder near the tail. The tail displays black or reddish brown bands. The chin and belly of the Gopher Snake are pale yellow, and the belly is stamped with numerous square or rectangular dark spots. Many individuals show a pronounced color change from head to tail. Body scales are keeled, and the anal plate is single. The pattern

Gopher Snake, adult, Goodhue County, Minnesota

Gopher Snake, adult head,
Goodhue County, Minnesota

of juvenile Gopher Snakes is similar to that of adults, but their over-all coloration is lighter.

The average adult Gopher Snake ranges in length from 95 to 183 centimeters (37 to 72 inches; Conant and Collins 1991). The largest known Minnesota Gopher Snake was a female from Wabasha County that measured 188 centimeters (74 inches).

The Fox Snake, which is often confused with the Gopher Snake, has an unmarked head with a rounded nose. The Fox Snake also has a divided anal plate. The Timber Rattlesnake has an unmarked head, a banded body pattern, and a black tail with a tan rattle.

Distribution

The Gopher Snake ranges from western Wisconsin and Illinois south to Texas and west to the Pacific Coast. Its range is extensive and includes the entire western United States, portions of southern Canada, and northern Mexico. In Minnesota, the Gopher Snake is found in the southern half of the state, and many of the records come from counties bordering the Mississippi, Minnesota, and St. Croix rivers. The isolated record from Polk County in northwest-ern Minnesota is a single specimen collected near Fertile in 1939.

Habitat

The Gopher Snake is a snake of open country. It prefers native prairies, old fields, pastures, oak savannas, and bluff prairies that are located on steep hillsides. This species thrives in sandy soil habitats where burrowing rodents are common. Overwintering occurs in mammal burrows well below the frost line or deep in rock fissures in bluff areas (Schroder 1950; Vogt 1981).

Life History

Emergence from overwintering sites occurs in late April or May. These sites may be shared with other species such as Racers, Rat Snakes, and Timber Rattlesnakes (Vogt 1981). Gopher Snakes are principally diurnal and can climb but spend much of the time foraging and resting in rodent burrows. They are fond of basking on warm sand, rock, or pavement. Their activity season ends in late September or early October.

In addition to eating gophers, these snakes take a variety of other small mammals including mice, voles, ground squirrels, and tree squirrels. Other food items include frogs, ground-nesting birds, and bird eggs. Larger rodents are seized in the mouth and quickly suffocated by coils of the snake's body before being swallowed. Rodents encountered in burrows are pressed against the tunnel wall by the snake until they succumb. The snake itself is at risk when trying to subdue a large rodent and may be badly bitten or, in rare instances, killed in the process (Haywood and Harris 1972). Eggs and small helpless prey are swallowed directly without constriction.

Gopher Snakes mate during May. During the breeding season, a male may engage in combat with another male to establish dominance (Shaw 1951). When a male finds a receptive female, he crawls alongside and on top of her in a jerking, spasmodic manner. Generally she lies still while elevating and slowly waving her tail. He may grasp her neck, back, or head with his mouth before positioning his vent adjacent to hers to achieve copulation. Copulation may take an hour or longer (Collins 1974).

During June or early July, females deposit a single clutch of 3 to 24 eggs (average of 12) in a self-excavated nest. The location of the nest may be out in the open or under a large rock or log in loose sandy soil. Communal nests have been reported, although they are not common (Burger and Zappalorti 1986). The whitish eggs are elliptical with rough, leathery shells, and they average 4.0 by 5.0 centimeters (1½ by 2 inches). Eggs often adhere to each other, and they gain in width and weight during the development period. Egg development periods of 56 to 100 days have been reported (Ernst and Barbour 1989). Hatchling length is 25.5 to 44 centimeters (10 to 17 inches). The skin is shed for the first time at seven to ten days of age.

When encountered in the wild, Gopher Snakes make every attempt to escape, often diving for the first available mammal burrow. If left without a retreat, they can put on an impressive display of fierceness. An agitated Gopher Snake coils, rapidly vibrates its tail, hisses loudly, and strikes repeatedly. In dry leaves the vibrating tail makes a sound similar to a rattlesnake. No other Minnesota snake can hiss as loudly. With open mouth, they forcefully expel air, causing the epiglottis, which covers the opening to the trachea, to vibrate. Their epiglottis is enlarged and may help amplify the sound (Martin and Huey 1971). Although nonvenomous, a large adult is capable of delivering a painful bite.

Adult Gopher Snakes have few predators, although it is probable that a large hawk or predatory mammal may occasionally take one. Young snakes fall prey to birds, mammals, and larger snakes such as Racers and Milk Snakes. The loss of Gopher Snakes to automobile traffic and habitat destruction is far more significant, and many snakes are needlessly destroyed by humans because of fear and misinformation.

Remarks

There are six recognized subspecies of *Pituophis catenifer* (Collins 1990). The subspecies of Gopher Snake found in Minnesota is the Bullsnake (*Pituophis c. sayi*). Currently, the taxonomy of this species is confusing. In an attempt to maintain consistency with names throughout the reptile accounts, we chose to follow Collins (1990) and to use the species name of *catenifer*. *Pituophis melanoleucus* is widely accepted by many authorities as the correct scientific name for the Gopher Snake (Conant and Collins 1991).

The Gopher Snake (Bullsnake) is an extremely beneficial predator eliminating numerous pocket gophers and ground squirrels. Rodents do substantial damage to crop fields, and the killing of a single snake creates hours of work by necessitating the trapping or poisoning of the rodents the snake would have consumed.

The name Bullsnake may have originated from the snake's "bullish" defensive behavior. Although unproved stories abound of Gopher Snakes eating rattlesnakes, it is unlikely that these snakes have an appetite for other snakes. Oldfield has witnessed the same overwintering den being used by *Pituophis* and Timber Rattlesnakes in Minnesota. The longevity record for a captive is just short of 22.5 years (Bowler 1977). The Minnesota Department of Natural Resources classifies this species as special concern primarily because of collection pressures generated by the pet trade (Coffin and Pfann-muller 1988).

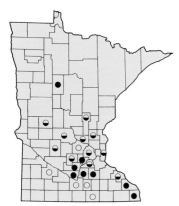

Brown Snake

Storeria dekayi

Description

The Brown Snake is a small, inoffensive earth-tone snake of Minnesota's woodlands. Ground color varies from grayish brown to reddish brown, and there is usually a light middorsal stripe about four scales in width bordered by a parallel row of small dark spots. These spots are often connected by a thin dark line that borders the middorsal stripe on either side, and a dark bar may connect adjacent spots across the stripe. A relatively large dark spot is located on each side of the neck, and there may be a smaller dark spot under each eye and a dark stripe behind the eye. The pale pink or cream-colored belly has pinpoint specks on the edges of the ventral plates. Dorsal scales are strongly keeled, and the anal plate is divided. Juvenile Brown Snakes have a light yellow or white band around the neck. The body pattern of juveniles is often indiscernible because of a widespread dark coloration.

The Brown Snake rarely exceeds 35.5 centimeters (14 inches) in total length. An average adult is 23 to 33 centimeters long (9 to 13 inches; Conant and Collins 1991).

The closely related Redbelly Snake normally has a bright red belly. Ringneck Snakes are easily confused with immature Brown Snakes, but Ringneck Snakes have smooth body scales.

Distribution

This species is found from Maine south to Florida and then west to Minnesota and Texas. The range of the Brown Snake is essentially the eastern half of the United States. Brown Snake records in Minnesota are from counties in the central and southeastern regions of the state. The snake is absent from the northern third and the southwest corner of the state.

Habitat

In Minnesota the Brown Snake prefers a moist environment in association with deciduous forests, especially woodland edges near clearings, marshes, and ponds. Lowland forests seem more suitable than upland areas with well-drained soils. Vogt (1981) reported that in Wisconsin old fields and vacant city lots are suitable habitat. Brown Snakes overwinter in deserted ant mounds, rock piles, and stone foundations. They are often found with garter snakes, Redbelly Snakes, and Smooth Green Snakes. The same overwintering site is used year after year (Minton 1972).

Life History

With warm weather in late April, Brown Snakes begin to emerge from winter retreats and may be found basking on rocks. Essentially diurnal during the spring and fall, they are active during evening hours in summer months. A very secretive snake, this little serpent spends much of its time under shelter such as rocks, logs, boards, and discarded rubbish. The home range is unusually small, but one individual traveled 374 meters (409 yards) in 30 days in Ontario (Freedman and Catling 1979). During the fall they may be found crossing highways on their way to overwintering sites.

Brown Snake, adult

Brown Snakes feed primarily on earthworms, slugs, and soft-bodied insect larvae. Other recorded food items for this species include snails, small frogs, amphibian eggs, small fish, and sow bugs (Wright and Wright 1957). They actively seek prey, using their sense of smell. If the prey is an earthworm, the snake seizes it midbody; then the snake works its mouth around to either end and swallows it whole.

Brown Snakes ordinarily reach sexual maturity by the fall of their second year. Breeding occurs the following spring shortly after emergence. Like females of other snake species, female Brown Snakes release pheromones, chemical odors that attract males. During August or early September, following a gestation period of 105 to 113 days, females give birth to an average litter of 14 (range of 3 to 41) (Fitch 1970). Newborn snakes are delivered in a thin transparent membrane from which they quickly escape. Their length at birth ranges from 9.5 to 10.5 centimeters (3¾ to 4⅛ inches).

When frightened, Brown Snakes flatten their bodies and discharge a mild musk, but generally they cannot be provoked to bite. This species is eaten by many predators including skunks, raccoons, weasels, opossums, shrews, hawks, robins, thrashers, toads, and other snakes.

Remarks

According to Conant and Collins (1991), there are five recognized subspecies of the Brown Snake. The subspecies found in Minnesota is the Texas Brown Snake (*Storeria dekayi texana*). In the past this species was referred to as DeKay's snake.

Redbelly Snake

Storeria occipitomaculata

Description

As the name indicates, this small, secretive colubrid possesses a crimson-colored belly. Dorsal ground color may be gray, brown, reddish brown, or black. Generally there is a wide, light middorsal stripe or, less commonly, four narrow dark stripes extending the length of the back. Usually the top of the head is darker than the back, and there may be three pale yellow or white spots on the nape of the neck. A white chin is followed by a deep red or orange red belly. Dorsal scales are markedly keeled, and the anal plate is divided. Immature Redbelly Snakes tend to be darker than adults. The spots on their neck are often fused forming a collar, and their belly coloration is less intense.

Adults reach a total length of 20 to 25 centimeters (8 to 10 inches; Conant and Collins 1991).

The bright red, unmarked ventral surface of the Redbelly Snake distinguishes it from its close relative the Brown Snake. Juvenile

Redbelly Snake, adult,
Anoka County, Minnesota

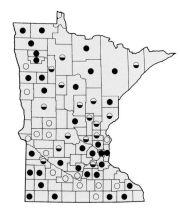

Ringneck Snakes are very similar in appearance to young Redbelly Snakes, but Ringneck Snakes have smooth body scales.

Distribution

The Redbelly Snake ranges from southern Canada and Maine south to northern Florida and west to eastern North Dakota in the north and Texas in the south. Large gaps in the range occur in the central states. There are disjunct populations in western South Dakota and eastern Wyoming. In Minnesota, this species has a statewide distribution, although it is more common in the northern half of the state.

Habitat

Redbelly Snakes are known for their preference for woodland habitat. It is not uncommon, however, to find them under ground cover in moist, grassy meadows. Karns (1992a) documented the occurrence of Redbelly Snakes in peatlands habitat in northern Minnesota.

Redbelly Snake, adult, Rice County, Minnesota

During spring and fall migration to winter retreats, they may be found in window wells and basements. Redbelly Snakes congregate to overwinter with other snake species in abandoned ant mounds (Lang 1969). Other possible winter retreats include rock crevices, old stone foundations, and deserted wells.

Life History

The activity season of the Redbelly Snake in Minnesota normally extends from late April to October. This snake is thought to be diurnal in the spring and fall and crepuscular or nocturnal during the summer. Because Redbelly Snakes are small and inconspicuously marked, they are difficult to see when crawling through leaves and twigs, and they may be more active during daylight hours than suspected. They forage in broad daylight during the summer in forest openings in northern Minnesota (Oldfield, personal observation).

Small, soft-bodied prey such as slugs, earthworms, beetle larvae, and isopods are preferred food items. Soft body parts of snails are extracted from their shells and consumed (Rossman and Myer 1990).

Redbelly Snakes are sexually mature at two years of age, and courtship may take place in spring, summer, or fall. Females are capable of storing viable sperm for several months before fertilization occurs. They give birth annually to a litter of 1 to 21 in August or early September. Breckenridge (1944) reported that a female captured in Pine County delivered a litter of 18 on 17 July. Newborn snakes are each covered with a thin transparent membrane that they promptly rupture. According to Ernst and Barbour (1989), their length at birth ranges from 7 to 11 centimeters (2¾ to 4⅜ inches).

This docile species can be handled without risk. It almost never attempts to bite, and if it did, it is unlikely that the tiny teeth would penetrate skin. When the snake is alarmed, a mild musk is discharged from glands at the base of the tail. On several occasions Redbelly Snakes have been reported to contort their body and stiffen out displaying their brightly colored abdomen in a behavior similar to death feigning (Jordon 1970). Redbelly Snakes have also been observed creating a "grin" by flattening their head and curling their upper lip to expose the teeth (Ernst and Barbour 1989).

A number of bird species and small predatory mammals consume Redbelly Snakes. Largemouth Bass, Milk Snakes, and Racers are also predators.

Remarks

Of the three recognized subspecies of Redbelly Snake, two are found in Minnesota. The Northern Redbelly Snake (*Storeria occipito-maculata occipitomaculata*) and the Black Hills Redbelly Snake (*Storeria o. pahasapae*) occur in Minnesota in a broad area of intergradation across the entire state (Ernst 1974). The Northern Redbelly Snake generally displays a light mark on the fifth upper labial and three well-defined light spots on the back of its neck. The Black Hills Redbelly Snake lacks a spot on the upper labial, and the nape spots are missing or poorly defined.

Redbelly Snakes may appear to be scarce in many areas. Lang (1969), however, captured and marked over 1,500 on 24 hectares (59 acres) in north-central Minnesota.

Plains Garter Snake

Thamnophis radix

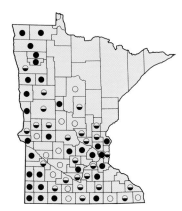

Description

The Plains Garter Snake, an occupant of Minnesota prairies, is a medium-sized striped snake. The dark brown, dark gray, or black ground color is partitioned by three light-colored stripes extending the length of the snake. The middorsal stripe is usually a deep yellow, and the side stripes are pale yellow with a greenish or bluish tint. The lateral stripes are located on the third and fourth scale rows above the belly plates. If the ground color is not too dark, two rows of alternating squarish spots may be discernible between the median and lateral stripes. Another row of dark spots is generally present between the belly plates and the lateral stripe. The top of the head is dark, and the pale greenish upper lip is marked with bold, black vertical bars along the edges of the labial scales. The underside of the snake is pale green or dingy gray. Dorsal and lateral body scales are keeled, and the anal plate is single. Juveniles are marked similar to adults.

The total length of adults ranges from 38 to 71 centimeters (15 to 28 inches; Conant and Collins 1991). Breckenridge (1944) reported an unusually large individual found in Anoka County in 1938 that measured 104 centimeters (41 inches).

Two striped snakes found in Minnesota that may be confused with the Plains Garter Snake are the Common Garter Snake and the Lined Snake. The Common Garter Snake lacks the dark upper lip bars, and its lateral stripes are on the second and third scale rows. Lined Snakes have a double row of half-moon spots on their abdomens.

Distribution

The Plains Garter Snake's range begins in western Indiana and expands westward across the Great Plains to the Rocky Mountains, reaching southern Canada in the north and northern New Mexico in the south. The distribution of the Plains Garter Snake in Minnesota includes the western, southern, and central counties. This species has not been reported from counties in the northeastern or north-central parts of the state.

Habitat

Plains Garter Snakes prefer open grasslands and sparsely wooded savannas. They are more frequently encountered along the edges of ponds, lakes, marshes, and streams in prairie habitats. Upland prairie distant from water is also utilized but less regularly. This species is not found in the northern coniferous forests. Abandoned mammal burrows (e.g., those of gophers and ground squirrels), deserted ant mounds, building foundations, and old wells are used as overwintering sites (Ernst and Barbour 1989). They frequently overwinter communally with other snake species such as Smooth Green Snakes and Redbelly Snakes (Lang 1969).

Life History

If warm weather permits, the Plains Garter Snake is active from mid-April through November. An individual was observed basking on an ant mound in Scott County on an unseasonably warm 14 November (Moriarty, personal observation). This species is principally diurnal, preferring air temperatures of 21° to 29° C (70° to 84° F). However, Ernst and Barbour (1989) reported observing this species feeding on Striped Chorus Frogs at night in Minnesota. Plains Garter Snakes maintain a small, restricted home range, moving less than 2 meters (6½ feet) per day (Seibert and Hagen 1947).

Plains Garter Snakes have a large appetite for amphibians and consume Gray Treefrogs, Western Chorus Frogs, American Toads, Northern Cricket Frogs, Northern Leopard Frogs, Wood Frogs, Tiger Salamanders, and tadpoles. They also eat grasshoppers, beetles, earthworms, slugs, fish, and small mammals (Ernst and Barbour 1989). Rodents may become a significant portion of their diet in areas distant from standing water.

Breeding normally occurs from mid-April through May, although Collins (1982) reported fall activity. Often several males court a single female by gliding alongside and nudging her with their noses while continually flicking their tongues. The male that gains the

Plains Garter Snake, adult, Nobles County, Minnesota

Plains Garter Snake, albino, Hennepin County, Minnesota

best position makes cloacal contact and achieves copulation while the receptive female remains stationary and elevates her tail. After a successful breeding, the male leaves a seminal plug in the cloaca of the female to inhibit copulation with other males (Ross and Crews 1977). Live birth is given to an average litter of 25 during late August and September. Litter size varies tremendously—a range of 5 to 92 is reported in the literature. Newborns range in length from 15 to 23.5 centimeters (5⅞ to 9¼ inches), and they may grow to 45 centimeters (17¾ inches) by the end of their first year.

When threatened, Plains Garter Snakes may hide their head under body coils and slowly wave their tail tip as a decoy (Jim Gerholdt, personal communication). If picked up, this species struggles to escape and sprays a pungent musk from glands near the base of the tail. It will attempt to bite but is not as aggressive as the Common Garter Snake.

Large birds and carnivorous mammals including hawks, bitterns, herons, foxes, coyotes, skunks, and raccoons are the most common predators. Habitat destruction and automobiles kill many more snakes than natural predators do.

Remarks

The two recognized subspecies of Plains Garter Snake look very similar and can be told apart only by scale counts. *Thamnophis radix radix* (Eastern Plains Garter Snake) has 154 or fewer ventral scales and usually less than 19 scale rows on the neck. This subspecies is found in southeastern Minnesota (Conant and Collins 1991). The remainder of the state is occupied by the Western Plains Garter Snake (*T. r. haydeni*), which has 155 or more ventral scales and 21 scale rows on the neck.

Common Garter Snake

Thamnophis sirtalis

Description

The most commonly encountered snake in Minnesota and the only species that many Minnesotans ever see in the wild is the Common Garter Snake. This harmless species is medium-sized with a slender build and three longitudinal yellow stripes that may be tinted blue, green, brown, or orange. The median stripe is generally a lighter hue than the lateral stripes. The lateral stripes are located on the second and third scale rows, counting up from the belly plates. The ground color is black, grayish brown, or olive. A double row of black spots may be apparent between the dorsal and lateral stripes.

Common Garter Snakes from southwestern Minnesota normally have prominent red bars along their sides between the stripes. Usually these bars are much reduced or absent on individuals from eastern and northern Minnesota. The top of the snake's head is dark, and the unmarked upper lips are light yellow or pale green. The chin is off-white, and the pale-colored belly is yellow, green, or blue. Dark spots may be present along the outside margins of the ventral plates. Body scales are keeled, and the anal plate is undivided. Young are marked similar to adults.

Common Garter Snake, adult, Clearwater County, Minnesota

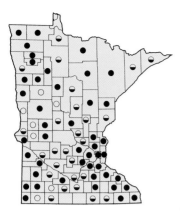

The average adult Common Garter Snake is 41 to 66 centimeters (16 to 26 inches) long (Conant and Collins 1991). An exceptionally large female from Fillmore County measured 104 centimeters (41 inches).

The similar-looking Plains Garter Snake has bold lip bars, and its lateral stripe is found on scale rows three and four. The Lined Snake has black half-moon spots on its belly.

Distribution

The Common Garter Snake has the widest distribution of any North American snake and lives farther north in Canada than any other serpent. This species is found from the East Coast to the West Coast and south to Florida and eastern Texas. It is not found in large areas of the arid Southwest. The Common Garter Snake has a statewide distribution in Minnesota and is probably found in every county, although several counties lack substantiated records.

Habitat

A habitat generalist, the Common Garter Snake resides in almost any vegetation association found in Minnesota including deciduous and coniferous forests, marshes, peatlands, and prairies. This species tolerates some degree of habitat alteration, for it is found on farmsteads, urban lots, golf courses, and cemeteries. It is strongly affiliated with water and is often found near ponds, streams, sloughs, and swampy areas. Suitable winter retreats include mammal burrows,

Common Garter Snake, adult, Rock County, Minnesota

building foundations, rock crevices in bluffs and quarries, and deserted ant mounds (Ernst and Barbour 1989). Large numbers of individuals may overwinter together. Congregations of approximately 8,000 snakes have been reported in limestone sinkholes in Canada (Gregory 1977).

Life History

Being cold-tolerant, the Common Garter Snake may be out basking shortly after snowmelt in early April and has been observed as late as 23 November (Breckenridge 1944). The species is considered to be primarily diurnal, but it may be active during the evening hours in spring and summer. Individuals may search for frogs and toads at night during breeding activities (Ernst and Barbour 1989). According to Aleksiuk (1976), active snakes have a body temperature range of 18° to 30° C (64° to 86° F). Common Garter Snakes may wander far afield to find summer feeding areas. Movements as great as 17.7 kilometers (11 miles) have been reported (Gregory and Stewart 1975).

Common Garter Snakes are not finicky eaters, and the list of acceptable food is extensive. Amphibians and earthworms are principal food items. Other food staples include fish, nestling birds, small mammals, arthropods, mollusks, and carrion. On rare occasions this species has been known to eat young snakes of other species (Ernst and Barbour 1989). The snake trails prey by scent, seizes it in the mouth, and swallows it. Although the bite of the Common Garter Snake is harmless to humans, there is some evidence that its saliva contains enzymes that help subdue and immobilize a struggling victim (Ernst and Barbour 1989).

Clusters of courting Common Garter Snakes can be found near overwintering sites in early spring. These writhing congregations are typically composed of a single female (usually the largest of the group) and a number of males. Each male attempts to maneuver into a position that will enable him to achieve copulation. The actual mating may last 15 to 20 minutes. The male leaves behind a copulatory plug in the female's cloaca that inhibits successful mating by other males. Gibson and Falls (1975) determined that despite the copulatory plug, a female may engage in multiple breedings. The female is capable of storing live sperm through the winter for fertilization of eggs the following spring. Females mature at two years of age and reproduce annually in Minnesota. Litter size ranges from 3 to 103 (Wright and Wright 1957), although 10 to 25 is typical. Newborns are 13 to 23 centimeters (5 to 9 inches) long.

When alarmed, the Common Garter Snake makes a dash for protective cover. This species is primarily terrestrial but readily slides into nearby water to escape predators. If cornered, an individual attempts to hide its head under body coils or flatten its neck and strike at the intruder. When captured, it struggles violently, bites repeatedly, discharges cloacal contents, and sprays a pungent musk. The musk of this species is strong and lingers on the captor's hands even after a thorough washing. If a person is bitten, the wound generally bleeds but causes no more discomfort than a minor scratch. Common Garter Snakes have many predators including mammals, birds, reptiles, amphibians, and fish.

Remarks

A broad zone of intergradation for two subspecies of the Common Garter Snake occurs across Minnesota extending from the northwest corner to the southeast corner (Conant and Collins 1991). The eastern part of the state is inhabited by the Eastern Garter Snake (*Thamnophis sirtalis sirtalis*), which generally lacks any red coloration. If there is red coloration, it occurs in small specks on the skin between scales along the snake's sides. As a rule *Thamnophis s. parietalis* (Red-sided Garter Snake) has bold red blotches along its sides between the median and lateral stripes. It is more likely to be encountered in the western part of the state.

It is not uncommon to hear people refer to the Common Garter Snake as a grass snake or gardener snake, probably because it is frequently found in gardens and yards.

Lined Snake

Tropidoclonion lineatum

Description

The Lined Snake is a small, striped snake of the prairies. Dorsal coloration is a drab gray brown, olive gray, or dark gray with three dirty white or pale yellow stripes running the length of the body. The middorsal stripe is narrow, and the lateral stripe occupies scale rows two and three. There may be a row of small black spots running alongside the middorsal stripe as well as another row following along the dorsal edge of the lateral stripe. The top of the small head has dark stippling on the same background color as the back. The ventral surface is white or pale yellow and is distinctly marked with a double

Lined Snake, adult

row of black or near black solid semicircles. Dorsal body scales are keeled, and the anal plate is single. Juvenile Lined Snakes have poorly defined stripes, but the halfmoon belly spots are distinct.

The total length of adult Lined Snakes ranges from 22 to 38 centimeters (8¾ to 15 inches; Conant and Collins 1991).

The larger garter snakes of Minnesota have a striped pattern similar to that of the Lined Snake, but they lack the double row of black spots on their abdomens.

Distribution

The fragmented distribution of the Lined Snake begins in extreme southeastern South Dakota, extends into central Iowa, and covers the Great Plains southward into central Texas. Isolated populations occur in Illinois, Iowa, Missouri, Colorado, and New Mexico. The sole province of the Lined Snake in Minnesota is Blue Mounds State Park and adjacent lands in Rock County. This species is found across the border in South Dakota in Minnehaha County.

Habitat

Lined Snakes prefer prairies, woodland edges, and open areas with scattered trees. In Minnesota their habitat is hilly prairie with large amounts of exposed rock. Elsewhere, they live in vacant city lots,

Lined Snake, underside

cemeteries, trash dumps, and along highways where there is abundant ground cover (Johnson 1987). Hamilton (1947) found seven Lined Snakes overwintering in Texas. They were coiled 7.5 to 20 centimeters (3 to 8 inches) deep in the soil with their heads protected in the center of their body coils. They evidently seek shelter below the frost line in rock crevices and burrows.

Life History

Emerging in late April, Lined Snakes return to their winter retreats by October. They may bask in the open during the day in the spring and again in early fall, but this species is normally nocturnal and spends daylight hours hidden under rocks, logs, bark, and other debris.

Lined Snakes feed almost exclusively on earthworms, locating them by smell and taste at night when the worms crawl out on the surface of the ground. Sow bugs are also eaten. Since this snake has a small head and mouth, its prey is restricted to appropriately sized, soft-bodied animals (Ernst and Barbour 1989).

Females mature in two years and may give birth annually. Mating generally takes place in the fall, and the female retains sperm until the following spring when fertilization occurs (Fox 1956). During the month of August, litters of 2 to 13 are born with a range in length of 7 to 13 centimeters (2¾ to 5⅛ inches). The young are born in thin transparent membranes from which they free themselves.

When threatened by an intruder, this small snake hides its head under its body. It often voids cloacal contents and sprays musk if disturbed but is very unlikely to bite. If it did bite, the resultant injury to a human finger would be inconsequential. Skunks, raccoons, weasels, and a variety of birds are known to eat these snakes (Ernst and Barbour 1989). Road-killed specimens have been found within Blue Mounds State Park.

Remarks

Of the four recognized subspecies, *Tropidoclonion lineatum lineatum* (Northern Lined Snake) is the one found in Minnesota (Conant and Collins 1991).

The Lined Snake was first discovered in 1972 (Bob Chance, personal communication) and is the most recent addition to Minnesota's reptile list. Because of its restricted range within the state, the Lined Snake is given special concern status by the Minnesota Department of Natural Resources (Coffin and Pfannmuller 1988). The population within Blue Mounds State Park is protected by law because of their location in the park.

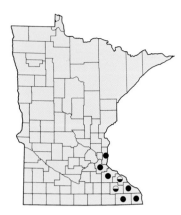

Timber Rattlesnake

Crotalus horridus

Description

The Timber Rattlesnake is a large, heavy-bodied rattlesnake native to the bluff and hill country of southeastern Minnesota. This snake has a broad head distinct from the narrow neck, and a large tan rattle on the end of its black tail. Dorsal ground color may be yellow, tan, brown, reddish brown, or, rarely, gray. On some individuals the dark coloration of the tail extends to include the posterior third of the body. Black or near black chevronlike cross bands form a pattern along the back, but several of these bands may be incomplete or broken on the front third of the body. Most snakes have a single row of light-colored scales bordering the dark cross bands. There may be a rust-colored middorsal stripe from the back of the head to the tail or even to the base of the rattle. In general the top of the head is the same ground color as the body and is unmarked except for a slightly darker nose. Frequently, a dark stripe extends from the eye to the angle of the mouth. The lips and chin are yellow or tan, and the belly is yellowish tan or light gray with a scattered stippling of dark gray or black that becomes heavier toward the tail. Dorsal body scales are strongly keeled, and the anal plate is single. A sensory pit is located between the eye and nostril on each side of the face, and the eyes have elliptical pupils in daylight.

VENOMOUS

*Timber Rattlesnake,
adult male,
Houston county, Minnesota*

Juvenile Timber Rattlesnakes are patterned like adults, but they tend to have a pinkish tan ground color and a prominent reddish mid-dorsal stripe. Newborns are gray with black bands until their first skin shedding, which occurs at 10 to 14 days of age.

Excluding the rattle, adult Timber Rattlesnakes range in length from 80 to 122 centimeters (31½ to 48 inches); adult females average 90 centimeters (35½ inches), and adult males average 110 centimeters (43¼ inches; Keyler and Oldfield 1992). Snakes that exceed 122 centimeters (48 inches) are rare. The largest known individual from Minnesota was a male from Houston County that measured 135 centimeters (53 inches) and weighed 1,760 grams (3 pounds 14 ounces; Keyler and Oldfield 1992).

In contrast to the Timber Rattlesnake, the Massasauga is a significantly smaller, blotched rattlesnake without a distinctly darker tail. Several species of harmless colubrids, including the Fox Snake, the Gopher Snake, the Northern Water Snake, and the Milk Snake, are regularly confused with the Timber Rattlesnake. None of these colubrids have facial pits, elliptical pupils, or a rattle.

Distribution

Much of the former range of the Timber Rattlesnake has been reduced by habitat loss and persecution. The snake was once found over much of the eastern United States excluding Michigan, upstate Maine, and the Florida peninsula. There are records for Timber Rattlesnakes in eight of Minnesota's southeastern counties; however, the likelihood of current viable populations in Washington or Dakota counties is remote. Currently, the most northerly active dens are known from Goodhue County, and they are widely scattered.

Habitat

In Minnesota the Timber Rattlesnake is found in the steeply dissected hills and valleys of the Mississippi River drainage. Forested hillsides with south- or southwest-facing rock outcrops and bluff prairies are critical habitat components. The snakes use limestone, dolomite, or sandstone bluffs and outcrops for winter retreats. Nearby forests, forest edges, and occasionally croplands serve as summer feeding grounds. This species overwinters in ancestral communal dens in rock fissures and crevices. Other snake species such as Racers, Rat Snakes, Milk Snakes, and Gopher Snakes may share its overwintering sites.

Life History

Timber Rattlesnakes occasionally bask near den openings in late April with favorable weather, but May is the prime emergence month in Minnesota. According to Brown (1982), New York populations disperse by mid-June, and individuals travel an average of 504 meters (551 yards) to their summer foraging areas. The maximum recorded distance of travel from the den is 5.6 kilometers (3.5 miles). They are active during the day in the spring and fall but become primarily nocturnal during summer months.

Although Timber Rattlesnakes are basically terrestrial, they are adept at climbing along rocky ledges and scaling bluff walls. Occasionally they are found in trees or vines up to 2 meters (6½ feet) off the ground (Oldfield and Dan Keyler, personal observation). They are also capable swimmers if the need arises.

Timber Rattlesnake, adult gray phase, Houston County, Minnesota

Small mammals are their preferred prey, which includes mice, shrews, moles, rats, chipmunks, squirrels, and young rabbits. Occasionally small birds, insects, and amphibians are also eaten (Wright and Wright 1957; Klauber 1972). A recent study in Pennsylvania (Reinert et al. 1984) found the Timber Rattlesnake to be a "sit-and-wait" ambush predator. A hungry snake spends several hours during the night coiled alongside a log waiting for an unsuspecting meal. Downed logs serve as runways for rodents. When prey comes into range, the snake's heat-sensing pits direct the strike. The rodent runs a short distance and quickly succumbs from the effects of the venom. The snake follows the scent of the victim and after catching up to it, swallows it whole.

Timber Rattlesnake, juvenile

Females are 5 to 6 years old before they give birth to their first litter (Martin 1966). Brown (1991) found females in New York State requiring 7 to 11 years to reach maturity, and they only reproduce every 3 or 4 years. Sexually mature males occasionally engage in a combat dance in April or May (Collins 1974; Klauber 1972). This rarely witnessed behavior includes two adult males elevating the front third of their bodies off the ground and attempting to push or throw their rival to the ground to establish dominance. Courtship and mating occur in late summer, and the female stores sperm over the winter for egg fertilization the following spring. Pregnant females remain within proximity of the den, taking advantage of open areas for periods of basking to hasten embryo development. A litter of 3 to 17 (average of 7) is born in late August or September. Newborn Timber Rattlesnakes are 20 to 36 centimeters (8 to 14 inches) long and remain with their mother for the first 10 to 14 days.

At birth they have a prebutton on the end of their tail, which gives way to a button (terminal segment of a complete rattle) when the skin is shed the first time. They gain a rattle segment with each subsequent shedding (about once a year in mature snakes). Since rattles are often missing segments, they do not provide a reliable method for determining the age of a snake.

Typically, the Timber Rattlesnake is a secretive, shy animal that remains motionless, depending upon cryptic coloration to avoid detection. If discovered, the snake often makes a rapid exit to protective cover and buzzes its rattle. When caught out in the open without a safe escape route, it will coil, flatten its body, and buzz continually. If harassed, it will either hide its head under body coils or launch a strike in the direction of the intruder.

The bite of the Timber Rattlesnake is dangerous, and human fatalities have resulted (Keyler 1983), but with prompt medical attention the prospect of death is unlikely. The symptoms of a bite include extreme pain, swelling, weakness, nausea, vomiting, difficult breathing, reduced blood pressure, and unconsciousness in severe cases. Available case histories indicate that approximately 25% of Timber Rattlesnake bites are "dry" bites in which no venom is injected (Dan Keyler, personal communication).

Juvenile snakes have many predators including hawks, owls, carnivorous mammals, and other snakes such as Racers and Milk Snakes. Humans are the dominant predators of adults, and they have contributed greatly to the decline of Timber Rattlesnakes.

Remarks

Additional common names for the Timber Rattlesnake include "ol' velvet-tail," "banded rattlesnake," and "bluff rattler." This species has been reported to survive just over 30 years in captivity (Bowler 1977).

Historically, dens supported large populations of Timber Rattlesnakes, but because of years of persecution by snake hunters, very few sizable dens remain. Many are entirely depleted of snakes. Bounty was paid by local governments to rattlesnake hunters in Minnesota until 1989, when a bill to repeal the bounty was signed into law. Special concern status is given the Timber Rattlesnake by the Minnesota Department of Natural Resources (Coffin and Pfannmuller 1988), but the only areas where the snake is protected are in several Minnesota state parks where resident populations exist. Because of its continued decline and vulnerability at dens, eight states furnish full protection (Brown 1993). Minnesota should reclassify this species to do likewise. The Timber Rattlesnake is a symbol of the wilderness, as is the timber wolf, and should be provided the opportunity for continued survival in the natural world (Oldfield and Keyler 1989).

VENOMOUS

Massasauga

Sistrurus catenatus

Description

The Massasauga is a small to medium-sized robust, spotted rattle-snake of river bottom floodplains. Ground color ranges from light gray to medium brown. A row of 26 to 40 large, dark brown or near black blotches extends down the back. The blotches are often outlined with a thin light line. Two or three additional rows of smaller alternating spots are found along each side of the body. The row nearest the belly blends into the dark, almost solid black abdominal scales that are lightly mottled with white or yellow. The snake's tail is ringed with large dark bands of the same color as the dorsal spots. There are two broad dark stripes that stretch from the top of the head out onto the neck. An additional dark stripe with a distinct white border goes from the eye near the jaw angle to the neck on each side of the face. The chin is dirty white. A heat-sensitive pit is located on each side of the face between the nostril and the eye. The vertical pupils form thin black lines in bright sunlight. Males have a proportionally longer tail than females, and the tail ends with a cornified rattle. Body scales are keeled, and the anal plate is undivided. Juvenile Massasaugas are patterned like adults but with lighter ground color, and the area between the bands on the tail is bright yellow.

Massasauga, adult

The total length of this species seldom exceeds 91 centimeters (36 inches) excluding the rattle. Most adults are 47 to 76 centimeters (18½ to 30 inches; Conant and Collins 1991).

All nonvenomous species in Minnesota that are likely to be confused with the Massasauga do not have rattles, facial pits, or vertical pupils. The only other snake in Minnesota with rattles and a vertical pupil is the larger Timber Rattlesnake, and it has cross bands and a solid-black tail.

Distribution

The range of the Massasauga in North America begins in southern Ontario and central New York and extends obliquely through the eastern deciduous forest onto the Great Plains into south Texas, New Mexico, and southeastern Arizona. There are disjunct populations in several states. Only Wabasha and Houston counties in Minnesota have Massasauga records, and these are notably few. Breckenridge (1944) mentioned only two specimens, both from Wabasha County. A scattering of unconfirmed sightings has occurred during the past 50 years. John Meltzer (personal communication) observed a courting pair in the Mississippi River bottoms in Houston County in 1986.

Habitat

The Massasauga prefers moist habitats such as marshes, bogs, swamps, and associated wetlands. In Wisconsin, Massasaugas are restricted to river bottom lowland forests and adjacent open fields (Vogt 1981). Massasaugas apparently do not den with other snakes during the winter. They overwinter in mammal burrows, old tree stumps, and rocky crevices. Maple and Orr (1968) discovered individuals overwintering singly in or near water in crayfish tunnels below the frost line in northeastern Ohio.

Life History

Prompted by spring flooding, Massasaugas emerge in late April in Wisconsin (Vogt 1981). During times of high water they may be found clinging to muskrat houses or other partially submerged brush piles and trees. As the water recedes, they move to meadows and open fields within the bottomlands. Reinert and Kodrich (1982) determined the mean home range for Massasaugas in Pennsylvania to be slightly less than 1 hectare (2½ acres). They are primarily diurnal during the spring and fall but resort to crepuscular and nocturnal activity during the summer. Gravid females can be found basking on humid, overcast days in late summer (Oldfield, personal observation). By mid-October they return to their overwintering sites to escape freezing temperatures.

Adult Massasaugas feed chiefly on small rodents such as voles, mice, and shrews. The heat-sensitive pits are used to detect endothermic prey, but sight and odor are also important stimuli. Normally, the prey is consumed after it dies from the effects of envenomation. Subadults feed on frogs, large insects, Brown Snakes, and juvenile Common Garter Snakes. The bright yellow coloration on the tail of a young Massasauga serves as a lure for frogs that often feed on moving, brightly colored insects (Schuett et al. 1984).

Females become reproductively mature by their third year, and most breeding activity takes place in the spring, although fall courtship has been reported. The Massasauga may not reproduce annually. Reinert (1981) in Pennsylvania and Seigel (1986) in Missouri have found evidence of a biennial reproductive cycle. The gravid female gives birth to 3 to 20 young during late August or early September. Newborns range in length from 18 to 25 centimeters (7 to 10 inches) and have a small prebutton on the end of their tail. Young shed their skin at five days of age, and the prebutton is replaced with a button (the terminal segment of a complete rattle). After several days of staying near their mother, young snakes begin life on their own (Bill Stark, personal communication).

Massasaugas generally remain motionless, depending upon cryptic coloration to prevent detection, but a nervous individual gives its location away by buzzing its rattle. Without an escape route, it holds its ground, vibrates its tail, and strikes if molested. Massasauga venom is potent, but because of the snake's modest size, relatively short fangs, and small venom glands, the bite is generally not life-threatening to humans.

Hawks, large wading birds, and small carnivorous mammals are natural predators. Persecution of the Massasauga and destruction of its habitat have resulted in a serious population decline across the United States.

Remarks

Three subspecies of the Massasauga are described, but only the Eastern Massasauga (*Sistrurus catenatus catenatus*) is found in Minnesota (Conant and Collins 1991).

The Massasauga has several local names including "swamp rattler," "black snapper," and "sauga." According to Vogt (1981), the name Massasauga is a Chippewa Indian word meaning "great river mouth." Captive longevity for this species is 14 years (Bowler 1977). This species is classified as endangered or threatened in nearly every state within its range. The Minnesota Department of Natural Resources currently classifies the Massasauga as special concern (Coffin and Pfannmuller 1988), but full protection for this rare species and its habitat is warranted.

SPECIES OF POSSIBLE OCCURRENCE

Six species of amphibians and reptiles are found in adjacent states within 10 kilometers (6.2 miles) of the Minnesota border. These species have yet to be found in the state, but it is likely that additional searching may document their occurrence.

The following species accounts are abbreviated and provide only a brief description of the species, its habitat, and potential range within the state. If anyone observes these species, he or she should immediately contact the Minnesota Nongame Wildlife Program (see address in Resources).

Spotted Salamander

Ambystoma maculatum

Description

The Spotted Salamander is a large mole salamander with a maximum length of 20 to 23 centimeters (8 to 9 inches). Individuals are gray black in color with yellow spots irregularly spaced on their back. Two distinct spots on the head are orange or a brighter yellow than those on the body. The ventral surface is light gray. The larger Tiger Salamander has yellow blotches on its dorsal and ventral surfaces and lacks orange spots near its head.

Habitat

Spotted Salamanders are found in coniferous and deciduous forests. They spend most of their time underground but can be found in early spring in woodland ponds, bogs, and wetlands.

Potential Range

Spotted Salamander, adult, Polk County, Wisconsin

If in Minnesota, Spotted Salamanders are likely to be found in Chisago or Washington counties along the St. Croix River. They are currently located in Interstate State Park, Polk County, Wisconsin. Moriarty has observed this salamander near the St. Croix River within 200 meters (219 yards) of the Minnesota border.

Four-toed Salamander

Hemidactylium scutatum

Description

The Four-toed Salamander has, as the name implies, four toes on each foot. Other terrestrial salamanders found in Minnesota have five toes on the hind feet. This small salamander measures 7 to 10 centimeters (3 to 4 inches) and is brown to red brown on top with a bright white belly. Numerous black spots are irregularly spaced on the ventral surface. The tail is obviously constricted at the base.

Habitat

Four-toed Salamanders are found in deciduous forests adjacent to springs, creeks, and small bogs. During the spring females can be found in sedge hummocks adjacent to or in the water. Adults spend the remainder of the year under logs, rocks, or sphagnum moss.

Potential Range

Four-toed Salamanders are most likely to be found in Chisago or Washington counties. They are currently found at Interstate State Park in Polk County, Wisconsin. They may also be found in Houston County because populations occur across the Mississippi River in Vernon County, Wisconsin.

Four-toed Salamander, adult
(Photo by John Moriarty)

Woodhouse's Toad

Bufo woodhousii

Description

Woodhouse's Toad is a medium-sized toad with a snout-vent length of 6 to 10 centimeters (2⅜ to 4 inches). They have a white belly with no flecking, a light dorsal stripe, and cranial ridges that touch the parotoid glands. Although Woodhouse's Toad appears similar

Woodhouse's Toad, adult

to the American Toad, the latter has flecking on the belly, and the cranial crests normally do not touch the parotoid glands. The breeding calls of the two species are also different. Woodhouse's Toad has a nasal "waaah" call, whereas the American Toad has a high-pitched musical trill (Johnson 1987).

Woodhouse's Toads and American Toads are known to hybridize where their ranges overlap (Johnson 1987), making distinguishing the two species very difficult.

Habitat

Woodhouse's Toad is found in a variety of prairie habitats, including both dry and mesic areas. Breeding takes place in shallow ponds and wetlands.

Potential Range

This species is likely to be found in the southwestern corner of the state in Rock, Nobles, or Pipestone counties. It may possibly be found along the western border as far north as Clay County. Currently there are records from border counties in North Dakota, South Dakota, and Iowa.

Plains Spadefoot

Spea bombifrons

Description

The Plains Spadefoot is a small toad reaching a snout-vent length of 5 centimeters (2 inches). The dorsal color is grayish with a reticulation of black and brown, and the belly is white and sometimes spotted. The Plains Spadefoot differs from toads of the genus *Bufo* by having large eyes with elliptical pupils and a horny spade on each hind foot.

Habitat

The Plains Spadefoot is found in arid, sandy grasslands. Individuals are highly fossorial and only come to the surface during wet periods. They use temporary ponds for breeding.

Potential Range

The Plains Spadefoot is most likely to be found in Rock County in the extreme southwestern corner of Minnesota. There is a record within 8 kilometers (5 miles) of the Minnesota border in Minnehaha County, South Dakota.

Plains Spadefoot, adult

Common Musk Turtle

Sternotherus odoratus

Description

The Common Musk Turtle is a small turtle, with a carapace length of 5 to 12 centimeters (2 to 4¾ inches). If discovered in Minnesota, it would be the smallest turtle in the state. This species has a smooth, high-domed carapace that is uniformly dark brown or black. Algae normally cover the shell, giving the turtle a fuzzy appearance. The plastron is reduced and hinged. An unusual feature is the presence of fleshy barbels on the chin and neck. The skin is black, and two light stripes are located on the side of the head.

Habitat

Common Musk Turtles are found in rivers, sloughs, lakes, and ponds with soft bottoms. They like areas with abundant submergent vegetation. They avoid hard-bottom ponds and lakes, fast-moving rivers, and ephemeral ponds (Vogt 1981).

Potential Range

If Common Musk Turtles are in Minnesota, they are probably in the backwaters of the Mississippi River south of Winona. There is also potential for finding them in the lower Root River, Crooked Creek, and Winnebago Creek drainages. Common Musk Turtles are frequently found in the lower Wisconsin River in Wisconsin. A 1992 record from Trempeleau County, Wisconsin, came from the edge of the Mississippi River and only 400 meters (437 yards) from the Minnesota border.

Common Musk Turtle, adult, Wisconsin

Slender Glass Lizard

Ophisaurus attenuatus

Description

The Slender Glass Lizard is long, slender, and legless. This snake-like lizard ranges in total length from 56 to 106 centimeters (22 to 42 inches); two-thirds of the length is tail. Coloration is tan to

Slender Glass Lizard, adult

brown with black dorsal stripes that fade with age. The tail separates easily when grabbed by a predator and the regenerated replacement is shorter than the original.

Habitat

Slender Glass Lizards are found in prairies, in open woods, and on rocky hillsides. In Wisconsin they are found on bluff prairies. This lizard prefers areas with loose soil or sand for burrowing.

Potential Range

Slender Glass Lizards are most likely to occur in southeastern Minnesota in Houston, Fillmore, or Winona counties. There is one record near the Mississippi River in La Crosse County, Wisconsin.

GLOSSARY

Amelanism a color condition in which black pigment is lacking.

Amniote a term applied to animals (reptiles, birds, and mammals) that have three extraembryonic membranes (amnion, chorion, and allantois) during their early development.

Amplexus the clasping behavior of amphibians during breeding.

Anal plate the scale just anterior to the cloacal opening in snakes.

Anuran a tailless amphibian; that is, a frog or toad.

Boss a swollen, rounded projection on top of the head or on the snout of some toad species.

Carapace the dorsal shell of turtles.

Caruncle a horny projection on the end of the snout of a hatching reptile used to slit open the egg during hatching.

Cline a gradual change in a species' characteristics across its geographic range.

Cloaca the common chamber where intestinal, urinary, and reproductive tracts empty.

Conspecific pertaining to the same species.

Cornified composed of a hard, horny substance such as keratin.

Costal referring to the area of the body near the ribs.

Costal groove the vertical furrow on the sides of some salamanders.

Cranial relating to the head.

Cranial crests ridges behind or between the eyes of some toad species.

Crepuscular active during twilight hours.

Diploid possessing the normal two sets of chromosomes.

Disjunct isolated or separated from the general range of the species.

Diurnal active during daylight.

Dorsal pertaining to the back or upper surface of the body.

Dorsolateral fold a ridge along the side of the back of some anurans.

Ecdysis the process of shedding the skin.

Ectotherm an animal whose body temperature is largely dependent upon its environment.

Eft the land-dwelling stage of a newt.

Egg tooth see Caruncle.

Estivation a period of inactivity during a warm season.

Facial pit the heat-sensitive organ between the eye and nostril of pit vipers.

Femoral pertaining to the area of the thigh.
Fossorial living underground or under surface cover.

Gravid pregnant.
Gular pertaining to the area of the throat.

Hemipenis one of the paired, extendable copulatory organs of male lizards and snakes.
Herpetology the study of amphibians and reptiles.

Intergradation the sharing of features between two or more subspecies producing an intermediate specimen.
Internasal positioned between the nasal openings.

Keel a narrow, elongated ridge found on the carapace of some turtle species and the scales of some snake species.

Larva the immature form of amphibians, usually possessing gills.
Lateral relating to the sides of an animal.

Marginal pertaining to the edge of a turtle's carapace.
Melanism a color condition in which black is the dominant pigment.
Melanophore a cell containing black pigment.
Metamorphosis the process of body transformation that occurs when an amphibian larva changes into an adult.
Middorsal the area in the middle of the back.
Morph the color, shape, structure, or form of an animal that is used to make its identification.

Nasal septum the membranous structure that separates the nostrils.
Naso-labial groove a groove from the nostril to the lip found in salamanders of the family Plethodontidae.
Neotenic having a condition found in some salamanders in which sexually mature adults retain characteristics of the larval stage.
Nocturnal active during the hours of darkness.

Ocelli circular or oval markings on an animal that may be made up of concentric rings.
Oviparous egg laying.

Parotoid glands large glands located behind the eyes of toads that produce toxic secretions.
Parthenogenesis reproduction without males by the development of an unfertilized egg.
Plastron the ventral shell of turtles.
Plates large scales of reptiles, especially those of the upper and lower shells of turtles.
Postocular behind the eye.
Prebutton the keratin structure on the end of the tail of a newborn rattlesnake.
Progenic having a condition found in some salamanders in which the larval form develops the ability to reproduce.

Rostral pertaining to the area of the snout or nose.
Rostrum snout or nose.

Scute the plates forming the upper and lower shells of turtles.
Septal pertaining to a partition or wall.
Serrate saw-toothed.
Smooth scales lacking a keel or ridge.
Snout-vent length (SVL) the distance from the tip of the snout to the cloacal opening.
Spectacle the clear scale that covers and protects a snake's eye.
Spermatophore a gelatinous structure containing sperm that is discharged from the cloaca of male salamanders during breeding activities.
Subspecies a geographic race of a species.
Sympatric occupying the same habitat or having broadly overlapping ranges.

Tadpole the aquatic larva of frogs and toads.
Thermoregulation the process of regulating body temperature by relying on the environment.
Tubercle a bump or projection on the skin.
Tympanum the rounded eardrum on the side of the head of frogs and toads.

Vent the external opening of the cloaca.
Ventral pertaining to the lower surface or belly.

RESOURCES

References in the text of this book can be found in the Literature Cited section. General references, some of which are also in the Literature Cited, are listed here. These references are separated into several groups: Minnesota, regional, North American, general, anuran calls, and photography. Additionally, a list of herpetological organizations is provided.

REFERENCE BOOKS

Regional (Upper Midwest)

Breckenridge, W. J. 1944. Reptiles and Amphibians of Minnesota. University of Minnesota Press, Minneapolis.

Coffin, B., and L. Pfannmuller. 1988. Minnesota's Endangered Flora and Fauna. University of Minnesota Press, Minneapolis.

Johnson, T. R. 1987. The Amphibians and Reptiles of Missouri. Missouri Department of Conservation, Jefferson City.

Karns, D. R. 1986. Field herpetology: Methods for the study of amphibians and reptiles in Minnesota. Bell Museum of Natural History Occasional Paper 18.

Preston, W. B. 1982. Amphibians and Reptiles of Manitoba. Manitoba Museum of Man and Nature, Winnipeg.

Smith, P. W. 1961. Amphibians and Reptiles of Illinois. Illinois Natural History Survey, Carbondale.

Vogt, R. C. 1981. Natural History of Amphibians and Reptiles of Wisconsin. Milwaukee Public Museum.

Wheeler, G. C., and J. Wheeler. 1966. Amphibians and Reptiles of North Dakota. University of North Dakota, Grand Forks.

North American

Behler, J. L., and F. W. King. 1979. Audubon Society Field Guide to North American Reptiles and Amphibians. Alfred Knopf, New York.

Bishop, S. C. 1947. Handbook of Salamanders. Comstock Press, Ithaca, N.Y.

Carr, A. 1952. Handbook of Turtles. Comstock Press, Ithaca, N.Y.

Conant, R., and Collins, J. T. 1991. A Field Guide to Reptiles and Amphibians of Eastern and Central North America. 3d ed. Houghton Mifflin, Boston.

Ernst, C. H., 1992. Venomous Reptiles of North America. Smithsonian Institution Press, Washington, D.C.

Ernst, C. H. and R. W. Barbour. 1972. Turtles of the United States. Kentucky University Press, Lexington.

Ernst, C. H., and R. W. Barbour. 1989. Snakes of Eastern North America. George Mason University Press, Fairfax, Va.

Smith, H. M. 1946. Handbook of Lizards. Comstock Press, Ithaca, N.Y.

Smith, H. M. 1978. A Guide to Field Identification: Amphibians of North America. Golden Press, New York.

Smith, H. M., and E. D. Brodie, Jr. 1982. A Guide to Field Identification: Reptiles of North America. Golden Press, New York.

Society for Study of Amphibians and Reptiles. 1962–93. Catalogue of American Amphibians and Reptiles. SSAR, Columbus, Ohio.

Stebbins, R. C. 1985. A Field Guide to Western Reptiles and Amphibians. 2d ed. Houghton Mifflin, Boston.

Wright, A. H. 1929. Synopsis and description of North American tadpoles. Proceedings of U.S. National Museum 74.

Wright, A. H., and A. A. Wright. 1949. Handbook of Frogs and Toads. Comstock Press, Ithaca, N.Y.

Wright, A. H., and A. A. Wright. 1957. Handbook of Snakes. Comstock Press, Ithaca, N.Y.

General

Alderton, D. 1989. Turtles and Tortoises of the World. Facts on File, New York.

Campbell, J. A., and E. D. Brodie. 1992. Biology of the Pit Vipers. Selva, Tyler, Tex.

Duellman, W. E., and L. Trueb. 1985. Amphibian Biology. McGraw-Hill, New York.

Ernst, C. H., and R. W. Barbour. 1989. Turtles of the World. Smithsonian Institution Press, Washington, D.C.

Halliday, T., and K. Adler. 1986. Encyclopedia of Reptiles and Amphibians. Facts on File, New York.

Harless, M., and H. Morlock, eds. 1979. Turtles: Perspectives and Research. Wiley and Sons, New York.

Mattison, C. 1986. Snakes of the World. Facts on File, New York.

Mattison, C. 1988. Frogs and Toads of the World. Facts on File, New York.

Mattison, C. 1989. Lizards of the World. Facts on File, New York.

Porter, K. R. 1972. Herpetology. W. B. Saunders, Philadelphia.

Seigel, R. A., J. T. Collins, and S. S. Novak. 1987. Snakes: Ecology and Evolutionary Biology. Macmillan, New York.

Zug, G. R. 1993. Herpetology: An Introductory Biology of Amphibians and Reptiles. Academic Press, San Diego.

Anuran Calls

Elliot, L. 1992. The Calls of Frogs and Toads. Chelsea Green Publishing, Post Mills, Vt. Cassette tape.

Wiewandt, T. 1982. Voices of the Night: The Calls of the Frogs and Toads of Eastern North America. Library of Natural Sounds, Ithaca, N.Y. Album or cassette tape.

Photography

Blaker, A. A. 1976. Field Photography: Beginning and Advanced Techniques. W. H. Freeman, San Francisco.

Freeman, M. 1981. The Complete Book of Wildlife and Nature Photography. Simon and Schuster, New York.

McDonald, J. 1992. The Complete Guide to Wildlife Photography: How to Get Close and Capture Animals on Film. Amphoto, New York.

Shaw, J. 1984. The Nature Photographer's Complete Guide to Professional Field Techniques. Amphoto, New York.

Shaw, J. 1987. John Shaw's Closeups in Nature. Amphoto, New York.

ORGANIZATIONS

Minnesota Herpetological Society
James Ford Bell Museum of Natural History
10 Church St. S.E.
Minneapolis, Minnesota 55455
Publications: monthly newsletter, occasional papers, care pamphlets

Minnesota Nongame Wildlife Program
Box 7, DNR Building
500 Lafayette Road
St. Paul, Minnesota 55155–4007

Chicago Herpetological Society
Chicago Academy of Science
2001 North Clark Street
Chicago, Illinois 60614
Publication: monthly bulletin

Society for the Study of Amphibians and Reptiles
Department of Zoology
Miami University
Oxford, Ohio 45056
Publications: Journal of Herpetology, Herpetological Review, Catalog of American Amphibians and Reptiles, Herpetological Circulars

Herpetologist's League
Section of Amphibians and Reptiles
Carnegie Museum of Natural History
4400 Forbes Ave.
Pittsburgh, Pennsylvania 15213
Publications: Herpetologica, Herpetological Monographs

American Society of Ichthyologists and Herpetologists
Florida State Museum
University of Florida
Gainesville, Florida 32611
Publications: Copeia

LITERATURE CITED

Alesksiuk, M. 1976. Metabolic and behavioural adjustments to temperature change in the red-sided garter snake (*Thamnophis sirtalis parietalis*): An integrated approach. Journal of Thermal Biology 1:153–56.

Baird, S. F. 1858. Descriptions of new genera and species of North American lizards in the Museum of the Smithsonian Institution. Proceedings Academy of Natural Sciences of Philadelphia 1858: 253–56.

Barbour, R. W. 1971. Amphibians and Reptiles of Kentucky. University Press of Kentucky, Lexington. 334 pp.

Behler, J. L., and F. W. King. 1979. Audubon Society Field Guide to North American Reptiles and Amphibians. Alfred Knopf, New York. 719 pp.

Bellis, E. D. 1957. An ecological study of the wood frog, *Rana sylvatica* Le Conte. Ph.D. thesis, University of Minnesota, Minneapolis. 169 pp.

Bishop, S. C. 1941. The salamanders of New York. New York State Museum Bulletin 364. 365 pp.

Blanchard, F. N. 1936. Eggs and natural nests of the eastern ringneck snake, *Diadophis punctatus edwardsii*. Paper of the Michigan Academy of Science. 22:521–37.

Bowler, J. K. 1977. Longevity of reptiles and amphibians in North America collections SSAR Herpetological Circular 6. 32pp.

Bragg, A. N. 1960. Is *Heterodon* venomous? Herpetologica 16:121–23.

Brecke, B., and J. J. Moriarty. 1989. Natural History Note. Longevity. *Emydoidea blandingii*. SSAR Herpetological Review 20:53.

Breckenridge, W. J. 1941. The amphibians and reptiles of Minnesota with special reference to the black-banded skink, *Eumeces septentrionalis* (Baird). Ph.D. thesis, University of Minnesota, Minneapolis. 398 pp.

———. 1943. The life history of the black-banded skink, *Eumeces septentrionalis* (Baird). American Midland Naturalist 29:591–606.

———. 1944. Reptiles and Amphibians of Minnesota. University of Minnesota Press, Minneapolis. 202 pp.

———. 1955. Observations on the life history of the softshelled turtle *Trionyx ferox,* with especial reference to growth. Copeia 1955:5–9.

———. 1960. A spiny soft-shelled turtle nest study. Herpetologica 16:284–85.

Breckenridge, W. J., and J. R. Tester. 1961. Growth, local movements and hibernation of the Manitoba toad, *Bufo hemiophrys*. Ecology 42:637–46.

Brooks, R. J., C. M. Shilton, G. P. Brown, and N. W. S. Quinn. 1992. Body size, age distribution and reproduction in a northern population of Wood Turtles (*Clem-*

mys insculpta). Canadian Journal of Zoology 70:462–69.

Brown, W. S. 1982. Overwintering body temperatures of Timber Rattlesnakes (*Crotalus horridus*) in northeastern New York. Journal of Herpetology 16:145–50.

———. 1991. Female reproductive ecology in a northern population of the Timber Rattlesnake, *Crotalus horridus*. Herpetologica 47:101–15.

———. 1993. Biology, status, and management of the Timber Rattlesnake (*Crotalus horridus*): A guide for conservation. SSAR Herpetological Circular 22. 78 pp.

Buech, R. R., M. D. Nelson, and B. J. Brecke. 1990. Progress Report: Wood Turtle (*Clemmys insculpta*) habitat use on the Cloquet River. A report to the Nongame Wildlife Program. St. Paul. 10 pp.

Bull, J. J., and R. C. Vogt. 1979. Temperature dependent sex determination in turtles. Science 206:1186–88.

Burger, J., and R. T. Zappalorti. 1986. Nest site selection by pine snakes, *Pitouphis melanoleucus*, in the New Jersey Pine Barrens. Copeia 1986: 116–21.

Burton, T.M. and G.E. Likens. 1975. Salamander populations and biomass in the Hubbard Brook Experimental Forest, New Hampshire. Copeia 1975:541–46.

Bury, R. B., and J. A. Whelan. 1984. Ecology and management of the bullfrog. U.S. Fish and Wildlife Service Resource Publication 155. 23 pp.

Cagle, F. R. 1953. Two new subspecies of *Graptemys pseudogeographica*. Occasional Paper of the Museum of Zoology, University of Michigan 546:1–17.

Cahn, A. R. 1937. The turtles of Illinois. Illinois Biological Monograph 35:1–218.

Caldwell, R. 1975. Observations on the winter activity of the red-backed salamander, *Plethodon cinereus*, in Indiana. Herpetologica 31:21–22.

Carr, A. F. 1952. Handbook of Turtles. Comstock Press, Ithaca, N.Y. 542 pp.

Cochran, P. A. 1981. The softshell turtles (*Genus Trionyx*) in Minnesota. Pages 15–18 in Ecology of reptiles and amphibians in Minnesota: Proceedings of a Symposium, Cass Lake, Minn. L. Elwell, K. Cram, and C. Johnson, eds. 64 pp.

———. 1982a. Geographic distribution. Anura. *Rana pipiens*. Herpetological Review 13:131.

———. 1982b. Geographic distribution. Serpentes. *Storeria occipitomaculata*. Herpetological Review 13:131.

———. 1982c. Geographic distribution. Serpentes. *Nerodia sipedon*. Herpetological Review 13:131.

———. 1982d. Life history notes. Anura. *Rana pipiens*. Predation. Herpetological Review 13:45–46.

———. 1983a. Geographic distribution. Testudines. *Chrysemys picta*. Herpetological Review 14:123–24.

———. 1983b. Geographic distribution. Anura. *Pseudacris triseriata*. Herpetological Review 14:122.

———. 1983c. Life history notes. Sauria. *Eumeces septentrionalis*. Agonistic behavior. Herpetological Review 14:119.

———. 1991. Distribution of the Mudpuppy (*Necturus maculosus*) in Minnesota in relation to postglacial events. Canadian Field-Naturalist 105:400–403.

Coffin, B., and L. Pfannmuller, eds. 1988. Minnesota's Endangered Flora and Fauna. University of Minnesota Press, Minneapolis. 464 pp.

Collins, J. T. 1974. Amphibians and Reptiles in Kansas. University of Kansas Museum of Natural History Public Education Series 1. 283 pp.

———. 1982. Amphibians and Reptiles in Kansas. 2d ed. University of Kansas Museum of Natural History Public Education Series 8. 356 pp.

———. 1990. Standard common and current scientific names for North American amphibians and reptiles. 3d ed. SSAR Herpetological Circular 19. 41 pp.

Conant, R. 1958. A Field Guide to Reptiles and Amphibians of the Eastern North America. Houghton Mifflin, Boston. 366 pp.

Conant, R., and Collins, J. T. 1991. A Field Guide to Reptiles and Amphibians of Eastern and Central North America. 3d ed. Houghton Mifflin, Boston. 450 pp.

Conway, C. H., and W. R. Fleming. 1960. Placental transmission of 22 131 Na and I in *Natrix*. Copeia 1960:53–55.

Cook, F. C. 1964. Communal egg-laying in the smooth green snake. Herpetologica 24:266.

Cook, F. R. 1983. An analysis of toads of the *Bufo americanus* group in a contact zone in central northern North America. National Museum of Canada Publication Natural Sciences 3. 89 pp.

Cooper, J. G. 1859. Report upon the reptiles collected on the survey. In Reports of explorations and surveys, to ascertain the most practical and economical route for a railroad from the Mississippi River to the Pacific Ocean, Vol. XII, Part 2.

Cope, E. D. 1889. The batrachia of North America. U.S. National Museum Bulletin 34. 525 pp.

———. 1900. The Crocodilians, Lizards, and Snakes of North America. Report. U.S. National Museum. 1141 pp.

DeGraaf, R. M., and D. D. Rudis. 1983. Amphibians and Reptiles of New England. University of Massachusetts Press, Amherst. 85 pp.

DeGraaff, R. M. 1991. The Book of the Toad. Park Street Press, Rochester, Vt. 208 pp.

Dole, J. W. 1965. Summer movements of adult leopard frogs, *Rana pipiens* (Schreber), in northern Michigan. Ecology 46:236–55.

Dorff, C. J. 1989. Blanding's Turtle (*Emydoidea blandingii*) Research: 1988 results/1989 plans. A report to the Nongame Wildlife Program, St. Paul.

Dunson, W. A. 1960. Relation of the rate of hyoid movement to body weight and temperature in diving soft-shell turtles. Comparative Biochemical Physiology 19:597–601.

Dymond, J. R., and F. E. J. Fry. 1932. Notes on the breeding habits of the green snake (*Liopeltis vernalis*). Copeia 1932:102.

Elwell, L., K. Cram, and C. Johnson, eds. 1981. Ecology of reptiles and amphibians in Minnesota. Proceedings of a symposium, Cass Lake, Minn. 64 pp.

Ernst, C. H. 1974. Taxonomic status of the red-bellied snake, *Storeria occipitomaculata*. Journal of Herpetology 8:347–50.

Ernst, C. H., and R. W. Barbour. 1972. Turtles of the United States. University Press Kentucky, Lexington. 347 pp.

————. 1989. Snakes of Eastern North America. George Mason University Press, Fairfax, Va. 282 pp.

Everman, B. W., and H. W. Clark. 1916. The turtles and bactrachians of the Lake Maxinkuckee region. Proceedings of Indiana Academy of Science. 1916:472–518.

Ewert, M. A. 1969. Seasonal movements of the toads *Bufo americanus* and *B. cognatus* in northwestern Minnesota. Ph.D. thesis, University of Minnesota, Minneapolis. 193 pp.

————. 1985. Assessment of the current distribution and abundance of the Wood Turtle (*Clemmys insculpta*) in Minnesota and along the St. Croix National Scenic Waterway in Wisconsin. Report to the Nongame Wildlife Program. St. Paul. 41 pp.

Farrell, R. F., and T. E. Graham. 1991. Ecological notes on the turtle *Clemmys insculpta* in northwestern New Jersey. Journal of Herpetology 25:1–9.

Ferguson, J. H., and R. M. Thornton. 1984. Oxygen storage capacity and tolerance of submergence of a non-aquatic reptile and an aquatic reptile. Comparative Biochemical Physiology 774:183–87.

Fishbeck, D. W. 1968. A study of some phases in the ecology of *Rana sylvatica* LeConte. Ph.D. thesis, University of Minnesota, Minneapolis. 159 pp.

Fitch, H. S. 1954. Life history and ecology of the five-lined skink, *Eumeces fasciatus*. University of Kansas Publications Museum of Natural History. 8:1–156.

————. 1958a. Home ranges, territories, and seasonal movements of vertebrates of the natural history reservation. University of Kansas Publications Museum of Natural History. 11:63–326.

————. 1958b. Natural history of the six-lined racerunner (*Cnemidophorus sexlineatus*). University of Kansas Publications Museum of Natural History. 11:11–62.

————. 1963a. Natural history of the racer *Coluber constrictor*. University of Kansas Publications Museum of Natural History. 15:351–468.

————. 1963b. Natural history of the black rat snake (*Elaphe o. obsoleta*) in Kansas. Copeia 1963:649–58.

————. 1970. Reproductive cycles in lizards and snakes. University of Kansas Museum of Natural History. Miscellaneous Publication 52:1–247.

Fleming, P. L. 1976. A study of the distribution and ecology of *Rana clamitans* Latreille. Ph.D. thesis, University of Minnesota, Minneapolis. 170 pp.

Fox, W. 1956. Seminal receptacles of snakes. Anatomy Record 124:519–40.

Freedman, W., and P. M. Catling. 1979. Movements of sympatric species of snakes at Amherstburg, Ontario. Canadian Field-Naturalist. 93:399–404.

Friedrich, G. W. 1934. Taxonomy and distribution of the fishes, amphibia, and reptiles of central Minnesota. Proceedings of the Minnesota Academy of Science 1:14–15.

Gerholdt, J., and B. L. Oldfield. 1987. Life History Notes: *Chelydra serpentina serpentina*. Size. Herpetological Review 18:73.

Gibbons, J. W. 1968a. Carapacial algae in a population of the painted turtle, *Chrysemys picta*. American Midland Naturalist 79:517–19.

————. 1968b. Population structure and survivorship in the painted turtle, *Chrysemys picta*. Copeia 1968:260–68.

Gibson, A. R., and J. B. Falls. 1975. Evidence for multiple insemination in the common garter snake, *Thamnophis sirtalis*. Canadian Journal of Zoology 53:1362–68.

Gill, D. E. 1978. The metapopulation ecology of the red-spotted newt, *Notophthalmus viridescens* (Rafinesque). Ecological Monographs 48:145–66.

Green, D. M. 1983. Allozyme variation through a clinal hybrid zone between the toads *Bufo americanus* and *Bufo hemiophrys* in southeastern Manitoba. Herpetologica 39:28–40.

Gregory, P. T. 1977. Life-history parameters of the red-sided garter snake (*Thamnophis sirtalis parietalis*) in one extreme environment, the Interlake Region of Manitoba. Publication in Zoology National Museum Natural Science Canada 13:1–44.

Gregory, P. T., and K. W. Stewart. 1975. Long-distance dispersal and feeding strategy of the red-sided garter snake (*Thamnophis sirtalis parietalis*) in the Interlake of Manitoba. Canadian Journal of Zoology 53:238–45.

Hamilton, W. J., Jr. 1932. The food and feeding habits of some eastern salamanders. Copeia 1932:83–86.

————. 1947. Hibernation of the lined snake. Copeia 1947:209–10.

————. 1948. The food and feeding behavior of the green frog, *Rana clamitans* (Latreille), in New York state. Copeia 1948: 203–7.

Hammer, D. A. 1969. Parameters of a marsh snapping turtle population, LaCreek Refuge, South Dakota.

Journal of Wildlife Management 33:995–1005.

Hammerson, G. A. 1982. Amphibians and Reptiles in Colorado. Colorado Division of Wildlife, Denver. 131 pp.

Harding, J. H., and T. J. Bloomer. 1979. The wood turtle, *Clemmys insculpta*. A natural history. HERP, Bulletin of the N.Y. Herpetological Society 15:9–26.

Harless, M., and H. Morlock. 1979. Turtles Perspectives and Research. Wiley and Sons, New York. 695 pp.

Haywood, C. A., and R. W. Harris. 1972. Fight between rock squirrel and bullsnake. Texas Journal of Science 22:427.

Healy, W. R. 1974. Populations consequences of alternative life histories in *Notophthalmus v. viridescens*. Copeia 1974(1): 221–29.

———. 1975. Breeding and postlarval migration of the red-spotted newt, *Notophthalmus v. viridescens,* in Massachusetts. Ecology 56:673–80.

Heatwole, H. 1962. Environmental factors influencing local distribution and activity of the salamander, *Plethodon cinereus*. Ecology 43:460–72.

Hedeen, S. E. 1970. The ecology and life history of the mink frog, *Rana septentrionalis* Baird. Ph.D. thesis, University of Minnesota, Minneapolis. 129 pp.

Hedges, S. B. 1986. An electrophorectic analysis of Holarctic hylid frog evolution. Systematic Zoology 35:1–21.

Henderson, C. 1979a. Guide to the reptiles and amphibians of northeast Minnesota—Region 2. Minnesota Department of Natural Resources. 5 pp.

———. 1979b. Guide to the reptiles and amphibians of east central Minnesota—Region 4E. Minnesota Department of Natural Resources. 5 pp.

———. 1979c. Guide to the reptiles and amphibians of lower west central Minnesota—Region 4W. Minnesota Department of Natural Resources. 5 pp.

Henderson, C. 1980a. Guide to the reptiles and amphibians of northwest Minnesota—Region 1S. Minnesota Department of Natural Resources. 5 pp.

———. 1980b. Guide to the reptiles and amphibians of central Minnesota—Region 3W. Minnesota Department of Natural Resources. 5 pp.

———. 1980c. Guide to the reptiles and amphibians of southwest Minnesota—Region 4S. Minnesota Department of Natural Resources. 3 pp.

———. 1980d. Guide to the reptiles and amphibians of southeast Minnesota—Region 5. Minnesota Department of Natural Resources. 5 pp.

———. 1980e. Guide to the reptiles and amphibians of metropolitan Minnesota—Region 6. Minnesota Department of Natural Resources. 5 pp.

———. 1980f. Guide to the reptiles and amphibians of northwest Minnesota—Region 1N. Minnesota Department of Natural Resources. 5 pp.

Hensley, M. 1964. The tiger salamander in northern Michigan. Herpetologica 20(3):203–4.

Highton, R., G. C. Maha, and L. R. Maxson. 1989. Biochemical evolution in the slimy salamanders of the *Plethodon glutinosus* complex in the eastern United States. Illinois Biological Monograph 57. 154 pp.

Hoppe, D. M. 1981. Chorus frogs and their colors. In Ecology of reptiles and amphibians in Minnesota: Proceedings of a symposium, Cass Lake, Minn. L. Elwell, K. Cram, and C. Johnson, eds. 64 pp.

Hoppe, D. M., and R. G. McKinnell. 1989. Report on 1987–1988 leopard frog surveys. A report to the Nongame Wildlife Program, St. Paul. 5 pp.

———. 1991a. Minnesota's mutant leopard frogs. Minnesota Volunteer. 54 (319):56–63.

———. 1991b. Distribution and prevalance of Kandiyohi Leopard Frog. A report to the Nongame Wildlife Program, St. Paul.

Hornfeldt, C. S., and D. E. Keyler. 1987. Review of the toxicity of hognose snakes. Occasional Paper, Minnesota Herpetological Society 1:85–90.

Huheey, J. E. 1958. Some feeding habits of the eastern hog-nose snake. Herpetologica 14:68.

James, J. E. 1966. Biology of the soft-shelled turtle, *Trionyx* sp., of the upper Mississippi River. M.S. thesis, Winona State College, Winona, Minn. 22 pp.

Jaslow, A. P., and R. C. Vogt. 1977. Identification and distribution of *Hyla versicolor* and *Hyla chrysoscelis* in Wisconsin. Herpetologica 33:201–5.

Johnson, B. K., and J. L. Christiansen. 1976. The food and food habits of Blanchard's cricket frog, *Acris crepitans blanchardi* (Amphibia, Anura, Hylidae), in Iowa Journal of Herpetology 10:63–74.

Johnson, T. R. 1987. The Amphibians and Reptiles of Missouri. Missouri Department of Conservation, Jefferson City. 368 pp.

Jones, D. 1981. Minnesota Herpetological Society: A progress report. In Ecology of reptiles and amphibians in Minnesota: Proceedings of a symposium, Cass Lake, Minn. L. Elwell, K. Cram, and C. Johnson, eds. 64 pp.

Jordon, R., Jr. 1970. Death-feigning in a captive red-bellied snake, *Storeria occipitomaculata* (Storer). Herpetologica 26: 466–68.

Karns, D. R. 1983. The role of low pH in the toxicity of bog water to amphibian embryos. Bulletin of the Ecological Society of America 64:188.

———. 1984. Toxic bog water in northern Minnesota peatlands: Ecological and evolutionary consequences for breeding amphibians. Ph.D. thesis, University of Minnesota, Minneapolis. 164 pp.

———. 1986. Field herpetology: Methods for the

study of amphibians and reptiles in Minnesota. Bell Museum of Natural History Occasional Paper 18. 88 pp.

———. 1992a. Amphibians and reptiles in peatlands. In The Patterned Peatlands of Minnesota, H. E. Wright, Jr., B. A. Coffin, and N. Aaseng, eds. University of Minnesota Press, Minneapolis.

———. 1992b. Effects of acidic bog habitats on amphibian reproduction in a northern Minnesota peatland. Journal of Herpetology 26: 401–12.

Kaufmann, J. H. 1989. The wood turtle stomp. Natural History 1989 (8): 8, 10, 12–13.

Keyler, D. E. 1983. Report on snakebite fatality. Minnesota Herpetological Society News 3(8): 2.

Keyler, D. E., and B. L. Oldfield. 1992. Timber rattlesnake survey on southeastern Minnesota state lands (1990–1991). A report to the Nongame Wildlife Program, St. Paul. 31 pp.

Klauber, L. M. 1972. Rattlesnakes: Their Habits, Life Histories, and Influence on Mankind. 2d. ed. 2 vols. University of California Press, Berkeley. 1533 pp.

Kleeberger, S. R., and J. K. Werner. 1982. Home range and homing behavior of *Plethodon cinereus* in Northern Michigan. Copeia 1982:409–15.

Kramer, D. C. 1974. Home range of the western chorus frog *Pseudacris triseriata triseriata*. Journal of Herpetology 8:245–46.

Kumpf, K. F. 1934. The courtship of *Ambystoma tigrinum*. Copeia 1934:7–10.

Lagler, K. F. 1940. A turtle loss? American Wildlife 29:41–44.

Lang, J. W. 1969. Hibernation and movements of *Storeria occipitomaculata* in northern Minnesota. Journal of Herpetology 3:196–97.

———. 1971. Overwintering of three species of snakes in northwestern Minnesota. M.S. thesis, University of North Dakota, Grand Forks. 98 pp.

———. 1982a. Distribution and abundance of the five-lined skink *Eumeces fasciatus* in Minnesota. Report to Minnesota Department of Natural Resources. 109 pp.

———. 1982b. The reptiles and amphibians of Minnesota: distribution maps, habitat preferences, and selected references. Report to Minnesota Department of Natural Resources. 109 pp.

———. 1983. Blue devils in rock valley: Our search for the five-lined skink. Minnesota Volunteer. 1983:40–46.

Lang, J. W., D. Karns, D. Wells, M. Nehl, and M. Pappas. 1982. Status report on Minnesota's amphibians and reptiles. Report to Endangered Species Advisory Committee, Minnesota Department of Natural Resources. 52 pp.

Legler, J. M. 1955. Observations on the sexual behavior of captive turtles. Llyodia 18:95–99.

Linck, M. H. 1988. *Emydoidea blandingii* survey within Ramsey County, Minnesota. A report to the Nongame Wildlife Program, St. Paul. 6 pp.

McAlister, W. H. 1963. A post-breeding concentration of the spring peeper. Herpetologica 19:293.

McComb, W. C., and R. E. Noble. 1981. Herpetofaunal use of natural tree cavities and nest boxes. Wildlife Society Bulletin 9:261–67.

McKinistry, D. M. 1978. Evidence of toxic saliva in some colubrid snakes of the United States. Toxicon 16:523–34.

Maple, W. T., and L. P. Orr. 1968. Overwintering adaptations of *Sistrurus catenatus* in northeastern Ohio. Journal of Herpetology 2:179–80.

Martin, W. F., and R. B. Huey. 1971. The function of the epiglottis in sound production (hissing) of *Pituophis melanoleucus*. Copeia 1971: 752–54.

Martin, W. H. 1966. Life history of the timber rattlesnake *Crotalus horridus*. Investigator's Annual Report. U.S.D.I. National Park Service, Shenandoah National Park.

Matthews, Y. 1990. Progress Report: Five-lined skink electrophorectic studies in Minnesota. A report to the Nongame Wildlife Program, St. Paul.

Mattison, C. 1987. The Care of Reptiles and Amphibians in Captivity. 2d ed. Blandford, London. 317 pp.

Merrell, D. J. 1965. The distribution of the dominant Burnsi gene in the leopard frog. Evolution 19:69–85.

———. 1970. Migration and gene dispersal in *Rana pipiens*. American Zoologist 10:47–52.

———. 1977. Life history of the leopard frog, *Rana pipiens,* in Minnesota. Bell Museum of Natural History Occasional Paper 15. 23 pp.

Meylan, P. A. 1987. The phylogenetic relationships of soft-shelled turtles (Family Trionychidae). Bulletin of the American Museum of Natural History 186:1–101.

Minton, S. A., Jr. 1972. Amphibians and reptiles of Indiana. Indiana Academy of Science Monograph 3. 346 pp.

Moll, E. O. 1973. Latitudinal and intersubspecific variation in reproduction of the painted turtle, *Chrysemys picta*. Herpetologica 29:307–18.

Moriarty, J. J. 1985. Amphibians and reptiles of the Missouri drainage of southwestern Minnesota. Occasional Paper, Minnesota Herpetological Society 1:2–12.

———. 1986. A survey of the amphibians and reptiles in southeastern Minnesota. Occasional Paper, Minnesota Herpetological Society 1:66–80.

———. 1988. Minnesota County Biological Survey: 1988 Herpetological Surveys. Minnesota Department of Natural Resources Biological Report Series No. 9. 43 pp.

———. 1990. Snapping turtle bites off more than it can chew. Minnesota Herpetological Society News 10(6):4.

————. 1991. Reintroduction of Bullsnakes into the Crow-Hassan Prairie Restoration. A report to the Nongame Wildlife Program, St. Paul. 23 pp.

Moriarty, J. J., and D. G. Jones. 1988. An annotated bibliography of Minnesota herpetology 1900–1985. Bell Museum of Natural History. 39 pp.

Mossman, M. J., and R. L. Hine. 1985. Wisconsin's frog and toad survey, 1984. Wisconsin Endangered Resources Report 16. 16 pp.

Munro, D. F. 1949. Gain in size and weight of *Heterodon* eggs during incubation. Herpetologica 5:133–34.

Natural Heritage Program. 1988. Minnesota County Biological Survey: Interim report. Minnesota Department of Natural Resouces, St. Paul. 9 pp.

Nehl, M. J. 1981. Species accounts for reptiles and amphibians—1981 field season. Unpublished report to Minnesota Nongame Wildlife Program, St. Paul. 65 pp.

Nelson, W. F. 1963. Natural history of the northern prairie skink, *Eumeces septentrionalis septentrionalis* (Baird). Ph.D. thesis, University of Minnesota, Minneapolis. 134 pp.

Obbard, M. 1985. Can we safely harvest snapping turtles in Ontario? Canadian Amphibians and Reptiles Conservation Society 23 (2):1–4.

Oldfield, B. L., and D. E. Keyler. 1989. Survey of Timber Rattlesnake (*Crotalus horridus*) distribution along the Mississippi River in western Wisconsin. Wisconsin Academy of Science Transactions 77: 27–34.

Oliver, J. A. 1955. The Natural History of North American Amphibians and Reptiles. Van Nostrand, Princeton, N. J. 359 pp.

Pallas, D. C. 1960. Observations on a nesting of the wood turtle, *Clemmys insculpta*. Copeia 1960:155–56.

Perry, P. S., and M. H. Dexter. 1989. Snakes and lizards of Minnesota. Nongame Wildlife Program, Minnesota Department of Natural Resources. 25 pp.

Peterson, H. W. 1956. A record of viviparity in a normally oviparous snake. Herpetologica 12:152.

Peterson, R. C., and R. W. Fritsch. 1986. Connecticut's venomous snakes. Connecticut Geology and Natural History Survey Bulletin 111. 48 pp.

Pettus, D., and G. M. Angleton. 1967. Comparative reproductive biology of montane and piedmont chorus frogs. Evolution 21:500–507.

Pfingsten, R. A., and F. L. Downs. 1989. Salamanders of Ohio. Bulletin of Ohio Biological Survey New Series Vol. 7. 315 pp.

Platt, D. R. 1969. Natural history of the hognose snakes *Heterodon platyrhinos* and *Heterodon nasicus*. University of Kansas Publications Museum Natural History 18:253–420.

Platz, J. E. 1989. Speciation within the chorus frog *Pseudacris triseriata*: Morphometric and mating call analyses of the boreal and western subspecies. Copeia 1989: 704–12.

Plummer, M. V., and D. B. Farrar. 1981. Sexual dietary differences in a population of *Trionyx muticus*. Journal of Herpetology 15:175–79.

Pope, C. H. 1939. Turtles of the United States and Canada. Knopf, New York. 343 pp.

Preston, W. B. 1982. Amphibians and reptiles of Manitoba. Manitoba Museum of Man and Nature, Winnipeg. 128 pp.

Ralin, D. B. 1968. Ecological and reproductive differentiation in the cryptic species of the *Hyla versicolor* complex (Hylidae). Southwest Naturalist 13:283–300.

Reinert, H. K. 1981. Reproduction by the massasauga (*Sistrurus catenatus catenatus*). American Midland Naturalist 105:393–95.

Reinert, H. K., D. Cundall, and L. M. Bushar. 1984. Foraging behavior of the timber rattlesnake, *Crotalus horridus*. Copeia 1984:976–81.

Reinert, H. K., and W. R. Kodrich. 1982. Movements and habitat utilization by the massasauga, *Sistrurus catenatus catenatus*. Journal of Herpetology 16:162–71.

Ross, P., Jr., and D. Crews. 1977. Influence of the seminal plug on mating behavior in the garter snake. Nature 267: 344–45.

Rossman, D. A., and P. A. Myer. 1990. Behavioral and morphological adaptations for snail extraction in the North American brown snakes (Genus *Storeria*). Journal of Herpetology 24:434–38.

Schmid, W. D. 1965. Some aspects of the water economies of nine species of amphibians. Ecology 46:261–69.

————. 1982. Survival of frogs in low temperature. Science 215:697–98.

Schroder, R. C. 1950. Hibernation of blue racers and bullsnakes in western Illinois. Natural History Miscellania 75:1–2.

Schuett, G. W., D. L. Clark, and F. Kraus. 1984. Feeding mimicry in the rattlesnake *Sistrurus catenatus*, with comments on the evolution of the rattle. Animal Behavior 32:625–26.

Seibert, H. C., and C. W. Hagen. 1947. Studies on a population of snakes in Illinois. Copeia 1947:6–22.

Seigel, R. A. 1986. Ecology and conservation of an endangered rattlesnake, *Sistrurus catenatus*, in Missouri, U.S.A. Biological Conservation 35:333–46.

Seigel, R. A., J. T. Collins, and S. S. Novak. 1987. Snakes: Ecology and Evolutionary Biology. MacMillian, New York. 529 pp.

Shaw, C. E. 1951. Male combat in American colubrid snakes with remarks on combat in other colubrid and elapid snakes. Herpetologica 7:149–68.

Shaw, J. 1987. John Shaw's Closeups in Nature. Amphoto, New York. 144 pp.

Slevin, J. R. 1951. A high birthrate for *Natrix sipedon sipedon* (Linnaeus). Herpetologica 7:132.

Smith, H. M. 1934. The amphibians of Kansas. American Midland Naturalist 15:377–528.

———. 1978. A Guide to Field Identification: Amphibians of North America. Golden Press, New York. 160 pp.

Smith, P. W. 1961. The amphibians and reptiles of Illinois. Illinois Natural History Survey Bulletin 28:1–298.

Somma, L. A. 1987. Maternal care of neonates in the Prairie Skink, *Eumeces septentrionalis.* Great Basin Naturalist. 47:536–37.

Stiles, R. B. 1938. The milk snakes in Minnesota. Copeia 1938:50.

Storey, K. B., and J. M. Storey. 1990. Frozen and alive. Scientific American 263:92–97

Swanson, G. 1935. A preliminary list of Minnesota amphibians. Copeia 1935:152–54.

Tester, J. R. 1963. Techniques for studying movements of vertebrates in the field. Pages 445–50 in Radioecology, V. Schultz, and A. W. Klement, Jr., eds. Reinhold Pub. Corp., N. Y.

———. 1964. Radio tracking of ducks, deer, and toads. Minnesota Journal of Science 7:9–15.

———. 1981. Growth, local movements and hibernation of the Manitoba Toad, *Bufo hemiophrys,* in northern Minnesota. Page 2 in Ecology of reptiles and amphibians in Minnesota: Proceedings of a symposium, Cass Lake, Minn. L. Elwell, K. Cram, and C. Johnson, eds. 64 pp.

Tester, J. R., and W. J. Breckenridge. 1964. Winter behavior patterns of the Manitoba toad, *Bufo hemiophrys,* in northwestern Minnesota. Annales Academiae Scientiarum Fennicae Series. A. IV Biology. 71: 423–31.

Tester, J. R., A. Parker, and D. B. Siniff. 1965. Experimental studies on habitat preferences and thermoregulation of *Bufo americanus, B. hemiophrys,* and *B. cognatus.* Journal of the Minnesota Academy of Science 33:27–32.

Verrell, P. 1982. The sexual behavior of the red-spotted newt *Notophthalmus viridescens* (Amphibia: Urodela: Salamandridae) Animal Behavior 30:1224–36.

Vogt, R. C. 1980. Natural history of the map turtles *Graptemys pseudogeographica* and *G. ouachitensis* in Wisconsin. Tulane Studies of Zoology and Botany 22:17–48.

———. 1981. Natural History of Amphibians and Reptiles of Wisconsin. Milwaukee Public Museum, Wis. 205 pp.

———. 1993. Systematics of the False Map Turtles (*Graptemys pseudogeographica* complex: Reptilia, Testudines, Emydidae). Annals of Carnegie Museum 62(1):1–46.

Waldman, B. 1982. Adaptive significance of communal oviposition in wood frogs (*Rana sylvatica*). Behavioral Ecology and Sociobiology 10:169–74.

Walker, C. F. 1946. Amphibians of Ohio, Part I: The frogs and toads. Ohio State Museum Science Bulletin 1(3):1–109.

Weed, A. C. 1922. New frogs from Minnesota. Proceedings Biological Society of Washington 35:107–10.

Wells, K. D. 1977. Territoriality and male mating success in the green frog (*Rana clamitans*). Ecology 58:750–62.

Wendt, K. M., and B. A. Coffin. 1988. Natural vegetation of Minnesota at the time of the public land survey 1847–1907. Minnesota Department of Natural Resources Biology Report No. 1. 6 pp.

Whitaker, J. O. 1971. A study of the western chorus frog, *Pseudacris triseriata,* in Vigo County, Indiana. Journal of Herpetology 5:127–50.

Whitford, P. C. 1991. Final report on Blanchard's Cricket Frog survey of southeastern Minnesota—1990/1991. A report to the Nongame Wildlife Program, St. Paul. 50 pp.

Wilbur, H. M., and J. P. Collins. 1973. Ecological aspects of amphibians metamorphosis. Science 182: 1305–14.

Williams, K. L. 1978. Systematics and Natural History of the American Milksnake, *Lampropeltis triangulum.* Milwaukee Public Museum Publications in Biology and Geology 2:1–258.

Williams, P. K. 1969. Ecology of *Bufo hemiophrys* and *B. americanus* tadpoles in northwestern Minnesota. M. S. thesis, University of Minnesota, Minneapolis. 56 pp.

Woolverton, E. 1961. Winter survival of hatchling painted turtles in northern Minnesota. Copeia 1961:109.

Wright, A. H. 1914. North American Anura: Life histories of the Anura of Ithaca, New York. Carnegie Institute Publication 197.

———. 1920. Frogs—Their natural history and utilization. U. S. Bureau of Fisheries. Document 888. 44 pp.

Wright, A. H., and A. A. Wright. 1949. Handbook of Frogs and Toads. Comstock Press, Ithaca, N. Y. 640 pp.

———. 1957. Handbook of Snakes. 2 vols. Comstock Press, Ithaca, N. Y. 1105 pp.

INDEX

BARNEY OLDFIELD was born in Colorado and grew up in the high desert of northwestern New Mexico, where he developed an interest in reptiles as a young boy. He graduated from veterinary school in 1972 at Colorado State University in Fort Collins. After a stint of small animal practice in New Mexico and two years in the Air Force, he moved to southeastern Minnesota in 1977 and entered the 90% dairy practice that he is engaged in to this day. While in Minnesota, he has conducted various field studies (three funded grants) for the Minnesota Department of Natural Resources, Wisconsin Department of Natural Resources, and The Nature Conservancy on the Timber Rattlesnake and the Wood Turtle. He has published one scientific paper on the Timber Rattlesnake and several lay articles on reptiles. A co-authored article on Timber Rattlesnakes was published in *The Minnesota Volunteer* (May-June 1992). Over the past ten years he has had numerous photographs of reptiles and amphibians published in various brochures, posters, magazines, and books. He also maintains an active public speaking schedule, giving slide presentations on native amphibians and reptiles.

JOHN MORIARTY was born and grew up in Connecticut. There he developed a strong interest in natural history. He went on to earn degrees in natural resource conservation and wildlife ecology from the University of Connecticut and the University of Kentucky, respectively. After moving to Minnesota in 1983, John began a series of reptile and amphibian surveys in the southeast and southwest regions of Minnesota. He spent several years working in the James Ford Bell Museum of Natural History's amphibian and reptile collections and is still associated with the museum as an honorary fellow. John worked for the Minnesota Department of Natural Resources as a herpetologist for the County Biological Survey, and worked on amphibian and reptile legislation. In his current position as a wildlife specialist with Hennepin Parks, he is conducting herpetological projects including Gopher Snake reintroductions, a Blanding's Turtles nesting study, and the initiation of a statewide frog and toad survey. Current and past projects have lead to numerous scientific and popular articles. He has served as vice-president and president of the Minnesota Herpetological Society and serves on several committees of the Society for the Study of Amphibians and Reptiles.